*The Raven
and Other Poems*

The Raven
and Other Poems

Edgar Allan Poe

ALMA CLASSICS

ALMA CLASSICS
an imprint of

ALMA BOOKS LTD
Thornton House
Thornton Road
Wimbledon Village
London SW19 4NG
United Kingdom
www.almaclassics.com

This edition of *The Raven and Other Poems* first published by
Alma Classics in 2023

Edited text, notes and extra material © Alma Books Ltd

Printed in Great Britain by CPI Group (UK) Ltd, Croydon CR0 4YY

ISBN: 978-1-84749-888-5

Contents

*The Raven
and Other Poems*

TAMERLANE
AND OTHER POEMS*
(1827)

BY A BOSTONIAN

> Young heads are giddy, and young hearts are warm,
> And make mistakes for manhood to reform.
>
> COWPER

TAMERLANE*

[1827 VERSION]

Preface

The greater part of the poems which compose this little volume were written in the year 1821–22, when the author had not completed his fourteenth year. They were of course not intended for publication – why they are now published concerns no one but himself. Of the smaller pieces very little need be said: they perhaps savour too much of egotism – but they were written by one too young to have any knowledge of the world but from his own breast.

In *Tamerlane* he has endeavoured to expose the folly of even *risking* the best feelings of the heart at the shrine of Ambition. He is conscious that in this there are many faults (besides that of the general character of the poem), which he flatters himself he could, with little trouble, have corrected, but, unlike many of his predecessors, has been too fond of his early productions to amend them in his *old* age.

He will not say that he is indifferent as to the success of these poems – it might stimulate him to other attempts – but he can safely assert that failure will not at all influence him in a resolution already adopted. This is challenging criticism – let it be so. *Nos hæc novimus esse nihil.**

I

I have sent for thee, holy friar,
But 'twas not with the drunken hope
Which is but agony of desire
To shun the fate, with which to cope
Is more than crime may dare to dream,
That I have call'd thee at this hour:
Such, Father, is not my theme –
Nor am I mad to deem that power
Of earth may shrive me of the sin
Unearthly pride hath revell'd in –   10
I would not call thee fool, old man,
But hope is not a gift of thine;
If I *can* hope (Oh God! I can),
It falls from an eternal shrine.

II

The gay wall of this gaudy tower
Grows dim around me – death is near.
I had not thought, until this hour
When passing from the earth, that ear
Of any, were it not the shade
Of one whom in life I made   20
All mystery but a simple name,
Might know the secret of a spirit
Bow'd down in sorrow and in shame...
Shame said'st thou?
                        Ay, I did inherit
That hated portion, with the fame,
The worldly glory, which has shown
A demon light around my throne,
Scorching my sear'd heart with a pain
Not hell shall make me fear again.

III

I have not always been as now...   30
The fever'd diadem on my brow
I claim'd and won usurpingly...
Ay... the same heritage hath given
Rome to the Caesar, this to me –
The heirdom of a kingly mind,
And a proud spirit, which hath striven
Triumphantly with humankind.

In mountain air I first drew life;
The mists of the Taglay have shed*
Nightly their dews on my young head;   40
And my brain drank their venom then,
When after day of perilous strife
With chamois, I would seize his den
And slumber, in my pride of power,
The infant monarch of the hour –
For, with the mountain dew by night,
My soul imbibed unhallow'd feeling;
And I would feel its essence stealing
In dreams upon me – while the light
Flashing from cloud that hover'd o'er   50
Would seem to my half-closing eye
The pageantry of monarchy!
And the deep thunder's echoing roar
Came hurriedly upon me, telling
Of war, and tumult, where my voice –
My *own* voice, silly child! – was swelling
(Oh, how would my wild heart rejoice
And leap within me at the cry)
The battle cry of victory!

   *   *   *   *   *

IV

The rain came down upon my head   60
But barely shelter'd, and the wind
Pass'd quickly o'er me, but my mind
Was maddening, for 'twas man that shed
Laurels upon me – and the rush,

The torrent of the chilly air
Gurgled in my pleased ear the crush
Of empires, with the captive's prayer,
The hum of suitors, the mix'd tone
Of flattery round a sovereign's throne.

The storm had ceased, and I awoke –   70
Its spirit cradled me to sleep,
And as it pass'd me by, there broke
Strange light upon me, though it were
My soul in mystery to steep:
For I was not as I had been –
The child of Nature, without care
Or thought, save of the passing scene...

V

My passions, from that hapless hour,
Usurp'd a tyranny, which men
Have deem'd, since I have reach'd to power   80
My innate nature – be it so:
But, Father, there lived one who, then...
Then, in my boyhood, when their fire
Burn'd with a still intenser glow
(For passion must with youth expire) –
Ev'n *then*, who deem'd this iron heart
In woman's weakness had a part.

I have no words, alas, to tell
The loveliness of loving well!
Nor would I dare attempt to trace   90
The breathing beauty of a face
Which, even to *my* impassion'd mind,
Leaves not its memory behind.
In spring of life have ye ne'er dwelt
Some object of delight upon,
With steadfast eye, till ye have felt
The earth reel, and the vision gone?
And I have held to memory's eye
One object... and but one – until
Its very form hath pass'd me by,   100
But left its influence with me still.

11

VI

'Tis not to thee that I should name...
Thou canst not – wouldst not dare to think
The magic empire of a flame
Which even upon this perilous brink
Hath fix'd my soul, though unforgiven,
By what it lost for passion: heaven.
I loved... and oh, how tenderly!
Yes! She [was] worthy of all love!
Such as in infancy was mine,   110
Though then its *passion* could not be:
'Twas such as angel minds above
Might envy – her young heart the shrine
On which my every hope and thought
Were incense, then a goodly gift:
For they were childish, without sin,
Pure as her young example taught;
Why did I leave it and, adrift,
Trust to the fickle star within?

VII

We grew in age and love together,   120
Roaming the forest and the wild –
My breast her shield in wintry weather –
And when the friendly sunshine smiled
And she would mark the opening skies,
I saw no heaven, but in her eyes...
Even childhood knows the human heart;
For when, in sunshine and in smiles,
From all our little cares apart,
Laughing at her half-silly wiles
I'd throw me on her throbbing breast   130
And pour my spirit out in tears,
She'd look up in my wilder'd eye...
There was no need to speak the rest –
No need to quiet her kind fears...
She did not ask the reason why.

The hallow'd memory of those years
Comes o'er me in these lonely hours,

And, with sweet loveliness, appears
As perfume of strange summer flowers –
Of flowers which we have known before   140
In infancy, which seen, recall
To mind... not flowers alone, but more:
Our earthly life, and love... and all.

VIII

Yes! She was worthy of all love!
Even such as from the accursed time
My spirit with the tempest strove,
When, on the mountain peak alone,
Ambition lent it a new tone,
And bade it first to dream of crime,
My frenzy to her bosom taught: 150
We still were young – no purer thought
Dwelt in a seraph's breast than *thine*;*
For passionate love is still divine:
I loved her as an angel might,
With ray of the all-living light
Which blazes upon Edis' shrine.*
It is not surely sin to name,
With such as mine, that mystic flame –
I had no being but in thee!
The world with all its train of bright   160
And happy beauty (for to me
All was an undefined delight),
The world – its joy, its share of pain
Which I felt not; its bodied forms
Of varied being, which contain
The bodiless spirits of the storms;
The sunshine and the calm; the ideal
And fleeting vanities of dreams,
Fearfully beautiful; the real
Nothings of midday waking life,   170
Of an enchanted life, which seems,
Now as I look back, the strife
Of some ill demon, with a power
Which left me in an evil hour –

All that I felt or saw or thought...
Crowding, confused became
(With thine unearthly beauty fraught)
Thou – and the nothing of a name.

IX

The passionate spirit which hath known
And deeply felt the silent tone   180
Of its own self-supremacy
(I speak thus openly to thee:
'Twere folly *now* to veil a thought
With which this aching breast is fraught);
The soul which feels its innate right;
The mystic empire and high power
Given by the energetic might
Of genius at its natal hour,
Which knows (believe me at this time,
When falsehood were a tenfold crime,   190
There *is* a power in the high spirit
To *know* the fate it will inherit) –
The soul, which knows such power, will still
Find *Pride* the ruler of its will.

Yes! I was proud – and ye who know
The magic of that meaning word,
So oft perverted, will bestow
Your scorn, perhaps, when ye have heard
That the proud spirit had been broken,
The proud heart burst in agony   200
At one upbraiding word or token
Of her, that heart's idolatry...
I was ambitious... have ye known
Its fiery passion?... Ye have not...
A cottager, I mark'd a throne
Of half the world as all my own,
And murmur'd at such lowly lot!
But it had pass'd me as a dream
Which, of light step, flies with the dew,
That kindling thought – did not the beam   210
Of Beauty, which did guide it through

14

The livelong summer day, oppress
My mind with double loveliness…
*   *   *   *   *

X

We walk'd together on the crown
Of a high mountain, which look'd down
Afar from its proud natural towers
Of rock and forest, on the hills –
The dwindled hills, whence amid bowers
Her own fair hand had rear'd around
Gush'd shoutingly a thousand rills,   220
Which, as it were, in fairy bound
Embraced two hamlets… those our own…
Peacefully happy – yet alone…
*   *   *   *   *

I spoke to her of power and pride –
But mystically, in such guise
That she might deem it naught beside
The moment's converse: in her eyes
I read (perhaps too carelessly)
A mingled feeling with my own;
The flush on her bright cheek, to me,   230
Seem'd to become a queenly throne
Too well that I should let it be
A light in the dark wild, alone.

XI

There, in that hour, a thought came o'er
My mind it had not known before:
To leave her while we both were young –
To follow my high fate among
The strife of nations, and redeem
The idle words which, as a dream
Now sounded to her heedless ear…   240
I held no doubt… I knew no fear
Of peril in my wild career:
To gain an empire, and throw down
As nuptial dowry… a queen's crown –

The only feeling which possessed,
With her own image, my fond breast...
Who, that had known the secret thought
Of a young peasant's bosom then,
Had deem'd him, in compassion, aught
But one whom fantasy had led   250
Astray from reason?... Among men
Ambition is chain'd down – nor fed
(As in the desert, where the grand,
The wild, the beautiful, conspire
With their own breath to fan its fire)
With thoughts such feeling can command,
Uncheck'd by sarcasm and scorn
Of those who hardly will conceive
That any should become "great" born
In their own sphere* – will not believe   260
That they shall stoop in life to one
Whom daily they are wont to see
Familiarly, whom Fortune's sun
Hath ne'er shone dazzlingly upon
Lowly... and of their own degree...

XII

I pictured to my fancy's eye
Her silent, deep astonishment,
When, a few fleeting years gone by
(For short the time my high hope lent
To its most desperate intent),   270
She might recall in him, whom Fame
Had gilded with a conqueror's name
(With glory, such as might inspire
Perforce a passing thought of one
Whom she had deem'd in his own fire
Wither'd and blasted – who had gone
A traitor, violate of the truth
So plighted in his early youth),
Her own Alexis, who should plight*
The love he plighted *then*... again,   280
And raise his infancy's delight,
The bride and queen of Tamerlane...

XIII

One noon of a bright summer's day,
I pass'd from out the matted bower
Where in a deep, still slumber lay
My Ada. In that peaceful hour,
A silent gaze was my farewell.
I had no other solace: then
To awake her and a falsehood tell
Of a feign'd journey were again   290
To trust the weakness of my heart
To her soft, thrilling voice; to part
Thus, haply, while in sleep she dream'd
Of long delight, nor yet had deem'd
Awake that I had held a thought
Of parting, were with madness fraught.
I knew not woman's heart, alas,
Though loved and loving... let it pass...

XIV

I went from out the matted bower
And hurried madly on my way,   300
And felt, with every flying hour
That bore me from my home, more gay.
There is of earth an agony
Which, ideal, still may be
The worst ill of mortality.
'Tis bliss, in its own reality –
Too real to *his* breast who lives
Not within himself but gives
A portion of his willing soul
To God, and to the great whole,   310
To him whose loving spirit will dwell
With Nature, in her wild paths, tell
Of her wondrous ways, and telling bless
Her overpowering loveliness!
A more than agony to him
Whose failing sight will grow dim
With its own living gaze upon
That loveliness around: the sun...
The blue sky... the misty light

Of the pale cloud therein, whose hue   320
Is grace to its heavenly bed of blue…
Dim, though looking on all bright!
O God! When the thoughts that may not pass
Will burst upon him, and alas,
For the flight on earth to fancy given,
There are no words – unless of heaven.

XV

*   *   *   *   *

Look round thee now on Samarcand,*
Is she not queen of earth? Her pride
Above all cities? In her hand
Their destinies? With all beside   330
Of glory which the world hath known?
Stands she not proudly and alone?
And who her sovereign? Timur, he*
Whom the astonish'd earth hath seen,
With victory on victory
Redoubling age! And more, I ween,
The Zinghis' yet re-echoing fame.*
And now what has he? What! A name.
The sound of revelry by night
Comes o'er me, with the mingled voice   340
Of many with a breast as light
As if 'twere not the dying hour
Of one in whom they did rejoice…
As in a leader, haply… Power
Its venom secretly imparts –
Nothing have I with human hearts.

XVI

When Fortune mark'd me for her own,
And my proud hopes had reach'd a throne
(It boots me not, good friar, to tell
A tale the world but knows too well,   350
How by what hidden deeds of might
I clamber'd to the tottering height),
I still was young – and well I ween

My spirit what it e'er had been.
My eyes were still on pomp and power,
My wilder'd heart was far away
In valleys of the wild Taglay,
In mine own Ada's matted bower.
I dwelt not long in Samarcand
Ere, in a peasant's lowly guise,   360
I sought my long-abandon'd land;
By sunset did its mountains rise
In dusky grandeur to my eyes –
But as I wander'd on the way,
My heart sunk with the sun's ray.
To him who still would gaze upon
The glory of the summer sun,
There comes, when that sun will from him part,
A sullen hopelessness of heart.
That soul will hate the evening mist   370
So often lovely, and will list
To the sound of the coming darkness (known
To those whose spirits hearken)* as one
Who in a dream of night *would* fly,
But cannot from a danger nigh.
What though the moon, the silvery moon,
Shine on his path, in her high noon?
Her smile is chilly, and *her* beam
In that time of dreariness will seem
As the portrait of one after death –   380
A likeness taken when the breath
Of young life and the fire o' the eye
Had lately been, but had pass'd by.
'Tis thus when the lovely summer sun
Of our boyhood his course hath run,
For all we live to know is known,
And all we seek to keep hath flown,
With the noonday beauty, which is all.
Let life, then, as the day flower fall* –
The transient, passionate day flower,   390
Withering at the evening hour.

XVII

I reach'd my home... my home no more...
For all was flown that made it so...
I pass'd from out its mossy door
In vacant idleness of woe.
There met me on its threshold stone
A mountain hunter I had known
In childhood, but he knew me not.
Something he spoke of the old cot:
It had seen better days, he said.   400
There rose a fountain once, and *there*
Full many a fair flower raised its head –
But she who rear'd them was long dead,
And in such follies had no part.
What was there left me *now*? Despair...
A kingdom for a broken heart.

FUGITIVE PIECES

To —

I saw thee on thy bridal day –
    When a burning blush came o'er thee,
Though happiness around thee lay,
    The world all love before thee.

And in thine eye the kindling light
    Of young passion free*
Was all on earth my chainèd* sight
    Of loveliness might* see.

That blush, I ween,* was maiden shame –
    As such it well may pass –   10
Though its glow hath raised a fiercer flame
    In the breast of him, alas,

Who saw thee on that bridal day,
    When that deep blush *would* come o'er thee –
Though happiness around thee lay,
    The world all love before thee…

Dreams

Oh, that my young life were a lasting dream,
My spirit not awakening till the beam
Of an eternity should bring the morrow!
Yes! Though that long dream were of hopeless sorrow,
'Twere better than the cold reality
Of waking life to him whose heart must be,
And hath been still, upon the lovely earth,
A chaos of deep passion from his birth.
But should it be, that dream eternally
Continuing, as dreams have been to me   10
In my young boyhood – should it thus be given,

'Twere folly still to hope for higher heaven.
For I have revell'd when the sun was bright
I' the summer sky in dreams of living light
And loveliness – have left my very heart
In climes of mine imagining, apart
From mine own home, with beings that have been
Of mine own thought... What more could I have seen?
'Twas once, and only once – and the wild hour
From my remembrance shall not pass – some power   20
Or spell had bound me: 'twas the chilly wind
Came o'er me in the night, and left behind
Its image on my spirit – or the moon
Shone on my slumbers in her lofty noon
Too coldly, or the stars... howe'er it was,
That dream was as that night wind... let it pass.

I *have been* happy, though in a dream.
I have been happy – and I love the theme:
Dreams! In their vivid colouring of life
As in that fleeting, shadowy, misty strife   30
Of semblance with reality which brings
To the delirious eye more lovely things
Of paradise and love – and all our own! –
Than young hope in his sunniest hour hath known.

Visit of the Dead

   *   *   *   *   *

Thy soul shall find itself alone –
Alone of all on earth, unknown
The cause, but none are near* to pry
Into thine hour of secrecy.
Be silent in that solitude,
Which is not loneliness – for then
The spirits of the dead, who stood
In life before thee, are again
In death around thee, and their will
Shall then o'ershadow thee: be still,   10
For the night,* though clear, shall frown,
And the stars shall look not down

From their thrones in the dark heaven,*
With light like hope to mortals given,
But their red orbs, without beam,
To thy withering heart* shall seem
As a burning, and a fever
Which would cling to thee for ever.
But 'twill leave thee, as each star
In the morning light afar   20
Will fly thee... and vanish –
But its *thought* thou canst not banish.
The breath of God will be still –
And the mist upon the hill,
By that summer breeze unbroken,
Shall charm thee, as a token,
And a symbol which shall be
Secrecy in thee.*

Evening Star

'Twas noontide of summer,
　　And midtime of night,
And stars, in their orbits,
　　Shone pale, through the light
Of the brighter, cold moon,
　　Mid planets her slaves,
Herself in the heavens,
　　Her beam on the waves.
　　　I gazed awhile
　　　On her cold smile –   10
Too cold... too cold for me...
　　　There pass'd, as a shroud,
　　　A fleecy cloud,
And I turn'd away to thee,
　　　Proud evening star,
　　　In thy glory afar,
And dearer thy beam shall be –
　　　For joy to my heart
　　　Is the proud part
Thou bearest in heaven at night,   20

And more I admire
Thy distant fire
Than that colder, lowly light.

Imitation

A dark, unfathom'd tide
Of interminable pride –
A mystery and a dream,
Should my early life seem.
I say that dream was fraught
With a wild and waking thought
Of beings that have been,
Which my spirit hath not seen,
Had I let them pass me by
With a dreaming eye!   10
Let none of earth inherit
That vision on my spirit –
Those thoughts I would control
As a spell upon his soul –
For that bright hope at last
And that light time have passed,
And my worldly rest hath gone
With a sigh as it pass'd on:
I care not though it perish
With a thought I then did cherish.   20

'In Youth Have I Known One with Whom the Earth'

How often we forget all time when lone
Admiring Nature's universal throne –
Her woods, her wilds, her mountains, the intense
Reply of HERS to OUR intelligence!

I

In youth have I known one with whom the earth
In secret communing held, as he with it,
In daylight, and in beauty from his birth –
Whose fervid, flickering torch of life was lit

From the sun and stars, whence he had drawn forth
A passionate light: such for his spirit was fit –
And yet that spirit knew not, in the hour
Of its own fervour, what had o'er it power.

II

Perhaps it may be that my mind is wrought
To a fever by the moonbeam that hangs o'er,   10
But I will half believe that wild light fraught
With more of sovereignty than ancient lore
Hath ever told – or is it of a thought
The unembodied essence, and no more,
That with a quickening spell doth o'er us pass
As dew of the night-time o'er the summer grass?

III

Doth o'er us pass when, as th' expanding eye
To the loved object, so the tear to the lid
Will start, which lately slept in apathy?
And yet it need not be (that object) hid   20
From us in life, but common – which doth lie
Each hour before us… but *then* only, bid
With a strange sound, as of a harp-string broken,
To awake us… 'Tis a symbol and a token

IV

Of what in other worlds shall be, and given
In beauty by our God to those alone
Who otherwise would fall from life and heaven
Drawn by their heart's passion, and that tone,
That high tone of the spirit which hath striven –
Though not with faith: with godliness, whose throne   30
With desperate energy 't hath beaten down,
Wearing its own deep feeling as a crown.

'A Wilder'd Being from My Birth'

A wilder'd being from my birth,
    My spirit spurn'd control,
But now, abroad on the wide earth,
    Where wanderest thou, my soul?*

In visions of the dark night
    I have dream'd of joy departed –
But a waking dream of life and light
    Hath left me broken-hearted.

And what is not a dream by day
    To him whose eyes are cast   10
On things around him with a ray
    Turn'd back upon the past?

That holy dream... that holy dream,
    While all the world were chiding,
Hath cheer'd me as a lovely beam
    A lonely spirit guiding...

What though that light through misty night
    So dimly shone afar?...*
What could there be more purely bright
    In Truth's day star?   20

'The Happiest Day, the Happiest Hour'

The happiest day, the happiest hour
    My sear'd and blighted heart hath known:
The highest hope of pride and power
    I feel hath flown.

Of power, said I? Yes! Such I ween,
    But they have vanish'd long, alas!
The visions of my youth have been...
    But let them pass.

And, pride, what have I now with thee?
    Another brow may even inherit   10
The venom thou hast pour'd on me –
    Be still, my spirit.

The happiest day, the happiest hour
    Mine eyes shall see – have ever seen –
The brightest glance of pride and power,
    I feel, have been.

But were that hope of pride and power
    Now offer'd with the pain
Even *then* I felt, that brightest hour
    I would not live again: 20

For on its wing was dark alloy,
    And, as it flutter'd, fell
An essence – powerful to destroy
    A soul that knew it well.

The Lake

In youth's spring* it was my lot
To haunt of the wide world* a spot
The which I could not love the less,
So lovely was the loneliness
Of a wild lake, with black rock bound,
And the tall pines that tower'd around.
But when the night had thrown her pall
Upon that spot, as upon all,
And the wind would pass me by
In its stilly melody,   10
My infant spirit would awake
To the terror of the lone lake.*
Yet the terror was not fright,
But a tremulous delight,
And a feeling undefined,
Springing from a darken'd mind.*
Death was in that poison'd wave,
And in its gulf a fitting grave
For him who thence could solace bring
To his dark* imagining –   20
Whose wildering thought could even make*
An Eden of that dim lake.

FROM
AL AARAAF, TAMERLANE
AND MINOR POEMS*
(1829)

AL AARAAF

¿Entiendes, Fabio, lo que voy diciendo?
*—Y cómo si lo entiendo. —Mientes, Fabio.**

What has night to do with sleep?*
COMUS

DEDICATION

Who drinks the deepest?... Here's to him.*

CLEVELAND

A star was discovered by Tycho Brahe* which burst forth, in a moment, with a splendour surpassing that of Jupiter, then gradually faded away and became invisible to the naked eye.

Science! Meet* daughter of old Time thou art,
   Who alterest all things with thy peering eyes!
Why prey'st thou thus upon the poet's heart,
   Vulture, whose wings are dull realities?
How should he love thee? Or how deem thee wise,
   Who wouldst not leave him in his wandering
To seek for treasure in the jewell'd skies,
   Albeit he soar* with an undaunted wing?
Hast thou not dragg'd Diana from her car,
   And driven the hamadryad from the wood   10
To seek a shelter in some happier star,
   The gentle naiad* from her fountain flood,*
The elfin from the green grass – and from me
   The summer dream beneath the shrubbery?*

AL AARAAF

Part One

Oh, nothing earthly save the ray
(Thrown back from flowers) of Beauty's eye,
As in those gardens where the day
Springs from the gems of Circassy –
Oh, nothing earthly save the thrill
Of melody in woodland rill –
Or (music of the passion-hearted)
Joy's voice so peacefully departed
That, like the murmur in the shell,
Its echo dwelleth and will dwell –   10
With nothing* of the dross of ours –
Yet all the beauty – all the flowers
That list our Love and deck our bowers –
Adorn yon world afar, afar –
The wandering star...

'Twas a sweet time for Nesace – for there
Her world lay lolling on the golden air,
Near four bright suns – a temporary rest –
A garden spot* in desert of the blessed.

Away – away – mid seas of rays that roll   20
Empyrean splendour o'er th' unchained soul –
The soul that scarce (the billows are so dense)
Can struggle to its destin'd eminence –
To distant spheres, from time to time, she rode,
And late to ours, the favour'd one of God –
But, now the ruler of an anchor'd realm,
She throws aside the sceptre – leaves the helm,
And, amid incense and high spiritual hymns,
Laves in quadruple light her angel limbs.

Now happiest, loveliest in yon lovely earth,   30
Whence sprang the "Idea of Beauty" into birth
(Falling in wreaths through many a startled star,
Like woman's hair mid pearls, until afar
It lit on hills Achaian,* and there dwelt),
She look'd into infinity – and knelt.
Rich clouds for canopies about her curled –
Fit emblems of the model of her world –
Seen but in beauty – not impeding sight
Of other beauty glittering through the light –
A wreath that twined each starry form around   40
And all the opal'd air in colour bound.

All hurriedly she knelt upon a bed
Of flowers: of lilies such as rear'd* the head
On the fair Capo Ducato,* and sprang
So eagerly around about to hang
Upon the flying footsteps of... deep pride –
Of her who lov'd a mortal* – and so died...
The sephalica, budding with young bees,
Uprear'd its purple stem around her knees –
And gemmy flower, of Trebizond misnam'd* –   50
Inmate of highest stars, where erst it sham'd
All other loveliness: its honeyed dew
(The fabled nectar that the heathen knew),
Deliriously sweet, was dropp'd from heaven,
And fell on gardens of the unforgiven
In Trebizond – and on a sunny flower
So like its own above that, to this hour,
It still remaineth, torturing the bee
With madness and unwonted reverie...
In heaven and all its environs the leaf   60
And blossom of the fairy plant in grief
Disconsolate linger – grief that hangs her head,
Repenting follies that full long have fled,
Heaving her white breast to the balmy air
Like guilty beauty, chasten'd and more fair –
Nyctanthes* too, as sacred as the light
She fears to perfume, perfuming the night –
And clytia,* pondering between many a sun,

While pettish tears adown her petals run,
And that aspiring flower* that sprang on earth   70
And died ere scarce exalted into birth,
Bursting its odorous heart in spirit to wing
Its way to heaven from garden of a king –
And Vallisnerian lotus* thither flown
From struggling with the waters of the Rhône –
And thy most lovely purple perfume, Zante,
Isola d'oro – Fior di Levante! *
And the nelumbo bud that floats for ever
With Indian Cupid down the holy river* –
Fair flowers, and fairy, to whose care is given   80
To bear the goddess' song, in odours, up to heaven:*

    "Spirit that dwellest where,
      In the deep sky,
    The terrible and fair
      In beauty vie!
    Beyond the line of blue –
      The boundary of the star
    Which turneth at the view
      Of thy barrier and thy bar –
    Of the barrier overgone   90
      By the comets who were cast
    From their pride and from their throne
      To be drudges till the last –
    To be carriers of fire
      (The red fire of their heart)
    With speed that may not tire
      And with pain that shall not part –
    Who livest – *that* we know –
      In eternity – we feel –
    But the shadow of whose brow   100
      What spirit shall reveal?
    Though the beings whom thy Nesace,
      Thy messenger, hath known
    Have dream'd for thy infinity
      A model of their own* –
    Thy will is done, O God!
      The star hath ridden high

Through many a tempest, but she rode
   Beneath thy burning eye,
And here, in thought, to thee –   110
   In thought that can alone
Ascend thy empire and so be
   A partner of thy throne –
By wingèd Fantasy,*
   My embassy* is given,
Till secrecy shall knowledge be
   In the environs of heaven."

She ceas'd, and buried then her burning cheek
Abash'd, amid the lilies there, to seek
A shelter from the fervour of his eye,   120
For the stars trembled at the Deity.
She stirr'd not, breath'd not, for a voice was there
How solemnly pervading the calm air! –
A sound of silence on the startled ear
Which dreamy poets name "the music of the sphere".
Ours is a world of words: quiet we call
"Silence" – which is the merest word of all.
Here* Nature speaks, and ev'n ideal things
Flap shadowy sounds from visionary wings –
But ah, not so when, thus, in realms on high   130
The eternal voice of God is passing by,
And the red winds are withering in the sky!
"What though in worlds which sightless* cycles run,
Link'd to a little system and one sun –
Where all my love is folly and the crowd
Still think my terrors but the thunder cloud,
The storm, the earthquake and the ocean wrath
(Ah, will they cross me in my angrier path?) –
What though in worlds which own a single sun
The sands of Time grow dimmer as they run?   140
Yet thine is my resplendency, so given
To bear my secrets through the upper heaven.
Leave tenantless thy crystal home, and fly,
With all thy train, athwart the moony sky –
Apart, like fireflies in Sicilian night* –
And wing to other worlds another light!

Divulge the secrets of thy embassy
To the proud orbs that twinkle – and so be
To every heart a barrier and a ban,
Lest the stars totter in the guilt of man!"   150

Up rose the maiden in the yellow night,
The single-moonèd eve! On earth we plight
Our faith to one love – and one moon adore:
The birthplace of young Beauty had no more.
As sprang that yellow star from downy hours,
Up rose the maiden from her shrine of flowers,
And bent o'er sheeny mountains and dim plain
Her way – but left not yet her Therasaean reign.*

Part Two

High on a mountain of enamell'd head –
Such as the drowsy shepherd on his bed   160
Of giant pasturage lying at his ease,
Raising his heavy eyelid, starts and sees
With many a mutter'd "hope to be forgiven"
What time* the moon is quadrated* in heaven –
Of rosy head, that towering far away
Into the sunlit ether caught the ray
Of sunken suns at eve – at noon of night,
While the moon danc'd with the fair stranger light –
Uprear'd upon such height arose a pile
Of gorgeous columns on th' unburthen'd air,   170
Flashing from Parian marble that twin smile
Far down upon the wave that sparkled there,
And nursled* the young mountain in its lair:
Of molten stars their pavement – such as fall*
Through the ebon* air, besilvering the pall
Of their own dissolution, while they die –
Adorning then the dwellings of the sky.
A dome, by linkèd light from heaven let down,
Sat gently on these columns as a crown –
A window of one circular diamond, there,   180
Look'd out above into the purple air,
And rays from God shot down that meteor chain

45

And hallow'd all the beauty twice again,
Save when, between th' Empyrean and that ring,
Some eager spirit flapp'd his dusky wing.
But on the pillars seraph eyes have seen
The dimness of this world: that greyish green
That Nature loves the best for Beauty's grave
Lurk'd in each cornice, round each architrave –
And every sculptur'd cherub thereabout   190
That from his marble dwelling ventur'd* out,
Seem'd earthly in the shadow of his niche –
Achaian* statues in a world so rich?
Friezes from Tadmor and Persepolis –
From Balbec,* and the stilly, clear abyss
Of beautiful Gomorrah! Oh, the wave
Is now upon thee – but too late to save!*

Sound loves to revel near* a summer night:
Witness the murmur of the grey twilight
That stole upon the ear, in Eyraco,*   200
Of many a wild star-gazer long ago –
That stealeth ever on the ear of him
Who, musing, gazeth on the distance dim,
And sees the darkness coming as a cloud –
Is not its form, its voice, most palpable and loud?*

But what is this?... It cometh... and it brings
A music with it... 'tis the rush of wings...
A pause... and then a sweeping, falling strain,
And Nesace is in her halls again.
From the wild energy of wanton haste   210
    Her cheeks were flushing, and her lips apart,
And zone* that clung around her gentle waist
    Had burst beneath the heaving of her heart.
Within the centre of that hall to breathe
She paus'd and panted, Zanthe! All beneath,
The fairy light that kiss'd her golden hair
And long'd to rest, yet could but sparkle there!

Young flowers were whispering in melody*
To happy flowers that night – and tree to tree;
Fountains were gushing music as they fell   220

In many a starlit grove or moonlit dell;
Yet silence came upon material things –
Fair flowers, bright waterfalls and angel wings –
And sound alone that from the spirit sprang
Bore burthen to the charm the maiden sang:

   "'Neath bluebell or streamer –
     Or tufted wild spray
   That keeps from the dreamer
     The moonbeam away* –
   Bright beings that ponder,   230
     With half-closing eyes,
   On the stars which your wonder
     Hath drawn from the skies
   Till they glance through the shade and
     Come down to your brow
   Like… eyes of the maiden
     Who calls on you now –
   Arise from your dreaming
     In violet bowers,
   To duty beseeming   240
     These star-litten hours,
   And shake from your tresses
     Encumber'd with dew
   The breath of those kisses
     That cumber them too!
   (Oh how, without you, Love,
     Could angels be blest?)
   Those kisses of true love
     That lull'd ye to rest,
   Up! – shake from your wing   250
     Each hindering thing!
   The dew of the night,
     It would weigh down your flight –
   And true love caresses…
     Oh, leave them apart!
   They are light on the tresses,
     But hang* on the heart.

   Ligeia! Ligeia!
     My beautiful one!

Whose harshest idea   260
　　Will to melody run,*
Oh, is it thy will
　　On the breezes to toss?
Or, capriciously still,
　　Like the lone albatross,*
Incumbent on night
　　(As she on the air),
To keep watch with delight
　　On the harmony there?

Ligeia! Wherever   270
　　Thy image may be,
No magic shall sever
　　Thy music from thee.
Thou hast bound many eyes
　　In a dreamy sleep,
But the strains still arise
　　Which *thy* vigilance keep:
The sound of the rain
　　Which leaps down to the flower
And dances again   280
　　In the rhythm of the shower,
The murmur that springs*
　　From the growing of grass
Are the music of things –
　　But are modell'd, alas!…
Away, then, my dearest,
　　Oh, hie thee away
To springs that lie clearest,
　　Beneath the moon ray –
To lone lake that smiles,   290
　　In its dream of deep rest,
At the many star isles
　　That enjewel its breast:
Where wild flowers, creeping,
　　Have mingled their shade,
On its margin is sleeping
　　Full many a maid –
Some have left the cool glade and

Have slept with the bee.*
Arouse them, my maiden,   300
    On moorland and lea –
Go, breathe on their slumber,
    All softly in ear,
The musical number
    They slumber'd to hear!
For what can awaken
    An angel so soon
Whose sleep hath been taken
    Beneath the cold moon,
As the spell which no slumber   310
    Of witchery may test,
The rhythmical number
    Which lull'd him to rest?"

Spirits in wing, and angels to the view,
A thousand seraphs burst th' Empyrean through,
Young dreams still hovering on their drowsy flight –
Seraphs in all but "Knowledge", the keen light
That fell refracted through thy bounds, afar
– O Death! – from eye of God upon that star.
Sweet was that error – sweeter still that death...   320
Sweet was that error, ev'n with *us* the breath
Of science dims the mirror of our joy –
To them 'twere the simoom,* and would destroy...
For what (to them) availeth it to know
That Truth is Falsehood – or that Bliss is Woe?
Sweet was their death – with them to die was rife
With the last ecstasy of satiate life...
Beyond that death no immortality,
But sleep that pondereth and is not "to be"* –
And there... oh, may my weary spirit dwell   330
Apart from Heaven's eternity, and yet how far from Hell!*
What guilty spirit, in what shrubbery dim,
Heard not the stirring summons of that hymn?
But two... they fell... for Heaven no grace imparts
To those who hear not for their beating hearts –
A maiden angel and her seraph lover –
Oh, where (and ye may seek the wide skies over)

Was Love, the blind, near sober Duty known?
Unguided Love hath fallen – mid "tears of perfect moan".*
He was a goodly spirit, he who fell –   340
A wanderer by mossy-mantled well,
A gazer on the lights that shine above,
A dreamer in the moonbeam by his love.
What wonder? For each star is eye-like there,
And looks so sweetly down on Beauty's hair –
And they, and every mossy spring were holy
To his love-haunted heart and melancholy.
The night had found (to him a night of woe),
Upon a mountain crag, young Angelo:*
Beetling it bends athwart the solemn sky,   350
And scowls on starry worlds that down beneath it lie.
Here sat he with his love – his dark eye bent
With eagle gaze along the firmament:
Now turn'd it upon her – but ever then
It trembled to one constant star* again.
"Ianthe, dearest, see how dim that ray!
How lovely 'tis to look so far away!
She seem'd not thus upon that autumn eve
I left her gorgeous halls – nor mourn'd to leave.
That eve... that eve – I should remember well –   360
The sunray dropp'd, in Lemnos,* with a spell
On th' arabesque carving of a gilded hall
Wherein I sat, and on the drap'ried wall,
And on my eyelids... Oh, the heavy light!
How drowsily it weigh'd them into night!
On flowers, before, and mist and love they ran
With Persian Saadi in his *Gulistan*...*
But oh, that light!... I slumber'd – Death, the while,
Stole o'er my senses in that lovely isle,
So softly that no single silken hair   370
Awoke that slept – or knew that it* was there.

The last spot of earth's orb I trod upon
Was a proud temple call'd the Parthenon* –
More beauty clung around her column'd wall
Than ev'n thy glowing bosom beats withal* –
And when old Time my wing did disenthral,

Thence sprang I, as the eagle from his tower,
And years I left behind me in an hour.
What time upon her airy bounds I hung,
One half the garden of her globe was flung   380
Unrolling as a chart unto my view –
Tenantless cities of the desert too!
Ianthe, beauty crowded on me then,
And half I wish'd to be again of men."

"My Angelo! And why of them to be?
A brighter dwelling place is there for thee,
And greener fields than in yon world above,
And woman's loveliness – and passionate love."

"But list, Ianthe! When the air so soft
Fail'd, as my pennon'd* spirit leapt aloft,   390
Perhaps my brain grew dizzy, but the world
I left so late was into chaos hurl'd –
Sprang from her station, on the winds apart,
And roll'd, a flame, the fiery heaven athwart.
Methought, my sweet one, then I ceas'd to soar
And fell – not swiftly as I rose before,
But with a downward, tremulous motion through
Light, brazen rays, this golden star unto!
Nor long the measure of my falling hours,
For nearest of all stars was thine to ours –   400
Dread star, that came, amid a night of mirth,
A red Daedalion* on the timid earth.

"We came, and to thy earth – but not to us
Be given our lady's bidding to discuss.
We came, my love – around, above, below,
Gay firefly of the night we come and go,
Nor ask a reason save the angel nod
She grants to us, as granted by her God –
But, Angelo, than thine grey Time unfurl'd
Never his fairy wing o'er fairier world!   410
Dim was its little disk, and angel eyes
Alone could see the phantom in the skies
When first Al Aaraaf knew her course to be
Headlong thitherward o'er the starry sea –

But when its glory swell'd upon the sky,
As glowing Beauty's bust beneath man's eye,
We paus'd before the heritage of men,
And thy star trembled, as doth Beauty then!"

Thus, in discourse, the lovers whiled away
The night that waned and waned and brought no day.   420
They fell – for Heaven to them no hope imparts,
Who hear not for the beating of their hearts.

TAMERLANE

[1829 VERSION]*

I

Kind solace in a dying hour!
　　Such, Father, is not (now) my theme –
I will not madly deem that power
　　　　Of earth may shrive me of the sin
　　　　Unearthly pride hath revell'd in –
　　I have no time to dote or dream:
You call it hope, that fire of fire!
It is but agony of desire:
If I *can* hope – Oh God, I can! –
　　Its fount is holier, more divine...　　　　　　　　10
I would not call thee fool, old man,
　　But such is not a gift of thine.

II

Know thou the secret of a spirit
　　Bow'd from its wild pride into shame.
Oh, yearning heart! I did inherit
　　Thy withering portion with the fame,
The searing glory which hath shone
Amid the jewels of my throne –
Halo of Hell! – and with a pain
Not Hell shall make me fear again...　　　　　　　　20
Oh, craving heart, for the lost flowers
And sunshine of my summer hours!
Th' undying voice of that dead time,
With its interminable chime,
Rings, in the spirit of a spell,
Upon thy emptiness – a knell.*

III

I have not always been as now:
The fever'd diadem on my brow
   I claim'd and won usurpingly –
Hath not the same fierce heirdom given   30
    Rome to the Caesar, this to me? –
      The heritage of a kingly mind
And a proud spirit which hath striven
      Triumphantly with human kind.

IV

On mountain soil I first drew life:
   The mists of the Taglay have shed*
   Nightly their dews upon my head,
And, I believe, the wingèd strife
And tumult of the headlong air
Have* nestl'd in my very hair.   40

V

So late from Heaven that dew, it fell
   (Mid dreams of an unholy night)
Upon me with the touch of Hell,
   While the red flashing of the light,
From clouds that hung like banners o'er,
   Appeared to my half-closing eye
   The pageantry of monarchy,
And the deep trumpet-thunder's roar
   Came hurriedly upon me, telling
     Of human battle, where my voice –   50
   My own voice, silly child! – was swelling
    (Oh, how my spirit would rejoice
And leap within me at the cry)
The battle cry of Victory!

VI

The rain came down upon my head
   Unshelter'd – and the heavy wind
   Was giant-like – so thou, my mind!*
It was but man, I thought, who shed

Laurels upon me, and the rush –
The torrent of the chilly air – 60
Gurgled within my ear the crush
    Of empires, with the captive's prayer –
The hum of suitors – and the tone
Of flattery round a sovereign's throne.

VII

My passions, from that hapless hour,
    Usurp'd a tyranny which men
Have deem'd, since I have reach'd to power,
    My innate nature – be it so:
    But, father, there liv'd one who, then,
Then – in my boyhood – when their fire 70
    Burn'd with a still intenser glow
(For passion must, with youth, expire),
    Ev'n *then* who knew this iron heart
    In woman's weakness had a part.*

VIII

I have no words – alas! – to tell
The loveliness of loving well!
Nor would I now attempt to trace
The more than beauty of a face
Whose lineaments, upon my mind,
Are... shadows on th' unstable wind. 80
Thus I remember having dwelt
    Some page of early lore upon,
With loitering eye, till I have felt
The letters, with their meaning, melt
    To fantasies – with none.*

IX

Oh, she was worthy of all love!*
    Love – as in infancy was mine –
'Twas such as angel minds above
    Might envy, her young heart the shrine
On which my every hope and thought 90

55

Were incense... then a goodly gift,
    For they were childish and upright –
Pure... as her young example taught.
    Why did I leave it, and, adrift,
        Trust to the fire within for light?

X

We grew in age – and love – together,
    Roaming the forest and the wild –
My breast her shield in wintry weather –
    And, when the friendly sunshine smil'd,
And she would mark the opening skies,   100
I saw no heaven but in her eyes.

XI

Young Love's first lesson is... the heart:
    For mid that sunshine and those smiles –
When, from our little cares apart
    And laughing at her girlish wiles,
I'd throw me on her throbbing breast*
    And pour my spirit out in tears –
There was no need to speak the rest,
    No need to quiet any fears
Of her...* who ask'd no reason why,   110
But turn'd on me her quiet eye!

XII

Yet *more* than worthy of the love
My spirit struggled with, and strove,
When, on the mountain peak, alone,
Ambition lent it a new tone* –
I had no being but in thee.
    The world, and all it did contain
In the earth, the air, the sea –
    Its joy, its little lot of pain
That was new pleasure... the ideal,*   120
    Dim vanities of dreams by night,
And dimmer nothings which were real

(Shadows – and a more shadowy light!) –
Parted upon their misty wings,
   And so, confusedly, became
    Thine image and... a name... a name!
Two separate, yet most intimate things.

XIII

I was ambitious – have you known
   The passion, Father? You have not.
A cottager, I mark'd a throne   130
Of half the world as all my own,
   And murmur'd at such lowly lot –
But, just like any other dream,
    Upon the vapour of the dew
My own had passed,* did not the beam
    Of Beauty which did while it through
The minute, the hour, the day, oppress
My mind with double loveliness.*

XIV

We walk'd together on the crown
Of a high mountain, which look'd down   140
Afar from its proud natural towers
   Of rock and forest on the hills –
The dwindled hills! – begirt* with bowers
   And shouting with a thousand rills.

XV

I spoke to her of power and pride,
   But mystically – in such guise
That she might deem it naught beside
   The moment's converse. In her eyes
I read, perhaps too carelessly,
    A mingled feeling with my own –   150
The flush on her bright cheek to me
    Seem'd to become a queenly throne
Too well that I should let it be
    Light in the wilderness alone.

XVI

I wrapp'd myself in grandeur then,
   And donn'd a visionary crown –
     Yet it was not that Fantasy
     Had thrown her mantle over me,
But that, among the rabble men,*
   Lion ambition is chain'd down,
And crouches to a keeper's hand...
Not so in deserts, where the grand,
The wild, the terrible conspire
With their own breath to fan his fire.

160

XVII

Look round thee now on Samarcand!* –
   Is she not queen of earth? Her pride
Above all cities? In her hand
   Their destinies? In all beside
Of glory which the world hath known?
Stands she not nobly and alone?
Falling, her veriest stepping stone
Shall form the pedestal of a throne –
And who her sovereign? Timur, he*
   Whom the astonished people saw
Striding o'er empires haughtily,
   A diadem'd outlaw!*

170

XVIII

Oh, human love! Thou spirit given,
On earth, of all we hope in heaven,
Which fall'st into the soul like rain
Upon the siroc-wither'd plain,*
And, failing in thy power to bless,
But leav'st the heart a wilderness!
Idea which bindest life around
With music of so strange a sound
And beauty of so wild a birth –
Farewell, for I have won the earth!

180

XIX

When Hope, the eagle that tower'd, could see
   No cliff beyond him in the sky,
His pinions were bent droopingly,
   And homeward turn'd his soften'd eye.   190

XX

'Twas sunset – when the sun will part,
There comes a sullenness of heart
To him who still would look upon
The glory of the summer sun.
That soul will hate the evening mist
So often lovely, and will list
To the sound of the coming darkness (known
To those whose spirits harken) as one
Who, in a dream of night, *would* fly
But *cannot* from a danger nigh.   200

XXI

What though the moon – the white moon –
Shed all the splendour of her noon?
Her smile is chilly, and *her* beam,
In that time of dreariness, will seem
(So like you gather in your breath)
A portrait taken after death.
And boyhood is a summer sun
Whose waning is the dreariest one –
For all we live to know is known,
And all we seek to keep hath flown.   210
Let life, then, as the day flower, fall
With the noonday beauty, which is all.*

XXII

I reach'd my home – my home no more,
   For all had flown who made it so.
I pass'd from out its mossy door,
   And, though my tread was soft and low,
A voice came from the threshold stone
Of one whom I had earlier known –

Oh, I defy thee, Hell, to show
On beds of fire that burn below,   220
An humbler heart, a deeper woe.*

XXIII

Father, I firmly do believe –
  I *know* – for Death, who comes for me
    From regions of the blessed afar,
Where there is nothing to deceive,
    Hath left his iron gate ajar,
   And rays of truth you cannot see
    Are flashing through Eternity...
I do believe that Eblis* hath
A snare in every human path –   230
Else how, when in the holy grove
I wandered of the idol, Love,
Who daily scents his snowy wings
With incense of burnt offerings
From the most unpolluted* things,
Whose pleasant bowers are yet so riven
Above with trellised rays from heaven
No mote may shun (no tiniest fly)
The lightning of his eagle eye –
How was it that Ambition crept,   240
  Unseen, amid the revels there,
Till, growing bold, he laughed and leapt
  In the tangles of Love's very hair?*

MISCELLANEOUS POEMS*

My nothingness, my wants,
My sins, and my contrition...
SOUTHEY'S PERS.*

And some flowers – *but* no bays.
MILTON*

Preface

I

Romance, who loves to nod and sing
With drowsy head and folded wing
Among the green leaves as they shake
Far down within some shadowy lake,
To me a painted paroquet*
Hath been – a most familiar bird –
Taught me my alphabet to say,
To lisp my very earliest word
While in the wild wood I did lie,
A child, with a most knowing eye.   10

II

Of late, eternal condor years*
So shake the very air on high
With tumult as they thunder by,
I hardly have had time for cares*
Through gazing on th' unquiet sky!
And when an hour with calmer wings
Its down upon my spirit flings,
That little time with lyre and rhyme
To while away (forbidden things!),
My heart would feel to be a crime   20
Did it not tremble with the strings!

To —

I

Should my early life seem
(As well it might) a dream,
Yet I build no faith upon
The king Napoleon –
I look not up afar
For my destiny in a star.

II

In parting from you now,
Thus much I will avow:
There are beings, and have been,
Whom my spirit had not seen   10
Had I let them pass me by
With a dreaming eye
If my peace hath fled away
In a night, or in a day –
In a vision, or in none...
Is it therefore the less gone?...

III

I am standing mid the roar
Of a weather-beaten shore,
And I hold within my hand
Some particles of sand –   20
How few, and how they creep
Through my fingers to the deep!
My early hopes? No: they
Went gloriously away,
Like lightning from the sky
At once – and so will I.

IV

So young? Ah, no, not now –
Thou hast not seen my brow,
But they tell thee I am proud.
They lie – they lie aloud...   30
My bosom beats with shame
At the paltriness of name
With which they dare combine
A feeling such as mine...
Nor Stoic? I am not.
In the terror of my lot,
I laugh to think how poor
That pleasure "to endure"!
What! Shade of Zeno!...* I!
Endure! No... no... defy.   40

To —

I

The bowers whereat, in dreams, I see
    The wantonest singing birds
Are lips – and all thy melody
    Of lip-begotten words...

II

Thine eyes, in heaven of heart enshrined,
    Then desolately fall –
Oh God! – on my funereal mind
    Like starlight on a pall...

III

Thy heart – *thy* heart!... I wake and sigh,
    And sleep to dream till day   10
Of the truth that gold can never buy –
    Of the trifles* that it may.

To the River —*

I

Fair river, in thy bright, clear flow
    Of labyrinth-like water,*
Thou art an emblem of the glow
      Of beauty – the unhidden heart,
      The playful maziness of art
In old Alberto's daughter...*

II

But when within thy wave she looks –
      Which glistens then, and trembles –
Why, then, the prettiest of brooks
      Her worshipper resembles: 10
For in his heart, as in thy stream,
    Her image deeply lies –
The heart which trembles at the beam,
    The scrutiny of her eyes.*

To M—

I

Oh, I care not that my earthly lot
    Hath little of Earth in it –
That years of love have been forgot
    In the fever of a minute –

II

I heed not that the desolate
    Are happier, sweet, than I –
But that *you* meddle with *my* fate,
    Who am a passer-by.

III

It *is* not that my founts of bliss
    Are gushing – strange! – with tears,   10
Or that the thrill of a single kiss
    Hath palsied many years –

IV

'Tis not that the flowers of twenty springs,
    Which have wither'd as they rose,
Lie dead on my heartstrings
    With the weight of an age of snows –

V

Nor that the grass (Oh, may it thrive!)
    On my grave is growing or grown –
But that, while I am dead yet alive
    I cannot be, lady, alone.   20

Fairy Land

Dim vales – and shadowy floods –
And cloudy-looking woods
Whose forms we can't discover
For the tears that drip all over.
Huge moons there wax and wane –
Again… again… again… –
Every moment of the night,
Forever changing places,
And they put out the starlight
With the breath from their pale faces.   10
About twelve by the moon dial,
One more *filmy* than the rest
(A sort* which, upon trial,
They have found to be the best)
Comes down… still down… and down
With its centre on the crown
Of a mountain's eminence,
While its wide circumference
In easy drapery falls

Over hamlets and rich halls,*   20
Wherever they may be –
O'er the strange woods... o'er the sea...
Over spirits on the wing...
Over every drowsy thing...
And buries them up quite
In a labyrinth of light...
And then, how deep – oh, deep! –
Is the passion of their sleep!
In the morning they arise,
And their moony covering   30
Is soaring in the skies,
With the tempests as they toss,
Like... almost any thing* –
Or a yellow albatross.
They use that moon no more
For the same end as before,
Videlicet a tent –
Which I think extravagant.
Its atomies, however,
Into a shower dissever,   40
Of which those butterflies,
Of earth, who seek the skies,
And so come down again
(The unbelieving things!),*
Have brought a specimen
Upon their quivering wings.

FROM
POEMS*
(1831)

TO
THE US CORPS OF CADETS
THIS VOLUME
IS RESPECTFULLY DEDICATED*

Tell wit how much it wrangles
In fickle points of niceness –
Tell wisdom it entangles
Itself in over-wiseness.*
SIR WALTER RALEIGH

Letter to Mr —

West Point, — 1831

DEAR B—,*

Believing only a portion of my former volume to be worthy a second edition, that small portion I thought it as well to include in the present book as to republish by itself. I have, therefore, herein combined *Al Aaraaf* and *Tamerlane* with other poems hitherto unprinted. Nor have I hesitated to insert from the "Minor Poems", now omitted, whole lines, and even passages, to the end that being placed in a fairer light, and the trash shaken from them in which they were embedded, they may have some chance of being seen by posterity.

* * *

It has been said that a good critique on a poem may be written by one who is no poet himself. This, according to *your* idea and *mine* of poetry, I feel to be false: the less poetical the critic, the less just the critique, and the converse. On this account, and because there are but few B—s in the world, I would be as much ashamed of the world's good opinion as proud of your own. Another than yourself might here observe "Shakespeare* is in possession of the world's good opinion, and yet Shakespeare is the greatest of poets. It appears then that the world judge correctly – why should you be ashamed of their favourable judgement?" The difficulty lies in the interpretation of the word "judgement", or "opinion". The opinion is the world's, truly, but it may be called theirs as a man would call a book his having bought it: he did not write the book, but it is his; they did not originate the opinion, but it is theirs. A fool, for example, thinks Shakespeare a great poet – yet the fool has never read Shakespeare. But the fool's neighbour, who is a step higher on the Andes of the mind, whose head (that is to say, his more exalted thought) is too far above the fool to be seen or understood, but whose feet (by which I mean his every-day actions) are sufficiently near to be discerned, and by means of which that superiority is ascertained, which *but* for them would never have been discovered – this neighbour asserts that Shakespeare is a great poet: the fool believes him, and it is henceforward his *opinion*. This neighbour's own opinion has, in like manner, been adopted from one above *him*, and so, ascendingly, to a few gifted individuals who kneel around the summit, beholding face to face the master spirit who stands upon the pinnacle.

You are aware of the great barrier in the path of an American writer. He is read, if at all, in preference to the combined and established wit of the world. I say "established", for it is with literature as with law or empire: an established name is an estate in tenure, or a throne in possession. Besides, one might suppose that books, like their authors, improve by travel: their having crossed the sea is, with us, so great a distinction. Our antiquaries abandon time for distance; our very fops glance from the binding to the bottom of the title page, where the mystic characters which spell "London", "Paris" or "Genoa" are precisely so many letters of recommendation.

* * *

I mentioned just now a vulgar error as regards criticism. I think the notion that no poet can form a correct estimate of his own writings is another. I remarked before that in proportion to the poetical talent would be the justice of a critique upon poetry. Therefore, a bad poet would, I grant, make a false critique, and his self-love would infallibly bias his little judgement in his favour – but a poet who is indeed a poet could not, I think, fail of making a just critique. Whatever should be deducted on the score of self-love might be replaced on account of his intimate acquaintance with the subject – in short, we have more instances of false criticism than of just where one's own writings are the test, simply because we have more bad poets than good. There are of course many objections to what I say: Milton is a great example of the contrary, but his opinion with respect to the *Paradise Regained* is by no means fairly ascertained. By what trivial circumstances men are often led to assert what they do not really believe! Perhaps an inadvertent word has descended to posterity. But, in fact, the *Paradise Regained** is little, if at all, inferior to the *Paradise Lost*, and is only supposed so to be because men do not like epics, whatever they may say to the contrary, and reading those of Milton in their natural order are too much wearied with the first to derive any pleasure from the second.

I dare say Milton preferred *Comus** to either – if so, justly.

As I am speaking of poetry, it will not be amiss to touch slightly upon the most singular heresy in its modern history – the heresy of what is called, very foolishly, the "Lake School".* Some years ago I might have been induced, by an occasion like the present, to attempt a formal refutation of their doctrine – at present it would be a work of supererogation.* The wise must bow to the wisdom of such men as Coleridge and Southey, but, being wise, have laughed at poetical theories so prosaically exemplified.

Aristotle, with singular assurance, has declared poetry the most philosophical of all writing* – but it required a Wordsworth to pronounce it the most metaphysical. He seems to think that the end of poetry is, or should be, instruction – yet it is a truism that the end of our existence is happiness; if so, the end of every separate part of our existence – every thing connected with our existence – should be still happiness. Therefore the end of instruction should be happiness – and happiness is another name for pleasure: therefore the end of instruction should be pleasure – yet we see the above-mentioned opinion implies precisely the reverse.

To proceed: *ceteris paribus*,* he who pleases is of more importance to his fellow men than he who instructs, since utility is happiness and pleasure is the end already obtained which instruction is merely the means of obtaining.

I see no reason, then, why our metaphysical poets should plume themselves so much on the utility of their works, unless indeed they refer to instruction with eternity in view – in which case, sincere respect for their piety would not allow me to express my contempt for their judgement, contempt which it would be difficult to conceal, since their writings are professedly to be understood by the few, and it is the many who stand in need of salvation. In such case, I should no doubt be tempted to think of the devil in *Melmoth*,* who labours indefatigably through three octavo volumes to accomplish the destruction of one or two souls, while any common devil would have demolished one or two thousand.

* * *

Against the subtleties which would make poetry a study – not a passion – it becomes the metaphysician to reason, but the poet to protest. Yet Wordsworth and Coleridge are men in years – the one imbued in contemplation from his childhood, the other a giant in intellect and learning. The diffidence, then, with which I venture to dispute their authority would be overwhelming, did I not feel, from the bottom of my heart, that learning has little to do with the imagination, intellect with the passions, or age with poetry.

> Trifles, like straws, upon the surface flow
> He who would search for pearls must dive below*

are lines which have done much mischief. As regards the greater truths, men oftener err by seeking them at the bottom than at the top: the depth lies in the huge abysses where wisdom is sought, not in the palpable palaces where she is found. The ancients were not always right in hiding the goddess in a well: witness the light which Bacon* has thrown upon philosophy – witness the principles of our divine faith, that moral mechanism by which the simplicity of a child may overbalance the wisdom of a man.

Poetry, above all things, is a beautiful painting whose tints, to minute inspection, are confusion worse confounded,* but start boldly out to the cursory glance of the connoisseur.

We see an instance of Coleridge's liability to err in his *Biographia Literaria** – professedly his literary life and opinions, but, in fact, a treatise *de omni scibili et quibusdam aliis.** He goes wrong by reason of his very profundity, and of his error we have a natural type in the contemplation of a star. He who regards it directly and intensely sees, it is true, the star, but it is the star without a ray – while he who surveys it less inquisitively is conscious of all for which the star is useful to us below: its brilliancy and its beauty.

* * *

As to Wordsworth, I have no faith in him. That he had in youth the feelings of a poet, I believe, for there are glimpses of extreme delicacy in his writings (and delicacy is the poet's own kingdom – his Eldorado), but they have the appearance of a better day recollected – and glimpses, at best, are little evidence of present poetic fire: we know that a few straggling flowers spring up daily in the crevices of the avalanche.

He was to blame in wearing away his youth in contemplation with the end of poetizing in his manhood. With the increase of his judgement, the light which should make it apparent has faded away. His judgement consequently is too correct. This may not be understood, but the old Goths of Germany would have understood it, who used to debate matters of importance to their state twice, once when drunk, and once when sober – sober that they might not be deficient in formality, drunk lest they should be destitute of vigour.

The long wordy discussions by which he tries to reason us into admiration of his poetry speak very little in his favour: they are full of such assertions as this (I have opened one of his volumes at random): "Of genius the only proof is the act of doing well what is worthy to be done, and what was never done before."* Indeed! Then it follows that in doing what is *un*worthy to be done, or what *has* been done before, no genius can be evinced – yet the picking of pockets is an unworthy act, pockets have been picked time immemorial, and Barrington, the pickpocket,* in point of genius, would have thought hard of a comparison with William Wordsworth the poet.

Again, in estimating the merit of certain poems, whether they be Ossian's or M'Pherson's,* can surely be of little consequence – yet, in order to prove their worthlessness, Mr W. has expended many pages in the controversy. *Tantæne animis?** Can great minds descend to such absurdity? But worse still: that he may bear down every argument in favour of these poems, he triumphantly drags forward a passage, in his abomination of which he expects the reader to sympathize. It is the beginning of the epic poem *Temora*.* "The blue waves of Ullin roll in light; the green hills are covered with day. Trees shake their dusky heads in the breeze." And this – this gorgeous, yet simple imagery, where all is alive and panting with immortality, than which earth has nothing more grand, nor paradise more beautiful – this, William Wordsworth, the author of *Peter Bell*,* has *selected* to dignify with his imperial contempt. We shall see what better he, in his own person, has to offer. *Imprimis*:

> And now she's at the pony's head,
> And now she's at the pony's tail,
> On that side now, and now on this,
> And almost stifled her with bliss,
> A few sad tears does Betty shed…
> She pats the pony, where or when
> She knows not, happy Betty Foy!…
> Oh, Johnny, never mind the doctor!*

Secondly:

> The dew was falling fast, the stars began to blink;
> I heard a voice; it said, "Drink, pretty creature, drink!"
> And, looking o'er the hedge, before me I espied
> A snow-white mountain lamb with a maiden at its side.
> No other sheep were near; the lamb was all alone;
> And by a slender cord was tethered to a stone.*

Now, we have no doubt this is all true; we *will* believe it – indeed we will, Mr W. Is it sympathy for the sheep you wish to excite? I love a sheep from the bottom of my heart.

* * *

But there *are* occasions, dear B—, there are occasions when even Wordsworth is reasonable. Even Stamboul,* it is said, shall have an end, and the most unlucky blunders must come to a conclusion. Here is an extract from his preface.

> Those who have been accustomed to the phraseology of modern writers, if they persist in reading this book to a conclusion [*impossible!*], will, no doubt, have to struggle with feelings of awkwardness [ha, ha, ha!]; they will look round for poetry [ha, ha, ha, ha!] and will be induced to enquire by what species of courtesy these attempts have been permitted to assume that title.

Ha, ha, ha, ha, ha!

Yet let not Mr. W. despair: he has given immortality to a wagon,* and the bee Sophocles has eternalized a sore toe, and dignified a tragedy with a chorus of turkeys.*

* * *

Of Coleridge I cannot speak but with reverence. His towering intellect! His gigantic power! To use an author quoted by himself, "*J'ay trouvé souvent que la plupart des sectes ont raison dans une bonne partie de ce qu'elles avancent, mais non pas tant en ce qu'elles nient*"* – and, to employ his own language, he has "imprisoned his own conceptions"* by the barrier he has erected against those of others. It is lamentable to think that such a mind should be buried in metaphysics, and, like the Nyctanthes,* waste its perfume upon the night alone. In reading that man's poetry, I tremble like one who stands upon a volcano – conscious, from the very darkness bursting from the crater, of the fire and the light that are weltering below.

* * *

What is Poetry? Poetry! That Proteus-like idea, with as many appellations as the nine-titled Corcyra!* Give me, I demanded of a scholar some time ago, give me a definition of poetry! "*Très volontiers*"* – and he proceeded to his library, brought me a Dr Johnson* and overwhelmed me with a definition. Shade of the immortal Shakespeare! I imagined to myself the scowl of your spiritual eye upon the profanity of that scurrilous Ursa Major.* Think of poetry, dear B—, think of poetry, and then think of... Dr Samuel Johnson! Think of all that is airy and fairy-like, and then of all that is hideous and unwieldy... think of his huge bulk – the Elephant! – and then... and then think of the *Tempest*... the *Midsummer Night's Dream*... Prospero... Oberon... and Titania!*

* * *

A poem, in my opinion, is opposed to a work of science by having, for its *immediate* object, pleasure, not truth; to romance, by having for its object an *indefinite* instead of a *definite* pleasure, being a poem only so far as this object is attained – romance presenting perceptible images with definite, poetry with *in*definite sensations – to which end music is an *essential*, since the comprehension of sweet sound is our most indefinite conception. Music, when combined with a pleasurable idea, is poetry; music without the idea is simply music; the idea without the music is prose from its very definitiveness.

What was meant by the invective against him who had no music in his soul?*

* * *

To sum up this long rigmarole, I have, dear B—, what you no doubt perceive, for the metaphysical poets, *as* poets, the most sovereign contempt. That they have followers proves nothing:

> No Indian prince has to his palace
> More followers than a thief to the gallows.*

Introduction*

Romance, who loves to nod and sing
With drowsy head and folded wing
Among the green leaves as they shake
Far down within some shadowy lake,
To me a painted paroquet*
Hath been – a most familiar bird –
Taught me my alphabet to say,
To lisp my very earliest word
While in the wild wood I did lie,
A child, with a most knowing eye.   10

Succeeding years, too wild for song,
Then roll'd like tropic storms along,
Where, though the garish lights that fly
Dying along the troubled sky
Lay bare through vistas thunder-riven,
The blackness of the general heaven,
That very blackness yet doth fling
Light on the lightning's silver wing.

For, being an idle boy lang syne*
Who read Anacreon* and drank wine,   20
I early found Anacreon rhymes
Were almost passionate sometimes,
And by strange alchemy of brain
His pleasures always turn'd to pain,
His naivety to wild desire,
His wit to love – his wine to fire.
And so, being young and dipp'd in folly,
I fell in love with melancholy,
And used to throw my earthly rest
And quiet all away in jest: 30
I could not love except where Death

Was mingling his with Beauty's breath –
Or Hymen,* Time and Destiny
Were stalking between her and me.

Oh, then the eternal condor years*
So shook the very heavens on high
With tumult as they thunder'd by,
I had no time for idle cares
Through gazing on the unquiet sky!
Or if an hour with calmer wing   40
Its down did on my spirit fling,
That little hour with lyre and rhyme
To while away (forbidden thing!),
My heart half fear'd to be a crime
Unless it trembled with the string.

But *now* my soul hath too much room –
Gone are the glory and the gloom:
The black hath mellow'd into grey,
And all the fires are fading away.

My draught of passion hath been deep: 50
I revell'd, and I now would sleep,
And after-drunkenness of soul
Succeeds the glories of the bowl –
An idle longing night and day
To dream my very life away.

But dreams – of those who dream as I,
Aspiringly – are damned, and die.
Yet should I swear I mean alone,
By notes so very shrilly blown,
To break upon Time's monotone,   60
While yet my vapid joy and grief
Are tintless of the yellow leaf,
Why, not an imp the greybeard hath
Will shake his shadow in my path –
And even the greybeard will o'erlook
Connivingly my dreaming book.

To Helen

Helen, thy beauty is to me
   Like those Nicean barks of yore,
That gently, o'er a perfumed sea,
   The weary, way-worn wanderer bore
   To his own native shore.*

On desperate seas long wont to roam,
   Thy hyacinth hair, thy classic face,
Thy naiad airs have brought me home
   To the glory that was Greece
And the grandeur that was Rome.   10

Lo! In yon brilliant window niche
   How statue-like I see thee stand,
   The agate lamp within thy hand!
Ah, Psyche, from the regions which
   Are Holy Land!

Israfel*

I

In heaven a spirit doth dwell
Whose heartstrings are a lute:
None sing so wild, so well
As the angel Israfel –
And the giddy stars are mute.

II

Tottering above
In her highest noon,
The enamoured moon
Blushes with love –
While, to listen, the red levin*   10
Pauses in heaven.

III

And they say (the starry choir
And all the listening things)
That Israfeli's fire
Is owing to that lyre
With those unusual strings.

IV

But the heavens that angel trod,
Where deep thoughts are a duty,
Where Love is a grown god,
Where houri glances are   20
(Stay! Turn thine eyes afar!)
Imbued with all the beauty
Which we worship in yon star.

V

Thou art not therefore wrong,
Israfeli, who despisest
An unimpassion'd song:
To thee the laurels belong,
Best bard – because the wisest.

VI

The ecstasies above
With thy burning measures suit –   30
Thy grief (if any), thy love,
With the fervour of thy lute…
Well may the stars be mute!

VII

Yes, heaven is thine – but this
Is a world of sweets and sours:
Our flowers are merely… flowers,
And the shadow of thy bliss
Is the sunshine of ours.

VIII

If I did dwell where Israfel
Hath dwelt, and he where I,   40
He would not sing one half as well –
One half as passionately –
And a stormier note than this would swell
From my lyre within the sky.

The Doomed City

Lo! Death hath rear'd himself a throne
In a strange city, all alone,
Far down within the dim west –
And the good and the bad, and the worst and the best,
Have gone to their eternal rest.

There shrines and palaces and towers
Are... not like anything of ours –
Oh no, oh no – *ours* never loom
To heaven with that ungodly gloom!
Time-eaten towers that tremble not!   10
Around, by lifting winds forgot,
Resignedly beneath the sky
The melancholy waters lie.

A heaven that God doth not contemn
With stars is like a diadem –
We liken our ladies' eyes to them –
But there, that everlasting pall!
It would be mockery to call
Such dreariness a heaven at all.

Yet though no holy rays come down   20
On the long night-time of that town,
Light from the lurid, deep sea
Streams up the turrets silently –
Up thrones, up long-forgotten bowers
Of sculptur'd ivy and stone flowers,
Up domes, up spires, up kingly halls,
Up fanes, up Babylon-like walls,
Up many a melancholy shrine

Whose entablatures intertwine
The mask, the viol and the vine.   30

There open temples, open graves,
Are on a level with the waves –
But not the riches there that lie
In each idol's diamond eye.
Not the gaily jewell'd dead
Tempt the waters from their bed,
For no ripples curl, alas,
Along that wilderness of glass –
No swellings hint that winds may be
Upon a far-off happier sea.   40
So blend the turrets and shadows there
That all seem pendulous in air,
While from the high towers of the town
Death looks gigantically down.

But lo! A stir is in the air!
The wave! There is a ripple there!
As if the towers had thrown aside,
In slightly sinking, the dull tide –
As if the turret tops had given
A vacuum in the filmy heaven.   50
The waves have now a redder glow –
The very hours are breathing low –
And when, amid no earthly moans,
Down, down that town shall settle hence,
Hell, rising from a thousand thrones,
Shall do it reverence,
And Death to some more happy clime
Shall give his undivided time.

Fairy Land*

Sit down beside me, Isabel,
Here, dearest, where the moonbeam fell
Just now so fairy-like and well.
Now thou art dress'd for paradise!
I am star-stricken with thine eyes!

My soul is lolling on thy sighs!
Thy hair is lifted by the moon
Like flowers by the low breath of June!
Sit down, sit down – how came we here?
Or is it all but a dream, my dear?   10

You know that most enormous flower –
That rose, that what-d'ye-call-it – that hung
Up like a Dog Star* in this bower…
Today (the wind blew, and) it swung
So impudently in my face,
So like a thing alive, you know,
I tore it from its pride of place
And shook it into pieces – so
Be all ingratitude requited.
The winds ran off with it delighted,   20
And, through the opening left, as soon
As she threw off her cloak, yon moon
Has sent a ray down with a tune.

And this ray is a *fairy* ray –
Did you not say so, Isabel?
How fantastically it fell
With a spiral twist and a swell,
And over the wet grass rippled away
With a tinkling like a bell!
In my own country, all the way   30
We can discover a moon ray
Which through some tatter'd curtain pries
Into the darkness of a room
Is by (the very source of gloom)
The motes, and dust, and flies,
On which it trembles and lies
Like joy upon sorrow!
Oh, *when* will come the morrow?
Isabel! Do you not fear
The night and the wonders here?   40
Dim vales, and shadowy floods,
And cloudy-looking woods
Whose forms we can't discover
For the tears that drip all over!

Huge moons – see! – wax and wane
Again... again... again...
Every moment of the night,
Forever changing places!
How they put out the starlight
With the breath from their pale faces!   50

Lo! One is coming down
With its centre on the crown
Of a mountain's eminence!
Down... still down... and down...
Now deep shall be – oh, deep! –
The passion of our sleep!
For that wide circumference
In easy drapery falls
Drowsily over halls,
Over ruin'd walls,   60
Over waterfalls,
(Silent waterfalls!),
O'er the strange woods, o'er the sea –
Alas! – over the sea!

Irene

'Tis now (so sings the soaring moon)
Midnight in the sweet month of June,
When wingèd visions love to lie
Lazily upon beauty's eye –
Or, worse, upon her brow – to dance
In panoply* of old romance,
Till thoughts and locks are left, alas,
A ne'er-to-be-untangled mass.

An influence dewy, drowsy, dim,
Is dripping from that golden rim –   10
Grey towers are mouldering into rest,
Wrapping the fog around their breast.
Looking like Lethe* – see! – the lake
A conscious slumber seems to take,
And would not for the world awake.

The rosemary sleeps upon the grave,
The lily lolls upon the wave,
And million bright pines to and fro
Are rocking lullabies as they go
To the lone oak that reels with bliss,   20
Nodding above the dim abyss.

All beauty sleeps – and lo! where lies
With casement open to the skies,
Irene, with her Destinies!*
Thus hums the moon within her ear:
"O lady sweet! How cam'st thou here?
Strange are thine eyelids – strange thy dress! –
And strange thy glorious length of tress!
Sure thou art come o'er far-off seas,
A wonder to our desert trees!   30
Some gentle wind hath thought it right
To open thy window to the night,
And wanton airs from the treetop
Laughingly through the lattice drop,
And wave this crimson canopy
Like a banner o'er thy dreaming eye!
Lady, awake! Lady, awake!
For the holy Jesus' sake!
For strangely, fearfully in this hall
My tinted shadows rise and fall!"   40

The lady sleeps – the *dead* all sleep,
At least as long as Love doth weep.
Entranc'd, the spirit loves to lie
As long as tears on Memory's eye,
But when a week or two go by,
And the light laughter chokes the sigh,
Indignant from the tomb doth take
Its way to some remember'd lake
Where oft, in life, with friends it went
To bathe in the pure element –   50
And there, from the untrodden grass
Wreathing for its transparent brow
Those flowers that say (ah hear them now!)
To the night winds as they pass,

"Ai! Ai! Alas!... Alas!",
Pores for a moment, ere it go,
On the clear waters there that flow,
Then sinks within (weigh'd down by woe)
Th' uncertain, shadowy heaven below.

* * *

The lady sleeps: oh, may her sleep   60
As it is lasting so be deep –
No icy worms about her creep!
I pray to God that she may lie
For ever with as calm an eye,
That chamber chang'd for one more holy –
That bed for one more melancholy!

Far in the forest, dim and old,
For her may some tall vault unfold,
Against whose sounding door she hath thrown,
In childhood, many an idle stone –   70
Some tomb which oft hath flung its black
And vampire-wingèd panels back,
Flutt'ring triumphant o'er the palls
Of her old family funerals.

A Paean

I

How shall the burial rite be read,
   The solemn song be sung –
The requiem for the loveliest dead
   That ever died so young?

II

Her friends are gazing on her,
   And on her gaudy bier,
And weep – oh, to dishonour
   Dead beauty with a tear!

III

They loved her for her wealth,
    And they hated her for her pride,   10
But she grew in feeble health,
    And they *love* her – that she died.

IV

They tell me (while they speak
    Of her "costly broider'd pall")
That my voice is growing weak,
    That I should not sing at all,

V

Or that my tone should be
    Tun'd to such solemn song
So mournfully – so mournfully
    That the dead may feel no wrong.   20

VI

But she is gone above,
    With young Hope at her side,
And I am drunk with love
    Of the dead who is my bride –

VII

Of the dead… dead who lies
    All perfum'd there
With the death upon her eyes
    And the life upon her hair.

VIII

Thus on the coffin loud and long
    I strike – the murmur sent   30
Through the grey chambers to my song
    Shall be the accompaniment.

IX

Thou died'st in thy life's June,
    But thou didst not die too fair –
Thou didst not die too soon,
    Nor with too calm an air.

X

From more than fiends on earth
    Thy life and love are riven,
To join the untainted mirth
    Of more than thrones in heaven –   40

XI

Therefore to thee this night
    I will no requiem raise,
But waft thee on thy flight
    With a paean of old days.

The Valley Nis*

Far away, far away,
Far away, as far at least
Lies that valley as the day
Down within the golden east…
All things lovely, are not they
Far away, far away?

It is called the Valley Nis,
And a Syriac tale there is
Thereabout which Time hath said
Shall not be interpreted.   10
Something about Satan's dart…
Something about angel wings…
Much about a broken heart…
All about unhappy things –
But "the Valley Nis" at best
Means "the valley of unrest".

Once it smil'd a silent dell
Where the people did not dwell,

Having gone unto the wars –
And the sly, mysterious stars,   20
With a visage full of meaning,
O'er the unguarded flowers were leaning,
Or the sunray dripp'd all red
Through the tulips overhead,
Then grew paler as it fell
On the quiet asphodel.*

Now the *unhappy* shall confess
Nothing there is motionless.
Helen, like thy human eye,
There th' uneasy violets lie;   30
There the reedy grass doth wave
Over the old forgotten grave;
One by one from the treetop
There the eternal dews do drop;
There the vague and dreamy trees
Do roll like seas in northern breeze
Around the stormy Hebrides;
There the gorgeous clouds do fly,
Rustling everlastingly,
Through the terror-stricken sky,   40
Rolling like a waterfall
O'er th' horizon's fiery wall;
There the moon doth shine by night
With a most unsteady light;
There the sun doth reel by day
"Over the hills and far away".

FROM
THE RAVEN AND OTHER POEMS*
(1845)

TO THE NOBLEST OF HER SEX —
TO THE AUTHOR OF
THE DRAMA OF EXILE —
TO MISS ELIZABETH BARRETT BARRETT,*
OF ENGLAND,
I DEDICATE THIS VOLUME,
WITH THE MOST ENTHUSIASTIC ADMIRATION
AND WITH THE MOST SINCERE ESTEEM.
E.A.P.

Preface

These trifles are collected and republished chiefly with a view to their redemption from the many improvements to which they have been subjected while going at random "the rounds of the press". If what I have written is to circulate at all, I am naturally anxious that it should circulate as I wrote it. In defence of my own taste, nevertheless, it is incumbent upon me to say that I think nothing in this volume of much value to the public or very creditable to myself. Events not to be controlled have prevented me from making, at any time, any serious effort in what, under happier circumstances, would have been the field of my choice. With me poetry has been not a purpose, but a passion – and the passions should be held in reverence: they must not – they cannot at will be excited with an eye to the paltry compensations, or the more paltry commendations, of mankind.

E.A.P.

The Raven[*]

Once upon a midnight dreary, while I pondered, weak and weary,
Over many a quaint and curious volume of forgotten lore,
While I nodded, nearly napping, suddenly there came a tapping,
As of someone gently rapping, rapping at my chamber door.
"'Tis some visitor," I muttered, "tapping at my chamber door –
              Only this, and nothing more."

Ah, distinctly I remember it was in the bleak December,
And each separate dying ember wrought its ghost upon the floor.
Eagerly I wished the morrow: vainly I had sought to borrow
From my books surcease of sorrow – sorrow for the lost Lenore,   10
For the rare and radiant maiden whom the angels name Lenore,
              Nameless here for evermore.

And the silken, sad, uncertain rustling of each purple curtain
Thrilled me, filled me with fantastic terrors never felt before –
So that now, to still the beating of my heart, I stood repeating
"'Tis some visitor entreating entrance at my chamber door:
Some late visitor entreating entrance at my chamber door –
              This it is, and nothing more."

Presently my soul grew stronger: hesitating then no longer,
"Sir," said I, "or madam, truly your forgiveness I implore.   20
But the fact is I was napping, and so gently you came rapping,
And so faintly you came tapping, tapping at my chamber door,
That I scarce was sure I heard you" – here I opened wide the door.
              Darkness there, and nothing more.

Deep into that darkness peering, long I stood there wondering, fearing,
Doubting, dreaming dreams no mortal ever dared to dream before –
But the silence was unbroken, and the darkness gave no token,
And the only word there spoken was the whispered word "Lenore!"
This I whispered, and an echo murmured back the word "Lenore!"
              Merely this, and nothing more.   30

Back into the chamber turning, all my soul within me burning,
Soon I heard again a tapping, somewhat louder than before.
"Surely," said I, "surely that is something at my window lattice:
Let me see, then, what thereat is, and this mystery explore –
Let my heart be still a moment and this mystery explore.
           'Tis the wind and nothing more!"

Open here I flung the shutter – when, with many a flirt and flutter,
In there stepped a stately raven of the saintly days of yore.
Not the least obeisance made he, not an instant stopped or stayed he,
But, with mien of lord or lady, perched above my chamber door,   40
Perched upon a bust of Pallas* just above my chamber door –
           Perched and sat, and nothing more.

Then this ebony bird beguiling my sad fancy into smiling
By the grave and stern decorum of the countenance it wore,
"Though thy crest be shorn and shaven, thou," I said, "art sure no craven,
Ghastly grim and ancient raven wandering from the nightly shore –
Tell me what thy lordly name is on the Night's Plutonian shore!"*
           Quoth the raven, "Nevermore."

Much I marvelled this ungainly fowl to hear discourse so plainly,
Though its answer little meaning, little relevancy bore,   50
For we cannot help agreeing that no living human being
Ever yet was blessed with seeing bird above his chamber door –
Bird or beast upon the sculptured bust above his chamber door –
           With such name as "Nevermore".

But the raven, sitting lonely on the placid bust, spoke only
That one word, as if his soul in that one word he did outpour.
Nothing further then he uttered – not a feather then he fluttered –
Till I scarcely more than muttered, "Other friends have flown before…
On the morrow *he* will leave me, as my hopes have flown before."
           Then the bird said, "Nevermore."   60

Startled at the stillness broken by reply so aptly spoken,
"Doubtless," said I, "what it utters is its only stock and store
Caught from some unhappy master whom unmerciful Disaster
Followed fast and followed faster till his songs one burden bore –
Till the dirges of his Hope that melancholy burden bore
           Of "Never – nevermore".

But the raven still beguiling all my sad soul into smiling,
Straight I wheeled a cushioned seat in front of bird and bust and door.
Then, upon the velvet sinking, I betook myself to linking
Fancy unto fancy, thinking what this ominous bird of yore –   70
What this grim, ungainly, ghastly, gaunt and ominous bird of yore –
                              Meant in croaking "Nevermore".

This I sat engaged in guessing, but no syllable expressing
To the fowl, whose fiery eyes now burned into my bosom's core,
This and more I sat divining, with my head at ease reclining
On the cushion's velvet lining that the lamplight gloated o'er –
But whose velvet violet lining with the lamplight gloating o'er
                              She shall press, ah, nevermore!

Then, methought, the air grew denser, perfumed from an unseen censer
Swung by angels whose faint footfalls tinkled on the tufted floor.   80
"Wretch," I cried, "thy God hath lent thee – by these angels he hath sent thee –
Respite, respite and nepenthe* from thy memories of Lenore!
Quaff, oh quaff this kind nepenthe and forget this lost Lenore!"
                              Quoth the raven, "Nevermore."

"Prophet!" said I. "Thing of evil!… Prophet still, if bird or devil!…
Whether Tempter sent, or whether tempest tossed thee here ashore,
Desolate yet all undaunted, on this desert land enchanted,
On this home by Horror haunted – tell me truly, I implore:
Is there – *is* there balm in Gilead?…* Tell me – tell me, I implore!"
                              Quoth the raven, "Nevermore."   90

"Prophet!" said I. "Thing of evil!… Prophet still, if bird or devil!
By that heaven that bends above us, by that God we both adore –
Tell this soul with sorrow laden if, within the distant Aidenn,*
It shall clasp a sainted maiden whom the angels name Lenore –
Clasp a rare and radiant maiden whom the angels name Lenore."
                              Quoth the raven, "Nevermore."

"Be that word our sign of parting, bird or fiend!" I shrieked, upstarting.
"Get thee back into the tempest and the Night's Plutonian shore!
Leave no black plume as a token of that lie thy soul hath spoken!
Leave my loneliness unbroken – quit the bust above my door!   100
Take thy beak from out my heart, and take thy form from off my door!"
                              Quoth the raven, "Nevermore."

And the raven, never flitting, still is sitting, still is sitting,
On the pallid bust of Pallas just above my chamber door.
And his eyes have all the seeming of a demon's that is dreaming,
And the lamplight o'er him streaming throws his shadow on the floor –
And my soul from out that shadow that lies floating on the floor
                    Shall be lifted... nevermore!

The Valley of Unrest*

Once it smiled a silent dell
Where the people did not dwell:
They had gone unto the wars,
Trusting to the mild-eyed stars,
Nightly, from their azure towers,
To keep watch above the flowers,
In the midst of which all day
The red sunlight lazily lay.
Now each visitor shall confess
The sad valley's restlessness.   10
Nothing there is motionless –
Nothing save the airs that brood
Over the magic solitude.
Ah, by no wind are stirred those trees
That palpitate like the chill seas
Around the misty Hebrides!
Ah, by no wind those clouds are driven
That rustle through the unquiet heaven
Uneasily, from morn till even,
Over the violets there that lie   20
In myriad types of the human eye –
Over the lilies there that wave
And weep above a nameless grave!
They wave: from out their fragrant tops
Eternal dews come down in drops.
They weep: from off their delicate stems
Perennial tears descend in gems.

Bridal Ballad

The ring is on my hand,
   And the wreath is on my brow;
Satins and jewels grand
Are all at my command,
   And I am happy now.

And my lord, he loves me well –
   But, when first he breathed his vow,
I felt my bosom swell,
For the words rang as a knell,
And the voice seemed *his* who fell   10
In the battle down the dell,
   And who is happy now.

But he spoke to reassure me,
   And he kissed my pallid brow,
While a reverie came o'er me,
And to the churchyard bore me,
And I sighed to him before me,
Thinking him dead D'Elormie,
   "Oh, I am happy now!"

And thus the words were spoken,   20
   And this the plighted vow,
And, though my faith be broken,
And, though my heart be broken,
Behold the golden token
   That *proves* me happy now!

Would God I could awaken!
   For I dream I know not how,
And my soul is sorely shaken
Lest an evil step be taken –
Lest the dead who is forsaken   30
   May not be happy now.

The Sleeper*

At midnight, in the month of June,
I stand beneath the mystic moon.
An opiate vapour, dewy, dim,
Exhales from out her golden rim,
And, softly dripping drop by drop
Upon the quiet mountaintop,
Steals drowsily and musically
Into the universal valley.
The rosemary nods upon the grave;
The lily lolls upon the wave;   10
Wrapping the fog about its breast,
The ruin moulders into rest;
Looking like Lethe* – see! – the lake
A conscious slumber seems to take,
And would not, for the world, awake.
All beauty sleeps – and lo! where lies
(Her casement open to the skies)
Irene, with her Destinies!*

Oh, lady bright! Can it be right,
This window open to the night?   20
The wanton airs, from the treetop,
Laughingly through the lattice drop –
The bodiless airs, a wizard rout,*
Flit through thy chamber in and out,
And wave the curtain canopy
So fitfully, so fearfully,
Above the closed and fringed lid
'Neath which thy slumb'ring soul lies hid,
That, o'er the floor and down the wall,
Like ghosts the shadows rise and fall!   30
Oh, lady dear, hast thou no fear?
Why and what art thou dreaming here?
Sure thou art come o'er far-off seas,
A wonder to these garden trees!
Strange is thy pallor – strange thy dress!
Strange, above all, thy length of tress,
And this all solemn silentness!

The lady sleeps! Oh, may her sleep,
Which is enduring, so be deep!
Heaven have her in its sacred keep!   40
This chamber changed for one more holy,
This bed for one more melancholy,
I pray to God that she may lie
For ever with unopened eye,
While the dim sheeted ghosts go by!

My love, she sleeps! Oh, may her sleep,
As it is lasting, so be deep!
Soft may the worms about her creep!
Far in the forest, dim and old,
For her may some tall vault unfold –   50
Some vault that oft hath flung its black
And wingèd panels fluttering back,
Triumphant, o'er the crested palls
Of her grand family funerals –
Some sepulchre, remote, alone,
Against whose portal she hath thrown,
In childhood, many an idle stone –
Some tomb from out whose sounding door
She ne'er shall force an echo more,
Thrilling to think, poor child of sin,   60
It was the dead who groaned within!

The Coliseum

Type* of the antique Rome! Rich reliquary
Of lofty contemplation left to Time
By buried centuries of pomp and power!
At length – at length, after so many days
Of weary pilgrimage and burning thirst
(Thirst for the springs of lore that in thee lie),
I kneel, an altered and an humble man,
Amid thy shadows, and so drink within
My very soul thy grandeur, gloom and glory!

Vastness, and age, and memories of Eld!*   10
Silence, and desolation, and dim night!

I feel ye now – I feel ye in your strength,
O spells more sure than e'er Judaean king
Taught in the gardens of Gethsemane!*
O charms more potent than the rapt Chaldee
Ever drew down from out the quiet stars!*

Here, where a hero fell, a column falls!
Here, where the mimic eagle glared in gold,
A midnight vigil holds the swarthy bat!
Here, where the dames of Rome their gilded hair   20
Waved to the wind, now wave the reed and thistle!
Here, where on golden throne the monarch lolled,
Glides, spectre-like, unto his marble home,
Lit by the wan light of the hornèd moon,
The swift and silent lizard of the stones!

But stay! These walls, these ivy-clad arcades,
These mouldering plinths, these sad and blackened shafts,
These vague entablatures, this crumbling frieze,
These shattered cornices, this wreck, this ruin,
These stones, alas, these grey stones – are they all,   30
All of the famed and the colossal left
By the corrosive Hours to Fate and me?

"Not all," the Echoes answer me. "Not all!
Prophetic sounds and loud arise for ever
From us, and from all Ruin, unto the wise,
As melody from Memnon to the Sun.*
We rule the hearts of mightiest men – we rule
With a despotic sway all giant minds.
We are not impotent – we pallid stones.
Not all our power is gone, not all our fame,   40
Not all the magic of our high renown,
Not all the wonder that encircles us,
Not all the mysteries that in us lie –
Not all the memories that hang upon
And cling around about us as a garment,
Clothing us in a robe of more than glory."

Lenore*

Ah, broken is the golden bowl – the spirit flown for ever!
Let the bell toll – a saintly soul floats on the Stygian river –
And, Guy De Vere, hast *thou* no tear? Weep now or nevermore!
See! On yon drear and rigid bier low lies thy love, Lenore!
Come! Let the burial rite be read, the funeral song be sung!
An anthem for the queenliest dead that ever died so young –
A dirge for her, the doubly dead, in that she died so young.

"Wretches! Ye loved her for her wealth and hated her for her pride,
And when she fell in feeble health, ye blessed her – that she died!
How *shall* the ritual then be read, the requiem how be sung   10
By you, by yours, the evil eye – by yours, the slanderous tongue
That did to death the innocence that died, and died so young?"

*Peccavimus** – but rave not thus, and let a Sabbath song
Go up to God so solemnly the dead may feel no wrong!
The sweet Lenore hath "gone before"* with Hope, that flew beside,
Leaving thee wild for the dear child that should have been thy bride –
For her, the fair and debonair, that now so lowly lies,
The life upon her yellow hair, but not within her eyes...
The life still there, upon her hair – the death upon her eyes.

"Avaunt! Tonight my heart is light. No dirge will I upraise,   20
But waft the angel on her flight with a paean of old days!
Let *no* bell toll – lest her sweet soul, amid its hallowed mirth,
Should catch the note, as it doth float up from the damnèd Earth.
To friends above, from fiends below, the indignant ghost is riven –
From Hell unto a high estate far up within the heaven,
From grief and groan, to a golden throne, beside the King of Heaven."

Catholic Hymn

At morn, at noon, at twilight dim,
Maria, thou hast heard my hymn!
In joy and woe, in good and ill,
Mother of God, be with me still!
When the Hours flew brightly by,
And not a cloud obscured the sky,
My soul, lest it should truant be,

Thy grace did guide to thine and thee.
Now, when storms of Fate o'ercast
Darkly my present and my past,   10
Let my future radiant shine
With sweet hopes of thee and thine!

Israfel*

In heaven a spirit doth dwell
   "Whose heartstrings are a lute":
None sing so wildly well
As the angel Israfel –
And the giddy stars (so legends tell),
Ceasing their hymns, attend the spell
   Of his voice, all mute.

Tottering above
   In her highest noon,
   The enamoured moon   10
Blushes with love –
      While, to listen, the red levin*
      (With the rapid Pleiads, even,
      Which were seven)*
      Pauses in heaven.

And they say (the starry choir
   And the other listening things)
That Israfeli's fire
Is owing to that lyre
   By which he sits and sings –   20
The trembling living wire
   Of those unusual strings.

But the skies that angel trod,
   Where deep thoughts are a duty,
Where Love's a grown-up god,
      Where the houri glances are
      Imbued with all the beauty
      Which we worship in a star.

Therefore, thou art not wrong,
    Israfeli, who despisest   30
An unimpassioned song:
To thee the laurels belong,
    Best bard, because the wisest!
Merrily live, and long!

The ecstasies above
    With thy burning measures suit –
Thy grief, thy joy, thy hate, thy love,
    With the fervour of thy lute...
    Well may the stars be mute!

Yes, heaven is thine – but this   40
    Is a world of sweets and sours,
    Our flowers are merely... flowers,
And the shadow of thy perfect bliss
    Is the sunshine of ours.

If I could dwell
Where Israfel
    Hath dwelt, and he where I,
He might not sing so wildly well
    A mortal melody,
While a bolder note than this might swell   50
    From my lyre within the sky.

Dream Land

By a route obscure and lonely,
Haunted by ill angels only,
Where an eidolon* named NIGHT
On a black throne reigns upright,
I have reached these lands but newly
From an ultimate, dim Thule* –
From a wild, weird clime that lieth, sublime,
        Out of SPACE – out of TIME.

Bottomless vales and boundless floods,
And chasms, and caves, and Titan woods,*   10
With forms that no man can discover

For the dews that drip all over;*
Mountains toppling evermore
Into seas without a shore;
Seas that restlessly aspire,
Surging, unto skies of fire;
Lakes that endlessly outspread
Their lone waters, lone and dead,
Their still waters, still and chilly,
With the snows of the lolling lily.   20

By the lakes that thus outspread
Their lone waters, lone and dead,
Their sad waters, sad and chilly,
With the snows of the lolling lily
By the mountains, near the river
Murmuring lowly, murmuring ever,
By the grey woods, by the swamp
Where the toad and the newt encamp,
By the dismal tarns* and pools
Where dwell the ghouls,   30
By each spot the most unholy,
In each nook most melancholy –
There the traveller meets aghast
Sheeted Memories of the Past,
Shrouded forms that start and sigh
As they pass the wanderer by,
White-robed forms of friends long given,
In agony, to the earth, and heaven.

For the heart whose woes are legion
'Tis a peaceful, soothing region –   40
For the spirit that walks in shadow
'Tis... oh, 'tis an Eldorado!
But the traveller, travelling through it,
May not – dare not openly view it.
Never its mysteries are exposed
To the weak human eye unclosed:
So wills its king, who hath forbid
The uplifting of the fringèd lid.
And thus the sad soul that here passes
Beholds it but through darkened glasses.   50

By a route obscure and lonely,
Haunted by ill angels only,
Where an eidolon named NIGHT
On a black throne reigns upright,
I have wandered home but newly
From this ultimate, dim Thule.

Sonnet – To Zante*

Fair isle, that from the fairest of all flowers
Thy gentlest of all gentle names dost take!
How many memories of what radiant hours
At sight of thee and thine at once awake!
How many scenes of what departed bliss!
How many thoughts of what entombèd hopes!
How many visions of a maiden that is
No more – no more upon thy verdant slopes!
No more! Alas, that magical, sad sound
Transforming all! Thy charms shall please *no more* –   10
Thy memory *no more*! Accursèd ground
Henceforth I hold thy flower-enamelled shore,
O hyacinthine isle! O purple Zante!
"Isola d'oro! Fior di Levante!"

The City in the Sea*

Lo! Death has reared himself a throne
In a strange city lying alone
Far down within the dim west,
Where the good and the bad and the worst and the best
Have gone to their eternal rest.
There shrines and palaces and towers
(Time-eaten towers that tremble not!)
Resemble nothing that is ours.
Around, by lifting winds forgot,
Resignedly beneath the sky   10
The melancholy waters lie.

No rays from the holy heaven come down
On the long night-time of that town,
But light from out the lurid sea
Streams up the turrets silently,
Gleams up the pinnacles far and free –
Up domes, up spires, up kingly halls,
Up fanes, up Babylon-like walls,
Up shadowy, long-forgotten bowers
Of sculptured ivy and stone flowers,   20
Up many and many a marvellous shrine
Whose wreathèd friezes intertwine
The viol, the violet and the vine.

Resignedly beneath the sky
The melancholy waters lie.
So blend the turrets and shadows there
That all seem pendulous in air,
While from a proud tower in the town
Death looks gigantically down.

There open fanes and gaping graves   30
Yawn level with the luminous waves,
But not the riches there that lie
In each idol's diamond eye,
Not the gaily jewelled dead
Tempt the waters from their bed,
For no ripples curl, alas,
Along that wilderness of glass,
No swellings tell that winds may be
Upon some far-off, happier sea,
No heavings hint that winds have been   40
On seas less hideously serene.

But lo, a stir is in the air!
The wave – there is a movement there!
As if the towers had thrown aside,
In slightly sinking, the dull tide –
As if their tops had feebly given
A void within the filmy heaven.
The waves have now a redder glow –
The hours are breathing faint and low –

And when, amid no earthly moans,   50
Down, down that town shall settle hence,
Hell, rising from a thousand thrones,
Shall do it reverence.

To One in Paradise

Thou wast all that to me, love,
    For which my soul did pine –
A green isle in the sea, love,
    A fountain and a shrine,
All wreathed with fairy fruits and flowers,
    And all the flowers were mine.

Ah, dream too bright to last!
    Ah, starry hope that didst arise
But to be overcast!
    A voice from out the future cries   10
"On! On!" – but o'er the past
    (Dim gulf!) my spirit hovering lies
Mute, motionless, aghast!

For alas, alas, with me
    The light of life is o'er!
    No more, no more, no more
(Such language holds the solemn sea
    To the sands upon the shore)
Shall bloom the thunder-blasted tree,
    Or the stricken eagle soar!   20

And all my days are trances,
    And all my nightly dreams
Are where thy dark eye glances,
    And where thy footstep gleams –
In what ethereal dances,
    By what eternal streams.

Eulalie – A Song

I dwelt alone
In a world of moan,
And my soul was a stagnant tide,
Till the fair and gentle Eulalie became my blushing bride –
Till the yellow-haired young Eulalie became my smiling bride.

Ah, less, less bright
The stars of the night
Than the eyes of the radiant girl!
And never a flake
That the vapour can make   10
With the moon tints of purple and pearl
Can vie with the modest Eulalie's most unregarded curl –
Can compare with the bright-eyed Eulalie's most humble and
                                          [careless curl.

Now Doubt, now Pain
Come never again,
For her soul gives me sigh for sigh,
And all day long
Shines, bright and strong,
Astarte within the sky,*
While ever to her dear Eulalie upturns her matron eye –   20
While ever to her young Eulalie upturns her violet eye.

To F—s S. O—d*

Thou wouldst be loved? Then let thy heart
    From its present pathway part not!
Being everything which now thou art,
    Be nothing which thou art not.
So with the world thy gentle ways,
    Thy grace, thy more than beauty,
Shall be an endless theme of praise,
    And love… a simple duty.

To F—*

Beloved! Amid the earnest woes
   That crowd around my earthly path
(Drear path, alas, where grows
Not even one lonely rose),
   My soul at least a solace hath
In dreams of thee – and therein knows
An Eden of bland repose.

And thus thy memory is to me
   Like some enchanted far-off isle
In some tumultuous sea –   10
Some ocean throbbing far and free
   With storms, but where meanwhile
Serenest skies continually
   Just o'er that one bright island smile.

Sonnet – Silence

There are some qualities, some incorporate* things,
   That have a double life, which thus is made
A type* of that twin entity which springs
   From matter and light, evinced in solid and shade.
There is a twofold *Silence*: sea and shore –
   Body and soul. One dwells in lonely places,
   Newly with grass o'ergrown; some solemn graces,
Some human memories and tearful lore,
Render him terrorless: his name's "No More".
He is the corporate* Silence: dread him not!   10
   No power hath he of evil in himself –
But should some urgent fate (untimely lot!)
   Bring thee to meet his shadow (nameless elf,
That haunteth the lone regions where hath trod
No foot of man), commend thyself to God!

The Conqueror Worm

Lo! 'Tis a gala night
    Within the lonesome latter years!
An angel throng, bewinged, bedight
    In veils, and drowned in tears,
Sit in a theatre, to see
    A play of hopes and fears,
While the orchestra breathes fitfully
    The music of the spheres.

Mimes, in the form of God on high,
    Mutter and mumble low,   10
And hither and thither fly –
    Mere puppets they, who come and go
At bidding of vast formless things
    That shift the scenery to and fro,
Flapping from out their condor* wings
    Invisible woe!

That motley drama, oh, be sure,
    It shall not be forgot!
With its phantom chased for evermore
    By a crowd that seize it not,   20
Through a circle that ever returneth in
    To the self-same spot,
And much of madness, and more of sin,
    And horror the soul of the plot.

But see, amid the mimic rout*
    A crawling shape intrude!
A blood-red thing that writhes from out
    The scenic solitude!
It writhes!... It writhes!... With mortal pangs
    The mimes become its food,   30
And the angels sob at vermin fangs
    In human gore imbued.

Out, out are the lights – out all!
    And, over each quivering form,
The curtain, a funeral pall,
    Comes down with the rush of a storm,
And the angels, all pallid and wan,

Uprising, unveiling, affirm
That the play is the tragedy *Man*,
    And its hero the Conqueror Worm.   40

The Haunted Place

In the greenest of our valleys,
    By good angels tenanted,
Once a fair and stately palace –
    Radiant palace – reared its head.
In the monarch Thought's dominion,
    It stood there!
Never seraph spread a pinion
    Over fabric half so fair!

Banners yellow, glorious, golden,
    On its roof did float and flow   10
(This – all this – was in the olden
    Time long ago),
And every gentle air that dallied,
    In that sweet day,
Along the ramparts plumed and pallid
    A wingèd odour went away.

Wanderers in that happy valley,
    Through two luminous windows, saw
Spirits moving musically
    To a lute's well-tunèd law   20
Round about a throne where, sitting
    (Porphyrogene!)*
In state his glory well befitting,
    The ruler of the realm was seen.

And all with pearl and ruby glowing
    Was the fair palace door,
Through which came flowing, flowing, flowing,
    And sparkling evermore,
A troop of echoes, whose sweet duty
    Was but to sing,   30
In voices of surpassing beauty,
    The wit and wisdom of their king.

But evil things, in robes of sorrow,
    Assailed the monarch's high estate
(Ah, let us mourn – for never morrow*
    Shall dawn upon him desolate!),
And round about his home the glory
    That blushed and bloomed
Is but a dim-remembered story
    Of the old time entombed.   40

And travellers now, within that valley,
    Through the red-litten windows see
Vast forms, that move fantastically
    To a discordant melody,
While, like a ghastly, rapid river,
    Through the pale door
A hideous throng rush out forever
    And laugh – but smile no more.

UNCOLLECTED POEMS

Poetry*

Last night, with many cares and toils oppress'd,
Weary, I laid me on a couch to rest...

[1824]

Oh, Tempora! Oh, Mores!*

Oh, times! Oh, manners! It is my opinion
That you are changing sadly your dominion –
I mean the reign of manners hath long ceased,
For men have none at all, or bad at least.
And as for times, although 'tis said by many
The "good old times" were far the worst of any,
Of which sound doctrine I believe each tittle,
Yet still I think these worse than them a little.

I've been a-thinking – isn't that the phrase?
I like your Yankee words and Yankee ways –   10
I've been a thinking whether it were best
To take things seriously or all in jest;
Whether with grim Heraclitus of yore
To weep, as he did, till his eyes were sore,
Or rather laugh with him, that queer philosopher,
Democritus of Thrace,* who used to toss over
The page of life and grin at the dog ears,
As though he'd say, "Why, who the devil cares?"

This is a question which, oh Heaven, withdraw
The luckless query from a Member's claw!   20
Instead of two sides, Bob has nearly eight,
Each fit to furnish forth four hours' debate.
What shall be done? I'll lay it on the table,

And take the matter up when I'm more able,
And in the mean time, to prevent all bother,
I'll neither laugh with one or cry with t'other,
Nor deal in flattery or aspersions foul,
But, taking one by each hand, merely growl.

Ah growl, say you, my friend – and pray, at what?
Why, really, sir, I almost had forgot –   30
But damn it, sir, I deem it a disgrace
That things should stare us boldly in the face,
And daily strut the street with bows and scrapes,
Who would be men by imitating apes.
I beg your pardon, reader, for the oath:
The monkey's made me swear, though something loath.
I'm apt to be discursive in my style,
But pray be patient: yet a little while
Will change me, and, as politicians do,
I'll mend my manners and my measures too.   40

Of all the cities – and I've seen no few,
For I have travelled, friend, as well as you –
I don't remember one, upon my soul,
But take it generally, upon the whole
(As Members say they like their logic taken,
Because divided it may chance be shaken),
So pat, agreeable and vastly proper
As this for a neat, frisky counter-hopper;*
Here he may revel to his heart's content,
Flounce like a fish in his own element,   50
Toss back his fine curls from his forehead fair
And hop o'er counters with a Vestris air,*
Complete at night what he began a.m.,
And, having cheated ladies, dance with them;
For at a ball what fair one can escape
The pretty little hand that sold her tape,
Or who so cold, so callous to refuse
The youth who cut the ribbon for her shoes!

One of these fish, par excellence the beau,
God help me, it has been my lot to know –   60
At least by sight, for I'm a timid man,

And always keep from laughing when I can.
But speak to him, he'll make you such grimace...
Lord! To be grave exceeds the power of face.*
The hearts of all the ladies are with him –
Their bright eyes on his Tom and Jerry brim*
And dovetailed coat, obtained at cost: while then,
Those eyes won't turn on anything like men.

His very voice is musical delight;
His form, once seen, becomes a part of sight –   70
In short, his shirt collar, his look, his tone is
The *beau idéal** fancied for Adonis.
Philosophers have often held dispute
As to the seat of thought in man and brute –
For that the power of thought attend the latter
My friend, the beau, hath made a settled matter,
And spite all dogmas current in all ages,
One settled fact is better than ten sages.

For he does think, although I'm oft in doubt
If I can tell exactly what about.   80
Ah, yes! His little foot and ankle trim –
'Tis there the seat of reason lies in him!
A wise philosopher would shake his head –
He then, of course, must shake his foot instead.
At me in vengeance shall that foot be shaken
(Another proof of thought, I'm not mistaken)
Because to his cat's eyes I hold a glass
And let him see himself a proper ass?
I think he'll take this likeness to himself,
But if he won't *he shall*, the stupid elf,   90
And lest the guessing throw the fool in fits,
I close the portrait with the name of *Pitts*.*

[1825?]

To Margaret*

Who hath seduced thee to this foul revolt	} Milton, *Par. Lost*, Bk. I
From the pure well of Beauty undefiled?	} Somebody
So banished from true wisdom to prefer	}
Such squalid wit to honourable rhyme?	} Cowper's *Task*, Book I
To write? To scribble? Nonsense and no more?	} Shakespeare
I will not write upon this argument:	} do. *Troilus & Cressida*
To write is human – not to write divine.*	} Pope, *Essay on Man*

[1827]

'When Wit and Wine and Friends Have Met'*

When wit and wine and friends have met,
And laughter crowns the festive hour
In vain I struggle to forget,
Still does my heart confess thy power,
    And fondly turn to thee!

But Octavia, do not strive to rob
My heart of all that soothes its pain,
The mournful hope that every throb
    Will make it break for thee!

[1827]

'From Childhood's Hour I Have Not Been'*

From childhood's hour I have not been
As others were; I have not seen
As others saw; I could not bring
My passions from a common spring.
From the same source I have not taken
My sorrow – I could not awaken
My heart to joy at the same tone –
And all I loved, *I* loved alone.
Then, in my childhood, in the dawn
Of a most stormy life, was drawn   10
From every depth of good and ill
The mystery which binds me still:

From the torrent, or the fountain,
From the red cliff of the mountain,
From the sun that round me rolled
In its autumn tint of gold,
From the lightning in the sky
As it passed me flying by,
From the thunder and the storm,
And the cloud that took the form   20
(When the rest of heaven was blue)
Of a demon in my view.

                                    [*c*.1829]

'It Was My Choice or Chance or Curse'*

It was my choice or chance or curse
To adopt the cause for better or worse,
And with my worldly goods and wit
And soul and body worship it.

                                    [1829]

'Elizabeth, It Surely Is Most Fit'*

Elizabeth, it surely is most fit
(Logic and common usage so commanding)
In thy own book that *first* thy name be writ,
Zeno* and other sages notwithstanding –
And *I* have other reasons for so doing
Besides my innate love of contradiction.
Each poet (*if* a poet) in pursuing
The Muses through their bowers of Truth or Fiction,
Has studied very little of his part,
Read nothing, written less – in short's a fool
Endued with neither soul, nor sense, nor art,   10
Being ignorant of one important rule
Employed in even the theses of the school
Called... I forget the heathenish Greek name
(Called anything, its meaning is the same):
"Always write *first* things uppermost in the heart."

                                    [*c*.1829]

'Elizabeth, It Is in Vain You Say'*

Elizabeth, it is in vain you say
"Love not" – thou sayest it in so sweet a way:
In vain those words from thee or L.E.L.*
Zantippe's talents* had enforced so well:
Ah, if that language from thy heart arise,
Breathe it less gently forth, and veil thine eyes!
Endymion, recollect, when Luna tried
To cure his love, was cured of all beside:
His folly, pride and passion – for he died.*

[1829?]

'As for Locke, He Is All in My Eye'*

As for Locke, he is all in my eye –
May the D—l right soon for his soul call.
He never was known to lie –
In bed at a reveille "roll-call".

John Locke* was a notable name;
Joe Locke is a greater – in short,
The former was well known to fame,
But the latter's well known "to report".

[1830–31]

Serenade*

So sweet the hour, so calm the time,
I feel it more than half a crime
When Nature sleeps and stars are mute,
To mar the silence ev'n with lute.
At rest on ocean's brilliant dyes
An image of Elysium lies:
Seven Pleiades* entranced in heaven
Form in the deep another seven;
Endymion, nodding from above,
Sees in the sea a second love;*   10
Within the valleys dim and brown,
And on the spectral mountain's crown

The wearied light is lying down;
And earth and stars and sea and sky
Are redolent of sleep, as I
Am redolent of thee and thine
Enthralling love, my Adeline.
But list, oh, list!... So soft and low
Thy lover's voice tonight shall flow
That, scarce awake, thy soul shall deem   20
My words the music of a dream.
Thus, while no single sound too rude
Upon thy slumber shall intrude,
Our thoughts, our souls – O God above! –
In every deed shall mingle, love.

[1833]

To —*

Sleep on, sleep on, another hour –
    I would not break so calm a sleep
To wake to sunshine and to show'r,
    To smile and weep.

Sleep on, sleep on, like sculptured thing,
    Majestic, beautiful art thou;
Sure seraph fans thee with his wing
    And fans thy brow.

We would not deem thee child of earth –
    For, oh, angelic is thy form! –   10
But that in heav'n thou hadst thy birth,
    Where comes no storm

To mar the bright, the perfect flow'r,
    But all is beautiful and still,
And golden sands proclaim the hour
    Which brings no ill.

Sleep on, sleep on, some fairy dream
    Perchance is woven in thy sleep –
But oh, thy spirit, calm, serene,
    Must wake to weep.   20

[1833]

Fanny*

The dying swan by northern lakes
   Sings its wild death song, sweet and clear,
And as the solemn music breaks
   O'er hill and glen dissolves in air –
Thus musical thy soft voice came,
Thus trembled on thy tongue my name.

Like sunburst* through the ebon cloud
   Which veils the solemn midnight sky,
Piercing cold evening's sable shroud,
   Thus came the first glance of that eye –   10
But like the adamantine rock,
My spirit met and braved the shock.

Let memory the boy recall
   Who laid his heart upon thy shrine:
When far away his footsteps fall,
   Think that he deem'd thy charms divine –
A victim on love's altar slain
By witching eyes which looked disdain.

                               [1833]

Epigram for Wall Street*

I'll tell you a plan for gaining wealth,
   Better than banking, trade or leases:
Take a banknote and fold it up,
   And then you will find your money in *creases*!
This wonderful plan, without danger or loss,
Keeps your cash in your hands, where nothing can trouble it –
And every time that you fold it across,
   'Tis as plain as the light of the day that you *double* it!

                               [1845]

Impromptu – To Kate Carol*

When from your gems of thought I turn
To those pure orbs, your heart to learn,
I scarce know which to prize most high –
The bright *i-dea*, or bright *dear-eye*.

                               [1845]

To —*

I would not lord it o'er thy heart –
    Alas, I cannot rule my own! –
Nor would I rob one loyal thought
    From him who there should reign alone.
We both have found a lifelong love,
Wherein our weary souls may rest,
Yet may we not, my gentle friend,
Be each to each the *second best*?

A love which shall be passion-free,
    Fondness as pure as it is sweet,   10
A bond where all the dearest ties
    Of brother, friend and *cousin* meet:
Such is the union I would frame,
    That thus we might be doubly blessed,
With Love to rule our hearts supreme
    And Friendship to be *second best*.

                  [1845]

The Divine Right of Kings*

The only king by right divine
Is Ellen King, and, were she mine,
I'd strive for liberty no more,
But hug the glorious chains I wore.

Her bosom is an ivory throne
Where tyrant virtue reigns alone –
No subject vice dare interfere
To check the power that governs here.

Oh, would she deign to rule my fate,
I'd worship kings and kingly state,   10
And hold this maxim all life long:
The King – *my* King – can do no wrong.

                  [1845]

Stanzas*

Lady! I would that verse of mine
    Could fling, all lavishly and free,
Prophetic tones from every line
    Of health, joy, peace, in store for thee!

Thine should be length of happy days,
    Enduring joys and fleeting cares,
Virtues that challenge envy's praise,
    By rivals loved and mourned by heirs;

Thy life's free course should ever roam
    Beyond this bounded earthly clime –   10
No billow breaking into foam
    Upon the rock-girt shore of Time;

The gladness of a gentle heart,
    Pure as the wishes breathed in prayer,
Which has in others' joys a part,
    While in its own all others share;

The fullness of a cultured mind,
    Stored with the wealth of bard and sage,
Which Error's glitter cannot blind,
    Lustrous in youth, undimmed in age;   20

The grandeur of a guileless soul,
    With wisdom, virtue, feeling fraught,
Gliding serenely to its goal
    Beneath the eternal sky of Thought –

These should be thine to guard and shield,
    And this the life thy spirit live,
Blessed with all bliss that earth can yield,
    Bright with all hopes that Heaven can give.

[1845]

'For Her These Lines Are Penned...'*

Valentine's Eve, 1846

For her these lines are penned whose luminous eyes,
Bright and expressive as the stars of Leda,*
Shall find her own sweet name that, nestling, lies
Upon this page, enwrapped from every reader.
Search narrowly these words, which hold a treasure
Divine – a talisman, an amulet
That must be worn *at heart*. Search well the measure,
The words, the letters themselves. Do not forget
The smallest point, or you may lose your labour.
And yet there is in this no Gordian knot*   10
Which one might not undo without a sabre
If one could merely understand the plot.
Upon the open page on which are peering
Such sweet eyes now, there lies, I say, *perdu*,*
A musical name oft uttered in the hearing
Of poets by poets – for the name is a poet's too.
In common sequence set the letters lying,
Compose a sound delighting all to hear –
Ah, this you'd have no trouble in descrying
Were you not something of a dunce, my dear –
And now I leave these riddles to their seer.   20

E.A.P.

[1846]

'Deep in Earth My Love Is Lying'*

Deep in earth my love is lying,
And I must weep alone.

[1847]

To Miss Louise Olivia Hunter*

Though I turn, I fly not –
  I cannot depart:
I would try, but try not
  To release my heart.

And my hopes are dying
While, on dreams relying,
    I am spelled by art.

Thus the bright snake coiling
    'Neath the forest tree
Wins the bird, beguiling,   10
    To come down and see:
Like that bird the lover
Round his fate will hover,
Till the blow is over
    And he sinks – like me.

                    [1847]

To M.L. S—*

Of all who hail thy presence as the morning;
Of all to whom thine absence is the night,
The blotting utterly from out high heaven
The sacred sun; of all who, weeping, bless thee
Hourly for hope, for life – ah, above all,
For the resurrection of deep-buried faith
In Truth, in Virtue, in Humanity;
Of all who, on Despair's unhallowed bed
Lying down to die, have suddenly arisen
At thy soft-murmured words, "Let there be light!" –   10
At the soft-murmured words that were fulfilled
In the seraphic glancing of thine eyes;
Of all who owe thee most, whose gratitude
Nearest resembles worship – oh, remember
The truest, the most fervently devoted,
And think that these weak lines are written by him,
By him who, as he pens them, thrills to think
His spirit is communing with an angel's.

                    [1847]

To —*

Not long ago, the writer of these lines,
In the mad pride of intellectuality,
Maintained the "power of words"* – denied that ever
A thought arose within the human brain
Beyond the utterance of the human tongue.
And now, as if in mockery of that boast,
Two words – two foreign, soft disyllables,*
Italian tones made only to be murmured
By angels dreaming in the moonlit "dew
That hangs like chains of pearl on Hermon Hill"* –   10
Have stirred from out the abysses of his heart
Unthought-like thoughts that are the souls of thought,
Richer, far wilder, far diviner visions*
Than even the seraph harper, Israfel,
Who has "the sweetest voice of all God's creatures",*
Could hope to utter. And I – my spells are broken!*
The pen falls powerless from my shivering hand.
With thy dear name as text, though bidden by thee,
I cannot write, I cannot speak or think* –
Alas, I cannot feel – for 'tis not feeling,   20
This standing motionless upon the golden
Threshold of the wide-open gate of dreams,*
Gazing, entranced, adown the gorgeous vista,
And thrilling as I see upon the right,
Upon the left, and all the way along
Amid empurpled vapours,* far away
To where the prospect terminates… *thee only*.
                         [1847–48]

Ulalume – A Ballad*

The skies, they were ashen and sober;
    The leaves, they were crispèd and sere –
    The leaves, they were withering and sere;
It was night, in the lonesome October
    Of my most immemorial year;
It was hard by the dim lake of Auber,
    In the misty mid region of Weir –

It was down by the dank tarn* of Auber,
In the ghoul-haunted woodland of Weir.

Here once, through an alley titanic*   10
Of cypress, I roamed with my soul –
Of cypress, with Psyche, my soul.
These were days when my heart was volcanic
As the scoriac* rivers that roll,
As the lavas that restlessly roll
Their sulphurous currents down Yaanek,
In the ultimate climes of the Pole –
That groan as they roll down Mount Yaanek
In the realms of the Boreal Pole.

Our talk had been serious and sober,   20
But our thoughts, they were palsied and sere –
Our memories were treacherous and sere;
For we knew not the month was October,
And we marked not the night of the year
(Ah, night of all nights in the year!);*
We noted not the dim lake of Auber
(Though once we had journeyed down here);
We remembered not the dank tarn of Auber,
Nor the ghoul-haunted woodland of Weir.

And now, as the night was senescent*   30
And star dials pointed to morn –
As the star dials hinted of morn –
At the end of our path a liquescent
And nebulous lustre was born,
Out of which a miraculous crescent
Arose with a duplicate horn –
Astarte's bediamonded crescent,*
Distinct with its duplicate horn.

And I said: "She is warmer than Dian;*
She rolls through an ether of sighs –   40
She revels in a region of sighs.
She has seen that the tears are not dry on
These cheeks where the worm never dies,
And has come past the stars of the Lion,*
To point us the path to the skies,

To the Lethean* peace of the skies –
Come up, in despite of the Lion,
   To shine on us with her bright eyes –
Come up, through the lair of the Lion,
   With love in her luminous eyes."   50

But Psyche, uplifting her finger,
   Said: "Sadly this star I mistrust –
   Her pallor I strangely mistrust.
Oh, hasten!... All, let us not linger!
   Oh, fly!... Let us fly – for we must!"
In terror she spoke; letting sink her
   Wings till they trailed in the dust,
In agony sobbed; letting sink her
   Plumes till they trailed in the dust –
   Till they sorrowfully trailed in the dust.   60

I replied: "This is nothing but dreaming.
   Let us on, by this tremulous light!
   Let us bathe in this crystalline light!
Its Sibyllic* splendour is beaming
   With Hope and in Beauty tonight...
   See!... It flickers up the sky through the night!
Ah, we safely may trust to its gleaming,
   And be sure it will lead us aright –
We surely may trust to a gleaming
   That cannot but guide us aright,   70
   Since it flickers up to heaven through the night."

Thus I pacified Psyche and kissed her,
   And tempted her out of her gloom –
   And conquered her scruples and gloom;
And we passed to the end of the vista,
   But were stopped by the door of a tomb –
   By the door of a legended* tomb –
And I said: "What is written, sweet sister,
   On the door of this legended tomb?"
   She replied: "Ulalume – Ulalume!...   80
   'Tis the vault of thy lost Ulalume!"

Then my heart, it grew ashen and sober
   As the leaves that were crispèd and sere –

As the leaves that were withering and sere –
And I cried: "It was surely October,
   On *this* very night of last year,
   That I journeyed… I journeyed down here! –
   That I brought a dread burden down here;
   On this night, of all nights in the year –
   Ah, what demon hath tempted me here?   90
Well I know, now, this dim lake of Auber –
   This misty mid region of Weir;
Well I know, now, this dank tarn of Auber –
   This ghoul-haunted woodland of Weir."*

              [1847]

An Enigma*

"Seldom we find," says Solomon Don Dunce,*
   "Half an idea in the profoundest sonnet.
Through all the flimsy things we see at once
   As easily as through a Naples bonnet –
   Trash of all trash! How *can* a lady don it?
Yet heavier far than your Petrarchan stuff* –
Owl-downy nonsense that the faintest puff
   Twirls into trunk paper the while you con it."
And, veritably, Sol is right enough.
The general tuckermanities* are arrant   10
Bubbles – ephemeral and *so* transparent…
   But *this* is now (you may depend upon it)
Stable, opaque, immortal – all by dint
Of the dear names that lie concealed within 't.

              [1847]

The Bells*

I

Hear the sledges with the bells –
    Silver bells!
What a world of merriment their melody foretells!
    How they tinkle, tinkle, tinkle,
      In the icy air of night!
    While the stars that oversprinkle
    All the heavens seem to twinkle
      With a crystalline delight,
    Keeping time, time, time,
    In a sort of Runic rhyme,*   10
To the tintinnabulation that so musically wells
    From the bells, bells, bells, bells,
      Bells, bells, bells –
From the jingling and the tinkling of the bells.

II

    Hear the mellow wedding bells,
      Golden bells!
What a world of happiness their harmony foretells!
    Through the balmy air of night,
    How they ring out their delight
      From the molten-golden notes,   20
      And, all in tune,
    What a liquid ditty floats
To the turtle dove that listens, while she gloats
      On the moon!
    Oh, from out the sounding cells,
What a gush of euphony voluminously wells!
      How it swells!
      How it dwells
    On the future! How it tells
    Of the rapture that impels   30
    To the swinging and the ringing
    Of the bells, bells, bells! –
    Of the bells, bells, bells, bells,
      Bells, bells, bells –
To the rhyming and the chiming of the bells!

III

Hear the loud alarum bells –
Brazen bells!
What a tale of terror, now, their turbulency tells!
In the startled ear of night,
How they scream out their affright! 40
Too much horrified to speak,
They can only shriek, shriek,
Out of tune,
In a clamorous appealing to the mercy of the fire –
In a mad expostulation with the deaf and frantic fire,
Leaping higher, higher, higher,
With a desperate desire,
And a resolute endeavour
Now… now to sit, or never,
By the side of the pale-faced moon. 50
Oh, the bells, bells, bells!
What a tale their terror tells
Of despair!
How they clang and clash and roar!
What a horror they outpour
In the bosom of the palpitating air!
Yet the ear, it fully knows,
By the twanging
And the clanging,
How the danger ebbs and flows – 60
Yes, the ear distinctly tells,
In the jangling
And the wrangling,
How the danger sinks and swells,
By the sinking or the swelling in the anger of the bells –
Of the bells,
Of the bells, bells, bells, bells,
Bells, bells, bells –
In the clamour and the clangour of the bells.

IV

Hear the tolling of the bells – 70
Iron bells!
What a world of solemn thought their monody compels!

In the silence of the night,
How we shiver with affright
At the melancholy menace of their tone!
For every sound that floats
From the rust within their throats
      Is a groan.
And the people – ah, the people,
They that dwell up in the steeple,   80
      All alone,
And who, tolling, tolling, tolling,
   In that muffled monotone,
Feel a glory in so rolling
   On the human heart a stone –
They are neither man nor woman,
They are neither brute nor human:
      They are ghouls –
   And their king it is who tolls,
   And he rolls, rolls, rolls, rolls,   90
      A paean from the bells!
And his merry bosom swells
   With the paean of the bells!
And he dances, and he yells,
Keeping time, time, time,
In a sort of Runic rhyme,
   To the paean of the bells,
      Of the bells,
Keeping time, time, time,
In a sort of Runic rhyme,   100
   To the throbbing of the bells,
Of the bells, bells, bells,
   To the sobbing of the bells,
Keeping time, time, time,
   As he knells, knells, knells,
In a happy Runic rhyme,
   To the rolling of the bells,
Of the bells, bells, bells,
   To the tolling of the bells –
Of the bells, bells, bells, bells,   110
   Bells, bells, bells –
To the moaning and the groaning of the bells.
                              [1849]

To Helen*

I saw thee once, once only, years ago:
I must not say *how* many – but *not* many.
It was a July midnight, and from out
A full-orbed moon that, like thine own soul soaring,
Sought a precipitate pathway up through heaven,
There fell a silvery-silken veil of light,
With quietude, and sultriness, and slumber,
Upon the upturn'd faces of a thousand
Roses that grew in an enchanted garden,
Where no wind dared to stir, unless on tiptoe;   10
Fell on the upturn'd faces of these roses
That gave out, in return for the love light,
Their odorous souls in an ecstatic death;
Fell on the upturn'd faces of these roses
That smiled and died in this parterre, enchanted
By thee, and by the poetry of thy presence.

Clad all in white, upon a violet bank
I saw thee half reclining, while the moon
Fell on the upturn'd faces of the roses,
And on thine own – upturn'd, alas, in sorrow!   20

Was it not Fate that, on this July midnight –
Was it not Fate (whose name is also Sorrow)
That bade me pause before that garden gate
To breathe the incense of those slumbering roses?
No footstep stirred: the hated world all slept,
Save only thee and me (Oh, Heaven – oh, God –
How my heart beats in coupling those two words!) –
Save only thee and me. I paused, I looked –
And in an instant all things disappeared.
(Ah, bear in mind this garden was enchanted!)   30
The pearly lustre of the moon went out;
The mossy banks and the meandering paths,
The happy flowers and the repining trees,
Were seen no more; the very roses' odours
Died in the arms of the adoring airs.
All, all expired save thee, save less than thou,
Save only the divine light in thine eyes –

Save but the soul in thine uplifted eyes.
I saw but them – they were the world to me.
I saw but them, saw only them for hours,   40
Saw only them until the moon went down.
What wild heart histories seemed to lie enwritten
Upon those crystalline, celestial spheres!
How dark a woe! Yet how sublime a hope!
How silently serene a sea of pride!
How daring an ambition! Yet how deep,
How fathomless a capacity for love!

But now, at length, dear Dian* sank from sight,
Into a western couch of thundercloud –
And thou, a ghost, amid the entombing trees   50
Didst glide away. *Only thine eyes remained*.
They *would not* go – they never yet have gone.
Lighting my lonely pathway home that night,
They have not left me (as my hopes have) since.
They follow me – they lead me through the years.
They are my ministers – yet I their slave.
Their office is to illumine and enkindle –
My duty *to be saved* by their bright light
And purified in their electric fire,
And sanctified in their Elysian fire.   60
They fill my soul with Beauty (which is Hope),
And are far up in heaven – the stars I kneel to
In the sad, silent watches of my night;
While even in the meridian glare of day
I see them still – two sweetly scintillant
Venuses, unextinguished by the sun!

[1848]

A Dream within a Dream*

Take this kiss upon the brow!
And, in parting from you now,
Thus much let me avow:
You are not wrong, who deem
That my days have been a dream –
Yet if hope has flown away

In a night, or in a day,
In a vision, or in none,
Is it therefore the less *gone*?
All that we see or seem   10
Is but a dream within a dream.

I stand amid the roar
Of a surf-tormented shore,
And I hold within my hand
Grains of the golden sand…
How few! Yet how they creep
Through my fingers to the deep
While I weep – while I weep!
O God! Can I not grasp
Them with a tighter clasp?   20
O God! Can I not save
One from the pitiless wave?
Is *all* that we see or seem
But a dream within a dream?

[1849]

For Annie*

Thank Heaven, the crisis,
    The danger is past,
And the lingering illness
    Is over at last –
And the fever called "living"
    Is conquered at last.

Sadly, I know
    I am shorn of my strength,
And no muscle I move
    As I lie at full length –   10
But no matter! I feel
    I am better at length.

And I rest so composedly,
    Now, in my bed,
That any beholder

Might fancy me dead –
Might start at beholding me,
   Thinking me dead.

The moaning and groaning,
   The sighing and sobbing   20
Are quieted now,
   With that horrible throbbing
At heart – ah, that horrible,
   Horrible throbbing!

The sickness, the nausea,
   The pitiless pain,
Have ceased, with the fever
   That maddened my brain –
With the fever called "living"
   That burned in my brain.   30

And oh, of all tortures
   That torture the worst
Has abated – the terrible
   Torture of thirst
For the naphthalene river
   Of Passion accursed:
I have drank of a water
   That quenches all thirst –

Of a water that flows,
   With a lullaby sound,   40
From a spring but a very few
   Feet underground,
From a cavern not very far
   Down underground.

And ah, let it never
   Be foolishly said
That my room, it is gloomy
   And narrow my bed!
For man never slept
   In a different bed –   50
And, to *sleep*, you must slumber
   In just such a bed.

My tantalized spirit
    Here blandly reposes,
Forgetting, or never
    Regretting its roses –
Its old agitations
    Of myrtles and roses.

For now, while so quietly
    Lying, it fancies   60
A holier odour
    About it, of pansies –
A rosemary odour,
    Commingled with pansies,
With rue and the beautiful
    Puritan pansies.

And so it lies happily,
    Bathing in many
A dream of the truth
    And the beauty of Annie –   70
Drowned in a bath
    Of the tresses of Annie.

She tenderly kissed me,
    She fondly caressed,
And then I fell gently
    To sleep on her breast –
Deeply to sleep
    From the heaven of her breast.

When the light was extinguished,
    She covered me warm,   80
And she prayed to the angels
    To keep me from harm –
To the queen of the angels
    To shield me from harm.

And I lie so composedly,
    Now, in my bed
(Knowing her love)
    That you fancy me dead –
And I rest so contentedly,

Now in my bed 90
(With her love at my breast)
 That you fancy me dead,
That you shudder to look at me,
 Thinking me dead.

But my heart, it is brighter
 Than all of the many
Stars in the sky,
 For it sparkles with Annie:
It glows with the light
 Of the love of my Annie – 100
With the thought of the light
 Of the eyes of my Annie.

      [1849]

Eldorado*

 Gaily bedight,
 A gallant knight,
In sunshine and in shadow,
 Had journeyed long,
 Singing a song,
In search of Eldorado.

 But he grew old –
 This knight so bold –
And o'er his heart a shadow
 Fell, as he found 10
 No spot of ground
That looked like Eldorado.

 And, as his strength
 Failed him at length,
He met a pilgrim shadow.
 "Shadow," said he,
 "Where can it be,
This land of Eldorado?"

  "Over the Mountains
  Of the Moon, 20

Down the Valley of the Shadow,
       Ride, boldly ride,"
       The shade replied,
"If you seek for Eldorado!"

[1849]

To My Mother*

Because I feel that, in the heavens above,
    The angels, whispering to one another,
Can find, among their burning terms of love,
    None so devotional as that of "Mother",
Therefore by that dear name I long have called you –
    You who are more than mother unto me,
And fill my heart of hearts, where Death installed you
    In setting my Virginia's spirit free.
My mother – my own mother, who died early –
    Was but the mother of myself, but you   10
Are mother to the one I loved so dearly,
    And thus are dearer than the mother I knew
By that infinity with which my wife
    Was dearer to my soul than its soul life.

[1849]

Annabel Lee*

It was many and many a year ago,
       In a kingdom by the sea,
That a maiden there lived whom you may know
       By the name of Annabel Lee –
And this maiden, she lived with no other thought
       Than to love and be loved by me.

I was a child and *she* was a child,
       In this kingdom by the sea,
But we loved with a love that was more than love,
       I and my Annabel Lee –   10
With a love that the wingèd seraphs of Heaven
       Coveted her and me.

And this was the reason that, long ago,
    In this kingdom by the sea,
A wind blew out of a cloud, chilling
    My beautiful Annabel Lee,
So that her high-born kinsmen came
    And bore her away from me,
To shut her up in a sepulchre
    In this kingdom by the sea.   20

The angels, not half so happy in heaven,
    Went envying her and me.
Yes! That was the reason (as all men know,
    In this kingdom by the sea)
That the wind came out of the cloud by night,
    Chilling and killing my Annabel Lee.

But our love, it was stronger by far than the love
    Of those who were older than we –
    Of many far wiser than we –
And neither the angels in heaven above   30
    Nor the demons down under the sea
Can ever dissever my soul from the soul
    Of the beautiful Annabel Lee.

For the moon never beams without bringing me dreams
    Of the beautiful Annabel Lee,
And the stars never rise but I feel the bright eyes
    Of the beautiful Annabel Lee.
And so, all the night-tide,* I lie down by the side
Of my darling, my darling, my life and my bride,
    In the sepulchre there by the sea –   40
    In her tomb by the sounding sea.

                     [1849]

THREE ESSAYS ON POETRY

THE POETIC PRINCIPLE*

In speaking of the poetic principle, I have no design to be either thorough or profound. While discussing, very much at random, the essentiality of what we call "poetry", my principal purpose will be to cite for consideration some few of those minor English or American poems which best suit my own taste, or which, upon my own fancy, have left the most definite impression. By "minor poems" I mean, of course, poems of little length. And here, in the beginning, permit me to say a few words in regard to a somewhat peculiar principle which, whether rightfully or wrongfully, has always had its influence in my own critical estimate of the poem. I hold that a long poem does not exist. I maintain that the phrase "a long poem" is simply a flat contradiction in terms.

I need scarcely observe that a poem deserves its title only inasmuch as it excites by elevating the soul. The value of the poem is in the ratio of this elevating excitement. But all excitements are, through a psychal necessity, transient. That degree of excitement which would entitle a poem to be so called at all cannot be sustained throughout a composition of any great length. After the lapse of half an hour, at the very utmost, it flags, fails – a revulsion ensues, and then the poem is, in effect and in fact, no longer such.

There are, no doubt, many who have found difficulty in reconciling the critical dictum that the *Paradise Lost* is to be devoutly admired throughout, with the absolute impossibility of maintaining for it, during perusal, the amount of enthusiasm which that critical dictum would demand. This great work, in fact, is to be regarded as poetical only when, losing sight of that vital requisite in all works of art, unity, we view it merely as a series of minor poems. If, to preserve its unity – its totality of effect or impression – we read it (as would be necessary) at a single sitting, the result is but a constant alternation of excitement and depression. After a passage of what we feel to be true poetry, there follows, inevitably, a passage of platitude which no critical prejudgement can force us to admire. But if, upon completing the work, we read it again, omitting the first book (that is to say, commencing with the second), we shall be surprised at now finding that admirable which we before condemned – that damnable which we had previously so much admired. It follows from all this that the ultimate, aggregate or absolute effect of even the best epic under the sun is a nullity – and this is precisely the fact.

In regard to the *Iliad*, we have, if not positive proof, at least very good reason for believing it intended as a series of lyrics – but, granting the epic intention, I can say only that the work is based in an imperfect sense of art. The modern epic is, of the supposititious ancient model, but an inconsiderate and blindfold imitation. But the day of these artistic anomalies is over. If, at any time, any very long poem *were* popular in reality, which I doubt, it is at least clear that no very long poem will ever be popular again.

That the extent of a poetical work is, *ceteris paribus*,* the measure of its merit seems undoubtedly, when we thus state it, a proposition sufficiently absurd – yet we are indebted for it to the quarterly reviews. Surely there can be nothing in mere *size*, abstractly considered – there can be nothing in mere *bulk*, so far as a volume is concerned – which has so continuously elicited admiration from these saturnine pamphlets! A mountain, to be sure, by the mere sentiment of physical magnitude which it conveys, *does* impress us with a sense of the sublime – but no man is impressed after *this* fashion by the material grandeur of even *The Columbiad*.* Even the quarterlies have not instructed us to be so impressed by it. As *yet*, they have not *insisted* on our estimating Lamartine* by the cubic foot, or Pollok* by the pound – but what else are we to *infer* from their continual prating about "sustained effort"? If by "sustained effort" any little gentleman has accomplished an epic, let us frankly commend him for the effort – if this indeed be a thing commendable – but let us forbear praising the epic on the effort's account. It is to be hoped that common sense, in the time to come, will prefer deciding upon a work of art rather by the impression it makes – by the effect it produces – than by the time it took to impress the effect, or by the amount of "sustained effort" which had been found necessary in effecting the impression. The fact is that perseverance is one thing and genius quite another – nor can all the quarterlies in Christendom confound them. By and by, this proposition, with many which I have been just urging, will be received as self-evident. In the mean time, by being generally condemned as falsities, they will not be essentially damaged as truths.

On the other hand, it is clear that a poem may be improperly brief. Undue brevity degenerates into mere epigrammatism. A *very* short poem, while now and then producing a brilliant or vivid, never produces a profound or enduring effect. There must be the steady pressing-down of the stamp upon the wax. De Béranger* has wrought innumerable things, pungent and spirit-stirring, but in general they have been too imponderous to stamp

themselves deeply into the public attention – and thus, as so many feath-
ers of fancy, have been blown aloft only to be whistled down the wind.

A remarkable instance of the effect of undue brevity in depressing a
poem – in keeping it out of the popular view – is afforded by the follow-
ing exquisite little serenade:

> I arise from dreams of thee
> > In the first sweet sleep of night,
> When the winds are breathing low
> > And the stars are shining bright.
> I arise from dreams of thee,
> > And a spirit in my feet
> Hath led me – who knows how? –
> > To thy chamber window, sweet!
>
> The wandering airs, they faint*
> > On the dark, the silent stream –
> The champak* odours fail
> > Like sweet thoughts in a dream.
> The nightingale's complaint,
> > It dies upon her heart –
> As I must on thine,
> > Belovèd as thou art!
>
> Oh, lift me from the grass!
> > I die! I faint! I fail!
> Let thy love in kisses rain
> > On my lips and eyelids pale.
> My cheek is cold and white, alas!
> > My heart beats loud and fast –
> Oh, press me to thine own again,
> > Where it will break at last!*

Very few, perhaps, are familiar with these lines – yet no less a poet than
Shelley is their author. Their warm, yet delicate and ethereal imagination
will be appreciated by all – but by none so thoroughly as by him who has
himself arisen from sweet dreams of one beloved to bathe in the aromatic
air of a southern midsummer night.

One of the finest poems by Willis* – the very best, in my opinion, which
he has ever written – has, no doubt, through this same defect of undue
brevity been kept back from its proper position, not less in the critical
than in the popular view.

The shadows lay along Broadway,
    'Twas near the twilight-tide* –
And slowly there a lady fair
    Was walking in her pride.
Alone walk'd she, but, viewlessly,
    Walk'd spirits at her side.

Peace charm'd the street beneath her feet,
    And Honour charm'd the air,
And all astir looked kind on her,
    And called her good as fair –
For all God ever gave to her
    She kept with chary care.

She kept with care her beauties rare
    From lovers warm and true,
For her heart was cold to all but gold,
    And the rich came not to woo –
But honour'd well are charms to sell
    If priests the selling do.

Now walking there was one more fair,
    A slight girl, lily-pale –
And she had unseen company
    To make the spirit quail:
'Twixt Want and Scorn she walk'd forlorn,
    And nothing could avail.

No mercy now can clear her brow
    For this world's peace to pray,
For, as love's wild prayer dissolved in air,
    Her woman's heart gave way!
But the sin forgiven by Christ in heaven
    By man is cursed alway!

In this composition we find it difficult to recognize the Willis who has written so many mere "verses of society". The lines are not only richly ideal, but full of energy, while they breathe an earnestness – an evident sincerity of sentiment – for which we look in vain throughout all the other works of this author.

While the epic mania – while the idea that, to merit in poetry, prolixity is indispensable – has, for some years past, been gradually dying out of the public mind by mere dint of its own absurdity, we find it succeeded by a heresy too palpably false to be long tolerated, but one which, in the brief period it has already endured, may be said to have accomplished more in the corruption of our poetical literature than all its other enemies combined. I allude to the heresy of the *didactic*. It has been assumed, tacitly and avowedly, directly and indirectly, that the ultimate object of all poetry is truth. Every poem, it is said, should inculcate a moral – and by this moral is the poetical merit of the work to be adjudged. We Americans especially have patronized this happy idea – and we Bostonians, very especially, have developed it in full. We have taken it into our heads that to write a poem simply for the poem's sake, and to acknowledge such to have been our design, would be to confess ourselves radically wanting in the true poetic dignity and force, but the simple fact is that, would we but permit ourselves to look into our own souls, we should immediately there discover that under the sun there neither exists nor *can* exist any work more thoroughly dignified, more supremely noble than this very poem, this poem per se, this poem which is a poem and nothing more – this poem written solely for the poem's sake.

With as deep a reverence for the true as ever inspired the bosom of man, I would nevertheless limit, in some measure, its modes of inculcation. I would limit to enforce them. I would not enfeeble them by dissipation. The demands of Truth are severe. She has no sympathy with the myrtles. All *that* which is so indispensable in song is precisely all *that* with which *she* has nothing whatever to do. It is but making her a flaunting paradox to wreathe her in gems and flowers. In enforcing a truth, we need severity rather than efflorescence of language. We must be simple, precise, terse. We must be cool, calm, unimpassioned. In a word, we must be in that mood which, as nearly as possible, is the exact converse of the poetical. *He* must be blind indeed who does not perceive the radical and chasmal differences between the truthful and the poetical modes of inculcation. He must be theory-mad beyond redemption who, in spite of these differences, shall still persist in attempting to reconcile the obstinate oils and waters of poetry and truth.

Dividing the world of mind into its three most immediately obvious distinctions, we have the pure intellect, taste and the moral sense. I place taste in the middle, because it is just this position which, in the mind, it occupies. It holds intimate relations with either extreme, but from the moral sense is separated by so faint a difference that Aristotle has not hesitated to place some of its operations among the virtues themselves. Nevertheless, we find the *offices* of the trio marked with a sufficient distinction. Just as the intellect concerns itself with truth, so taste informs us of the beautiful, while the moral sense is regardful of duty. Of this latter, while Conscience teaches the obligation and Reason the expediency, Taste contents herself with displaying the charms, waging war upon Vice solely on the ground of her deformity, her disproportion, her animosity to the fitting, to the appropriate, to the harmonious – in a word, to Beauty.

An immortal instinct, deep within the spirit of man, is thus, plainly, a sense of the Beautiful. This it is which administers to his delight in the manifold forms and sounds and odours and sentiments amid which he exists. And just as the lily is repeated in the lake or the eyes of Amaryllis in the mirror, so is the mere oral or written repetition of these forms and sounds and colours and odours and sentiments a duplicate source of delight. But this mere repetition is not poetry. He who shall simply sing, with however glowing enthusiasm, or with however vivid a truth of description, of the sights and sounds and odours and colours and sentiments which greet *him* in common with all mankind – he, I say, has yet failed to prove his divine title. There is still a something in the distance which he has been unable to attain. We have still a thirst unquenchable, to allay which he has not shown us the crystal springs. This thirst belongs to the immortality of man. It is at once a consequence and an indication of his perennial existence. It is the desire of the moth for the star.* It is no mere appreciation of the beauty before us – but a wild effort to reach the Beauty above. Inspired by an ecstatic prescience of the glories beyond the grave, we struggle, by multiform combinations among the things and thoughts of time, to attain a portion of that Loveliness whose very elements, perhaps, appertain to eternity alone. And thus when by poetry – or when by music, the most entrancing of the poetic moods – we find ourselves melted into tears, we weep then not (as the Abate Gravina supposes) through excess of pleasure,* but through a certain petulant, impatient sorrow at our inability to grasp *now*, wholly, here on earth, at once and for ever, those divine and rapturous joys of which *through* the poem, or *through* the music, we attain to but brief and indeterminate glimpses.

The struggle to apprehend the supernal Loveliness – this struggle, on the part of souls fittingly constituted – has given to the world all *that* which it (the world) has ever been enabled at once to understand and *to feel* as poetic.

The poetic sentiment, of course, may develop itself in various modes: in painting, in sculpture, in architecture, in the dance – very especially in music, and very peculiarly, and with a wide field, in the composition of the landscape garden. Our present theme, however, has regard only to its manifestation in words. And here let me speak briefly on the topic of rhythm. Contenting myself with the certainty that music, in its various modes of metre, rhythm and rhyme, is of so vast a moment in poetry as never to be wisely rejected, is so vitally important an adjunct that he is simply silly who declines its assistance, I will not now pause to maintain its absolute essentiality. It is in music, perhaps, that the soul most nearly attains the great end for which, when inspired by the poetic sentiment, it struggles: the creation of supernal Beauty. It *may* be, indeed, that here this sublime end is, now and then, attained *in fact*. We are often made to feel, with a shivering delight, that from an earthly harp are stricken notes which *cannot* have been unfamiliar to the angels. And thus there can be little doubt that, in the union of poetry with music in its popular sense, we shall find the widest field for the poetic development. The old bards and minnesingers had advantages which we do not possess – and Thomas Moore,* singing his own songs, was, in the most legitimate manner, perfecting them as poems.

To recapitulate, then: I would define, in brief, the poetry of words as the *rhythmical creation of Beauty*. Its sole arbiter is taste. With the intellect or with the conscience, it has only collateral relations. Unless incidentally, it has no concern whatever either with duty or with truth.

A few words, however, in explanation. *That* pleasure which is at once the most pure, the most elevating and the most intense is derived, I maintain, from the contemplation of the Beautiful. In the contemplation of Beauty we alone find it possible to attain that pleasurable elevation, or excitement, *of the soul* which we recognize as the "poetic sentiment", and which is so easily distinguished from truth, which is the satisfaction of the reason, or from passion, which is the excitement of the heart. I make Beauty, therefore (using the word as inclusive of the sublime), I make Beauty the province of the poem, simply because it is an obvious rule of art that effects should be made to spring as directly as possible from their causes – no one as yet having been weak enough to deny that the peculiar elevation in question is at least *most readily* attainable in the poem. It by no means follows, however, that the incitements of passion or the precepts of duty, or even the lessons of truth, may not be introduced into a poem, and with advantage, for they may subserve, incidentally, in various ways, the general purposes of the work – but the true artist will always contrive to tone them down in proper subjection to that *Beauty* which is the atmosphere and the real essence of the poem.

I cannot better introduce the few poems which I shall present for your consideration than by the citation of the Proem to Mr Longfellow's *Waif:**

The day is done, and the darkness
   Falls from the wings of Night,
As a feather is wafted downward
   From an eagle in his flight.

I see the lights of the village
   Gleam through the rain and the mist,
And a feeling of sadness comes o'er me
   That my soul cannot resist –

A feeling of sadness and longing
   That is not akin to pain,
And resembles sorrow only
   As the mist resembles the rain.

Come, read to me some poem,
   Some simple and heartfelt lay,
That shall soothe this restless feeling
   And banish the thoughts of day.

Not from the grand old masters,
   Not from the bards sublime,
Whose distant footsteps echo
   Through the corridors of Time.

For, like strains of martial music,
   Their mighty thoughts suggest
Life's endless toil and endeavour –
   And tonight I long for rest.

Read from some humbler poet
   Whose songs gushed from his heart
As showers from the clouds of summer,
   Or tears from the eyelids start –

Who, through long days of labour
   And nights devoid of ease,
Still heard in his soul the music
   Of wonderful melodies.

Such songs have power to quiet
   The restless pulse of care,
And come like the benediction
   That follows after prayer.

> Then read from the treasured volume
> > The poem of thy choice,
> And lend to the rhyme of the poet
> > The beauty of thy voice.
>
> And the night shall be filled with music,
> > And the cares that infest the day
> Shall fold their tents, like the Arabs,
> > And as silently steal away.

With no great range of imagination, these lines have been justly admired for their delicacy of expression. Some of the images are very effective. Nothing can be better than

> > the bards sublime,
> Whose distant footsteps echo
> Down the corridors of Time.

The idea of the last quatrain is also very effective. The poem, on the whole, however, is chiefly to be admired for the graceful *insouciance* of its metre, so well in accordance with the character of the sentiments, and especially for the *ease* of the general manner. This "ease", or naturalness, in a literary style, it has long been the fashion to regard as ease in appearance alone – as a point of really difficult attainment. But not so: a natural manner is difficult only to him who should never meddle with it – to the unnatural. It is but the result of writing with the understanding, or with the instinct, that *the tone*, in composition, should always be that which the mass of mankind would adopt – and must perpetually vary, of course, with the occasion. The author who, after the fashion of the *North American Review*,* should be, upon *all* occasions, merely "quiet", must necessarily, upon *many* occasions, be simply silly or stupid – and has no more right to be considered "easy" or "natural" than a Cockney exquisite,* or than the Sleeping Beauty in the waxworks.

Among the minor poems of Bryant,* none has so much impressed me as the one which he entitles 'June'. I quote only a portion of it:*

> > There, through the long, long summer hours,
> > > The golden light should lie,
> > And thick young herbs and groups of flowers
> > > Stand in their beauty by.
> > The oriole* should build and tell
> > His love tale close beside my cell;
> > > The idle butterfly

Should rest him there, and there be heard
The housewife bee and hummingbird.

And what if cheerful shouts at noon
  Come, from the village sent,
Or songs of maids, beneath the moon,
  With fairy laughter blent?
And what if, in the evening light,
Betrothèd lovers walk in sight
  Of my low monument?
I would the lovely scene around
Might know no sadder sight nor sound.

I know, I know I should not see
  The season's glorious show,
Nor would its brightness shine for me,
  Nor its wild music flow –
But if, around my place of sleep,
The friends I love should come to weep,
  They might not haste to go:
Soft airs, and song, and light, and bloom,
Should keep them lingering by my tomb.

These to their soften'd hearts should bear
  The thought of what has been,
And speak of one who cannot share
  The gladness of the scene,
Whose part in all the pomp that fills
The circuit of the summer hills
  Is… that his grave is green –
And deeply would their hearts rejoice
To hear again his living voice.

The rhythmical flow, here, is even voluptuous – nothing could be more melodious. The poem has always affected me in a remarkable manner. The intense melancholy which seems to well up, perforce, to the surface of all the poet's cheerful sayings about his grave, we find thrilling us to the soul – while there is the truest poetic elevation in the thrill. The impression left is one of a pleasurable sadness. And if, in the remaining compositions which I shall introduce to you, there be more or less of a similar tone always apparent, let me remind you that (how or why we know not) this certain taint of sadness is inseparably connected with all the higher manifestations of true Beauty. It is, nevertheless,

A feeling of sadness and longing
    That is not akin to pain,
And resembles sorrow only
    As the mist resembles the rain.

The taint of which I speak is clearly perceptible even in a poem so full of brilliancy and spirit as the 'Health' of Edward Coote Pinkney:*

I fill this cup to one made up
    Of loveliness alone –
A woman, of her gentle sex
    The seeming paragon,
To whom the better elements
    And kindly stars have given
A form so fair that, like the air,
    'Tis less of earth than heaven.

Her every tone is music's own,
    Like those of morning birds,
And something more than melody
    Dwells ever in her words;
The coinage of her heart are they,
    And from her lips each flows
As one may see the burden'd bee
    Forth issue from the rose.

Affections are as thoughts to her,
    The measures of her hours;
Her feelings have the fragrancy,
    The freshness of young flowers;
And lovely passions, changing oft,
    So fill her, she appears
The image of themselves by turns –
    The idol of past years!

Of her bright face one glance will trace
    A picture on the brain,
And of her voice in echoing hearts
    A sound must long remain –
But memory, such as mine of her,
    So very much endears,
When death is nigh, my latest sigh
    Will not be life's, but hers.

> I filled this cup to one made up
>   Of loveliness alone –
> A woman, of her gentle sex
>   The seeming paragon.
> Her health! And would on earth there stood
>   Some more of such a frame,
> That life might be all poetry,
>   And weariness a name.

It was the misfortune of Mr Pinkney to have been born too far south.*
Had he been a New Englander, it is probable that he would have been
ranked as the first of American lyrists by that magnanimous cabal which
has so long controlled the destinies of American Letters in conducting the
thing called the *North American Review*. The poem just cited is especially
beautiful, but the poetic elevation which it induces we must refer chiefly
to our sympathy in the poet's enthusiasm. We pardon his hyperboles for
the evident earnestness with which they are uttered.

It was by no means my design, however, to expatiate upon the *merits*
of what I should read you. These will necessarily speak for themselves.
Boccalini, in his *Advertisements from Parnassus*, tells us that Zoilus once
presented Apollo a very caustic criticism upon a very admirable book –
whereupon the god asked him for the beauties of the work. He replied
that he only busied himself about the errors. On hearing this, Apollo,
handing him a sack of unwinnowed wheat, bade him pick out *all the
chaff* for his reward.*

Now, this fable answers very well as a hit at the critics – but I am by no
means sure that the god was in the right. I am by no means certain that the
true limits of the critical duty are not grossly misunderstood. Excellence,
in a poem especially, may be considered in the light of an axiom, which
need only be properly *put* to become self-evident. It is *not* excellence if it
require to be demonstrated as such – and thus, to point out too particularly
the merits of a work of art is to admit that they are *not* merits altogether.

Among the *Melodies** of Thomas Moore is one whose distinguished
character as a poem proper seems to have been singularly left out of view.
I allude to his lines beginning "Come, rest in this bosom". The intense
energy of their expression is not surpassed by anything in Byron. There
are two of the lines in which a sentiment is conveyed that embodies the
all in all of the divine passion of Love – a sentiment which, perhaps, has
found its echo in more, and in more passionate, human hearts than any
other single sentiment ever embodied in words:

Come, rest in this bosom, my own stricken deer:
Though the herd have fled from thee, thy home is still here –
Here still is the smile, that no cloud can o'ercast,
And a heart and a hand all thy own to the last.

Oh, what was love made for, if 'tis not the same
Through joy and through torment, through glory and shame?
I know not, I ask not, if guilt's in that heart:
I but know that I love thee, whatever thou art.

Thou hast call'd me thy angel in moments of bliss,
And thy angel I'll be, mid the horrors of this –
Through the furnace, unshrinking, thy steps to pursue,
And shield thee, and save thee, or perish there too.

It has been the fashion of late days to deny Moore imagination, while granting him fancy, a distinction originating with Coleridge – than whom no man more fully comprehended the great powers of Moore. The fact is that the fancy of this poet so far predominates over all his other faculties, and over the fancy of all other men, as to have induced, very naturally, the idea that he is fanciful *only*. But never was there a greater mistake. Never was a grosser wrong done the fame of a true poet. In the compass of the English language I can call to mind no poem more profoundly, more weirdly *imaginative*, in the best sense, than the lines commencing "I would I were by that dim lake"* – which are the composition of Thomas Moore. I regret that I am unable to remember them.

One of the noblest – and, speaking of fancy, one of the most singularly fanciful of modern poets – was Thomas Hood.* His 'Fair Ines' had always, for me, an inexpressible charm:

Oh, saw ye not fair Ines?
She's gone into the west,
To dazzle when the sun is down
And rob the world of rest.
She took our daylight with her,
The smiles that we love best,
With morning blushes on her cheek
And pearls upon her breast.

Oh, turn again, fair Ines,
Before the fall of night,
For fear the moon should shine alone,

And stars unrivall'd bright.
And blessèd will the lover be
That walks beneath their light,
And breathes the love against thy cheek
I dare not even write!

Would I had been, fair Ines,
That gallant cavalier
Who rode so gaily by thy side
And whisper'd thee so near!
Were there no bonny dames at home,
Or no true lovers here,
That he should cross the seas to win
The dearest of the dear?

I saw thee, lovely Ines,
Descend along the shore
With bands of noble gentlemen
And banners waved before –
And gentle youth and maidens gay,
And snowy plumes they wore:
It would have been a beauteous dream,
If it had been no more!

Alas, alas, fair Ines,
She went away with song,
With music waiting on her steps
And shoutings of the throng.
But some were sad and felt no mirth,
But only music's wrong,
In sounds that sang "Farewell, Farewell"
To her you've loved so long.

Farewell, farewell, fair Ines!
That vessel never bore
So fair a lady on its deck,
Nor danced so light before –
Alas for pleasure on the sea,
And sorrow on the shore!
The smile that blessed one lover's heart
Has broken many more!

'The Haunted House', by the same author, is one of the truest poems
ever written – one of the *truest*, one of the most unexceptional, one of
the most thoroughly artistic, both in its theme and in its execution. It is,
moreover, powerfully ideal – imaginative. I regret that its length renders
it unsuitable for the purposes of this lecture. In place of it, permit me to
offer the universally appreciated 'Bridge of Sighs'.

> One more unfortunate,
> Weary of breath,
> Rashly importunate,
> Gone to her death!
>
> Take her up tenderly,
> Lift her with care –
> Fashion'd so slenderly,
> Young, and so fair!
>
> Look at her garments
> Clinging like cerements,*
> Whilst the wave constantly
> Drips from her clothing –
> Take her up instantly,
> Loving, not loathing.
>
> Touch her not scornfully,
> Think of her mournfully,
> Gently and humanly,
> Not of the stains of her –
> All that remains of her
> Now is pure womanly.
>
> Make no deep scrutiny
> Into her mutiny
> Rash and undutiful –
> Past all dishonour,
> Death has left on her
> Only the beautiful.
>
> Still, for all slips of hers,
> One of Eve's family,
> Wipe those poor lips of hers
> Oozing so clammily.
> Loop up her tresses

Escaped from the comb,
Her fair auburn tresses,
Whilst wonderment guesses:
Where was her home?

Who was her father?
Who was her mother?
Had she a sister?
Had she a brother?
Or was there a dearer one
Still, and a nearer one
Yet, than all other?

Alas, for the rarity
Of Christian charity
Under the sun!
Oh, it was pitiful!
Near a whole city full,
Home she had none.

Sisterly, brotherly,
Fatherly, motherly,
Feelings had changed:
Love, by harsh evidence,
Thrown from its eminence –
Even God's providence
Seeming estranged.

Where the lamps quiver
Sor far in the river,
With many a light
From window and casement
From garret to basement,
She stood, with amazement,
Houseless by night.

The bleak wind of March
Made her tremble and shiver;
But not the dark arch
Or the black flowing river:
Mad from life's history,
Glad to death's mystery,

Swift to be hurl'd –
Anywhere, anywhere
Out of the world!

In she plunged boldly,
No matter how coldly
The rough river ran –
Over the brink of it,
Picture it, think of it,
Dissolute man!
Lave in it, drink of it
Then, if you can!

Take her up tenderly,
Lift her with care –
Fashion'd so slenderly,
Young, and so fair!
Ere her limbs frigidly
Stiffen too rigidly,
Decently, kindly,
Smooth, and compose them –
And her eyes, close them,
Staring so blindly!

Dreadfully staring
Through muddy impurity,
As when with the daring
Last look of despairing
Fixed on futurity.

Perishing gloomily,
Spurred by contumely,
Cold inhumanity,
Burning insanity,
Into her rest –
Cross her hands humbly,
As if praying dumbly,
Over her breast!
Owning her weakness,
Her evil behaviour,
And leaving, with meekness,
Her sins to her Saviour!

The vigour of this poem is no less remarkable than its pathos. The versification, although carrying the fanciful to the very verge of the fantastic, is nevertheless admirably adapted to the wild insanity which is the thesis of the poem.

Among the minor poems of Lord Byron is one which has never received from the critics the praise which it undoubtedly deserves:

> Though the day of my destiny's over
>   And the star of my fate hath declined,
> Thy soft heart refused to discover
>   The faults which so many could find;
> Though thy soul with my grief was acquainted,
>   It shrunk not to share it with me,
> And the love which my spirit hath painted,
>   It never hath found but in *thee*.
>
> Then when nature around me is smiling,
>   The last smile which answers to mine,
> I do not believe it beguiling,
>   Because it reminds me of thine;
> And when winds are at war with the ocean,
>   As the breasts I believed in with me,
> If their billows excite an emotion,
>   It is that they bear me from *thee*.
>
> Though the rock of my last hope is shivered
>   And its fragments are sunk in the wave,
> Though I feel that my soul is delivered
>   To pain, it shall not be its slave.
> There is many a pang to pursue me:
>   They may crush, but they shall not contemn –
> They may torture, but shall not subdue me:
>   'Tis of *thee* that I think – not of them.
>
> Though human, thou didst not deceive me;
>   Though woman, thou didst not forsake;
> Though loved, thou forborest to grieve me;
>   Though slandered, thou never couldst shake –
> Though trusted, thou didst not disclaim me;
>   Though parted, it was not to fly;
> Though watchful, 'twas not to defame me,
>   Nor mute, that the world might belie.

Yet I blame not the world, nor despise it,
  Nor the war of the many with one –
If my soul was not fitted to prize it,
  'Twas folly not sooner to shun.
And if dearly that error hath cost me,
  And more than I once could foresee,
I have found that, whatever it lost me,
  It could not deprive me of *thee*.

From the wreck of the past, which hath perished,
  Thus much I at least may recall:
It hath taught me that which I most cherished
  Deserved to be dearest of all.
In the desert a fountain is springing,
  In the wide waste there still is a tree,
And a bird in the solitude singing,
  Which speaks to my spirit of *thee*.*

Although the rhythm, here, is one of the most difficult, the versification could scarcely be improved. No nobler *theme* ever engaged the pen of poet. It is the soul-elevating idea that no man can consider himself entitled to complain of fate while, in his adversity, he still retains the unwavering love of woman.

From Alfred Tennyson* – although in perfect sincerity I regard him as the noblest poet that ever lived – I have left myself time to cite only a very brief specimen. I call him, and *think* him, the noblest of poets *not* because the impressions he produces are, at *all* times, the most profound, *not* because the poetical excitement which he induces is, at *all* times, the most intense, but because it *is*, at all times, the most ethereal – in other words, the most elevating and most pure. No poet is so little of the earth, earthy. What I am about to read is from his last long poem, *The Princess*:

Tears, idle tears, I know not what they mean,
Tears from the depth of some divine despair
Rise in the heart, and gather to the eyes,
In looking on the happy autumn fields,
And thinking of the days that are no more.

Fresh as the first beam glittering on a sail,
That brings our friends up from the underworld,
Sad as the last which reddens over one
That sinks with all we love below the verge –
So sad, so fresh, the days that are no more.

Ah, sad and strange as in dark summer dawns
The earliest pipe of half-awaken'd birds
To dying ears, when unto dying eyes
The casement slowly grows a glimmering square –
So sad, so strange, the days that are no more.

Dear as remember'd kisses after death,
And sweet as those by hopeless fancy feign'd
On lips that are for others – deep as love,
Deep as first love, and wild with all regret…
Oh, death in life, the days that are no more.*

Thus, although in a very cursory and imperfect manner, I have endeavoured to convey to you my conception of the poetic principle. It has been my purpose to suggest that, while this principle itself is, strictly and simply, the human aspiration for supernal Beauty, the manifestation of the principle is always found in *an elevating excitement of the soul*, quite independent of that passion which is the intoxication of the heart – or of that truth which is the satisfaction of the reason. For, in regard to passion, alas, its tendency is to degrade rather than to elevate the soul. Love, on the contrary, Love – the true, the divine Eros, the Uranian, as distinguished from the Dionaean Venus* – is unquestionably the purest and truest of all poetical themes. And in regard to truth (if, to be sure, through the attainment of a truth we are led to perceive a harmony where none was apparent before), we experience, at once, the true poetical effect – but this effect is referable to the harmony alone, and not in the least degree to the truth which merely served to render the harmony manifest.

We shall reach, however, more immediately a distinct conception of what the true poetry is by mere reference to a few of the simple elements which induce in the poet himself the true poetical effect. He recognizes the ambrosia which nourishes his soul in the bright orbs that shine in heaven, in the volutes of the flower, in the clustering of low shrubberies, in the waving of the grain fields, in the slanting of tall, eastern trees, in the blue distance of mountains, in the grouping of clouds, in the twinkling of half-hidden brooks, in the gleaming of silver rivers, in the repose of sequestered lakes, in the star-mirroring depths of lonely wells. He perceives it in the songs of birds, in the harp of Aeolus,* in the sighing of the night wind, in the repining voice of the forest, in the surf that complains to the shore, in the fresh breath of the woods, in the scent of the violet, in the voluptuous perfume of the hyacinth, in the suggestive odour that comes to him, at eventide, from far-distant, undiscovered islands, over dim oceans, illimitable and unexplored. He owns it in all noble thoughts, in all unworldly motives, in all holy impulses, in all chivalrous, generous and self-sacrificing deeds. He feels it in the beauty of woman, in the grace of her step, in the lustre of her eye, in the melody of her voice, in her soft laughter, in her sigh, in the harmony of the rustling of her robes. He deeply feels it in her winning endearments, in her burning enthusiasms, in her gentle charities, in her meek and devotional endurances – but, above all (ah, far above all), he kneels to it, he worships it in the faith, in the purity, in the strength, in the altogether divine majesty... of her *love*.

Let me conclude by the recitation of yet another brief poem – one very different in character from any that I have before quoted. It is by Motherwell,* and is called 'The Song of the Cavalier'. With our modern and altogether rational ideas of the absurdity and impiety of warfare, we are not precisely in that frame of mind best adapted to sympathize with the sentiments, and thus to appreciate the real excellence of the poem. To do this fully, we must identify ourselves, in fancy, with the soul of the old cavalier.

> Then mounte, then mounte, brave gallants, all,
>   And don your helmes amaine!
> Deathe's couriers, Fame and Honour, call
>   Us to the field againe.
>
> No shrewish teares shall fill our eye
>   When the sword hilt's in our hand –
> Heart-whole* we'll part, and no whit sighe
>   For the fayrest of the land.
> Let piping swaine and craven wight
>   Thus weepe and puling crye:
> Our business is like men to fight,
>   And hero-like to die!

THE PHILOSOPHY OF COMPOSITION*

Charles Dickens, in a note now lying before me, alluding to an examination I once made of the mechanism of *Barnaby Rudge*,* says: "By the way, are you aware that Godwin wrote his *Caleb Williams* backwards?* He first involved his hero in a web of difficulties, forming the second volume, and then, for the first, cast about him for some mode of accounting for what had been done."

I cannot think this the *precise* mode of procedure on the part of Godwin – and indeed what he himself acknowledges is not altogether in accordance with Mr Dickens's idea – but the author of *Caleb Williams* was too good an artist not to perceive the advantage derivable from at least a somewhat similar process. Nothing is more clear than that every plot worth the name must be elaborated to its denouement before anything be attempted with the pen. It is only with the denouement constantly in view that we can give a plot its indispensable air of consequence, or causation, by making the incidents, and especially the tone at all points, tend to the development of the intention.

There is a radical error, I think, in the usual mode of constructing a story. Either history affords a thesis, or one is suggested by an incident of the day, or, at best, the author sets himself to work in the combination of striking events to form merely the basis of his narrative – designing, generally, to fill in with description, dialogue or authorial comment whatever crevices of fact or action may, from page to page, render themselves apparent.

I prefer commencing with the consideration of an *effect*. Keeping originality *always* in view – for he is false to himself who ventures to dispense with so obvious and so easily attainable a source of interest – I say to myself, in the first place: "Of the innumerable effects, or impressions, of which the heart, the intellect or (more generally) the soul is susceptible, what one shall I, on the present occasion, select?" Having chosen a novel, first, and secondly a vivid effect, I consider whether it can best be wrought by incident or tone – whether by ordinary incidents and peculiar tone or the converse, or by peculiarity both of incident and tone – afterward looking about me (or rather within) for such combinations of event or tone as shall best aid me in the construction of the effect.

I have often thought how interesting a magazine paper might be written by any author who would (that is to say, who could) detail, step by step, the processes by which any one of his compositions attained its ultimate point of completion. Why such a paper has never been given to the world, I am much at a loss to say – but, perhaps, the authorial vanity has had more to do with the omission than any one other cause. Most writers, poets in especial, prefer having it understood that they compose by a species of fine frenzy, an ecstatic intuition, and would positively shudder at letting the public take a peep behind the scenes at the elaborate and vacillating crudities of thought, at the true purposes seized only at the last moment, at the innumerable glimpses of idea that arrived not at the maturity of full view, at the fully matured fancies discarded in despair as unmanageable, at the cautious selections and rejections, at the painful erasures and interpolations – in a word, at the wheels and pinions, the tackle for scene-shifting, the stepladders and demon traps, the cock's feathers, the red paint and the black patches which, in ninety-nine cases out of the hundred, constitute the properties of the literary *histrio*.*

I am aware, on the other hand, that the case is by no means common in which an author is at all in condition to retrace the steps by which his conclusions have been attained. In general, suggestions, having arisen pell-mell, are pursued and forgotten in a similar manner.

For my own part, I have neither sympathy with the repugnance alluded to, nor, at any time, the least difficulty in recalling to mind the progressive steps of any of my compositions – and, since the interest of an analysis, or reconstruction, such as I have considered a desideratum, is quite independent of any real or fancied interest in the thing analysed, it will not be regarded as a breach of decorum on my part to show the modus operandi by which someone of my own works was put together. I select 'The Raven' as most generally known. It is my design to render it manifest that no one point in its composition is referable either to accident or intuition – that the work proceeded, step by step, to its completion with the precision and rigid consequence of a mathematical problem.

Let us dismiss as irrelevant to the poem, per se, the circumstance – or say the necessity – which, in the first place, gave rise to the intention of composing *a* poem that should suit at once the popular and the critical taste.

We commence, then, with this intention.

The initial consideration was that of extent. If any literary work is too long to be read at one sitting, we must be content to dispense with the immensely important effect derivable from unity of impression – for, if two sittings be required, the affairs of the world interfere, and every thing like totality is at once destroyed. But since, *ceteris paribus*,* no poet can afford to dispense with *any thing* that may advance his design, it but remains to be seen whether there is, in extent, any advantage to counterbalance the loss of unity which attends it. Here I say no, at once. What we term a long poem is, in fact, merely a succession of brief ones – that is to say, of brief poetical effects. It is needless to demonstrate that a poem is such only inasmuch as it intensely excites, by elevating, the soul, and all intense excitements are, through a psychal necessity, brief. For this reason, at least one half of the *Paradise Lost* is essentially prose, a succession of poetical excitements interspersed, *inevitably*, with corresponding depressions – the whole being deprived, through the extremeness of its length, of the vastly important artistic element: totality, or unity, of effect.

It appears evident, then, that there is a distinct limit, as regards length, to all works of literary art: the limit of a single sitting – and that, although in certain classes of prose composition, such as *Robinson Crusoe** (demanding no unity), this limit may be advantageously overpassed, it can never properly be overpassed in a poem. Within this limit, the extent of a poem may be made to bear mathematical relation to its merit: in other words, to the excitement or elevation – again, in other words, to the degree of the true poetical effect which it is capable of inducing, for it is clear that the brevity must be in direct ratio of the intensity of the intended effect. This with one proviso: that a certain degree of duration is absolutely requisite for the production of any effect at all.

Holding in view these considerations, as well as that degree of excitement which I deemed not above the popular (while not below the critical) taste, I reached at once what I conceived the proper *length* for my intended poem – a length of about one hundred lines. It is, in fact, a hundred and eight.

My next thought concerned the choice of an impression, or effect, to be conveyed – and here I may as well observe that, throughout the construction, I kept steadily in view the design of rendering the work *universally* appreciable. I should be carried too far out of my immediate topic were I to demonstrate a point upon which I have repeatedly insisted, and which, with the poetical, stands not in the slightest need of demonstration – the point, I mean, that Beauty is the sole legitimate province of the poem. A few words, however, in elucidation of my real meaning, which some of my friends have evinced a disposition to misrepresent. That pleasure which is at once the most intense, the most elevating and the most pure is, I believe, found in the contemplation of the beautiful. When, indeed, men speak of Beauty, they mean, precisely, not a quality, as is supposed, but an effect: they refer, in short, just to that intense and pure elevation of *soul – not* of intellect, or of heart – upon which I have commented, and which is experienced in consequence of contemplating "the beautiful". Now, I designate Beauty as the province of the poem merely because it is an obvious rule of art that effects should be made to spring from direct causes, that objects should be attained through means best adapted for their attainment – no one as yet having been weak enough to deny that the peculiar elevation alluded to is *most readily* attained in the poem. Now, the object, truth, or the satisfaction of the intellect, and the object passion, or the excitement of the heart, are, although attainable to a certain extent in poetry, far more readily attainable in prose. Truth, in fact, demands a precision and passion, a *homeliness* (the truly passionate will comprehend me), which are absolutely antagonistic to that Beauty which, I maintain, is the excitement, or pleasurable elevation, of the soul. It by no means follows from anything here said that passion, or even truth, may not be introduced, and even profitably introduced, into a poem – for they may serve in elucidation or aid the general effect, as do discords in music, by contrast – but the true artist will always contrive, first, to tone them into proper subservience to the predominant aim, and, secondly, to enveil them, as far as possible, in that Beauty which is the atmosphere and the essence of the poem.

Regarding, then, Beauty as my province, my next question referred to the *tone* of its highest manifestation – and all experience has shown that this tone is one of *sadness*. Beauty of whatever kind, in its supreme development, invariably excites the sensitive soul to tears. Melancholy is thus the most legitimate of all the poetical tones.

The length, the province and the tone being thus determined, I betook myself to ordinary induction, with the view of obtaining some artistic piquancy which might serve me as a keynote in the construction of the poem – some pivot upon which the whole structure might turn. In carefully thinking over all the usual artistic effects – or more properly *points*, in the theatrical sense – I did not fail to perceive immediately that no one had been so universally employed as that of the *refrain*. The universality of its employment sufficed to assure me of its intrinsic value, and spared me the necessity of submitting it to analysis. I considered it, however, with regard to its susceptibility of improvement, and soon saw it to be in a primitive condition. As commonly used, the *refrain*, or burden, not only is limited to lyric verse, but depends for its impression upon the force of monotone – both in sound and thought. The pleasure is deduced solely from the sense of identity – of repetition. I resolved to diversify, and so vastly heighten, the effect, by adhering, in general, to the monotone of sound, while I continually varied that of thought: that is to say, I determined to produce continuously novel effects, by the variation *of the application* of the *refrain* – the *refrain* itself remaining, for the most part, unvaried.

These points being settled, I next bethought me of the *nature* of my *refrain*. Since its application was to be repeatedly varied, it was clear that the *refrain* itself must be brief, for there would have been an insurmountable difficulty in frequent variations of application in any sentence of length. In proportion to the brevity of the sentence would, of course, be the facility of the variation. This led me at once to a single word as the best *refrain*.

The question now arose as to the *character* of the word. Having made up my mind to a *refrain*, the division of the poem into stanzas was, of course, a corollary – the *refrain* forming the close to each stanza. That such a close, to have force, must be sonorous and susceptible of protracted emphasis admitted no doubt – and these considerations inevitably led me to the long *o* as the most sonorous vowel, in connection with *r* as the most producible consonant.

The sound of the *refrain* being thus determined, it became necessary to select a word embodying this sound, and at the same time in the fullest possible keeping with that melancholy which I had predetermined as the tone of the poem. In such a search it would have been absolutely impossible to overlook the word "nevermore". In fact, it was the very first which presented itself.

The next desideratum was a pretext for the continuous use of the one word "nevermore". In observing the difficulty which I at once found in inventing a sufficiently plausible reason for its continuous repetition, I did not fail to perceive that this difficulty arose solely from the preassumption that the word was to be so continuously or monotonously spoken by *a human* being – I did not fail to perceive, in short, that the difficulty lay in the reconciliation of this monotony with the exercise of reason on the part of the creature repeating the word. Here, then, immediately arose the idea of a *non*-reasoning creature capable of speech – and, very naturally, a parrot, in the first instance, suggested itself, but was superseded forthwith by a raven, as equally capable of speech and infinitely more in keeping with the intended *tone*.

I had now gone so far as the conception of a raven – the bird of ill omen – monotonously repeating the one word "nevermore" at the conclusion of each stanza in a poem of melancholy tone and in length about one hundred lines. Now, never losing sight of the object *supremeness*, or perfection, at all points, I asked myself: "Of all melancholy topics, what, according to the *universal* understanding of mankind, is the *most* melancholy?" Death was the obvious reply. "And when," I said, "is this most melancholy of topics most poetical?" From what I have already explained at some length, the answer, here also, is obvious: "When it most closely allies itself to *Beauty*: the death, then, of a beautiful woman is, unquestionably, the most poetical topic in the world – and equally is it beyond doubt that the lips best suited for such topic are those of a bereaved lover."

I had now to combine the two ideas of a lover lamenting his deceased mistress and a raven continuously repeating the word "nevermore" – I had to combine these bearing in mind my design of varying, at every turn, the *application* of the word repeated – but the only intelligible mode of such combination is that of imagining the raven employing the word in answer to the queries of the lover. And here it was that I saw at once the opportunity afforded for the effect on which I had been depending – that is to say, the effect of the *variation of application*. I saw that I could make the first query propounded by the lover, the first query to which the Raven should reply "nevermore" – that I could make this first query a commonplace one, the second less so, the third still less, and so on, until at length the lover, startled from his original *nonchalance* by the melancholy character of the word itself, by its frequent repetition and by a consideration of the ominous reputation of the fowl that uttered it, is at length excited to superstition, and wildly propounds queries of a far different character – queries whose solution he has passionately at heart; propounds them half in superstition and half in that species of despair which delights in self-torture; propounds them not altogether because he believes in the prophetic or demoniac character of the bird (which, reason assures him, is merely repeating a lesson learned by rote), but because he experiences a frenzied pleasure in so modelling his questions as to receive from the *expected* "nevermore" the most delicious because the most intolerable of sorrow. Perceiving the opportunity thus afforded me (or, more strictly, thus forced upon me in the progress of the construction), I first established in mind the climax, or concluding query: that to which "nevermore" should be in the last place an answer – that query in reply to which this word "nevermore" should involve the utmost conceivable amount of sorrow and despair.

Here then the poem may be said to have its beginning: at the end, where all works of art should begin – for it was here, at this point of my preconsiderations, that I first put pen to paper in the composition of the stanza:

"Prophet!" said I. "Thing of evil!… Prophet still, if bird or devil!
By that heaven that bends above us, by that God we both adore –
Tell this soul with sorrow laden if, within the distant Aidenn,
It shall clasp a sainted maiden whom the angels name Lenore –
Clasp a rare and radiant maiden whom the angels name Lenore."
                              Quoth the raven, "Nevermore."

I composed this stanza, at this point, first that, by establishing the climax, I might the better vary and graduate, as regards seriousness and importance, the preceding queries of the lover, and, secondly, that I might definitely settle the rhythm, the metre and the length and general arrangement of the stanza – as well as graduate the stanzas which were to precede so that none of them might surpass this in rhythmical effect. Had I been able, in the subsequent composition, to construct more vigorous stanzas, I should, without scruple, have purposely enfeebled them, so as not to interfere with the climacteric effect.

And here I may as well say a few words of the versification. My first object (as usual) was originality. The extent to which this has been neglected, in versification, is one of the most unaccountable things in the world. Admitting that there is little possibility of variety in mere *rhythm*, it is still clear that the possible varieties of metre and stanza are absolutely infinite – and yet, *for centuries no man, in verse, has ever done, or ever seemed to think of doing, an original thing*. The fact is, originality (unless in minds of very unusual force) is by no means a matter, as some suppose, of impulse or intuition. In general, to be found, it must be elaborately sought, and, although a positive merit of the highest class, demands in its attainment less of invention than negation.

Of course, I pretend to no originality in either the rhythm or metre of the 'Raven'. The former is trochaic – the latter is octameter acatalectic, alternating with heptameter catalectic* repeated in the *refrain* of the fifth verse, and terminating with tetrameter catalectic. Less pedantically, the feet employed throughout (trochees) consist of a long syllable followed by a short: the first line of the stanza consists of eight of these feet, the second of seven and a half (in effect two thirds), the third of eight, the fourth of seven and a half, the fifth the same, the sixth three and a half. Now, each of these lines, taken individually, has been employed before, and what originality the 'Raven' has is in their *combination into stanza*: nothing even remotely approaching this combination has ever been attempted. The effect of this originality of combination is aided by other unusual and some altogether novel effects, arising from an extension of the application of the principles of rhyme and alliteration.

The next point to be considered was the mode of bringing together the lover and the raven – and the first branch of this consideration was the locale. For this the most natural suggestion might seem to be a forest, or the fields – but it has always appeared to me that a close *circumscription of space* is absolutely necessary to the effect of insulated incident: it has the force of a frame to a picture; it has an indisputable moral power in keeping concentrated the attention, and, of course, must not be confounded with mere unity of place.

I determined, then, to place the lover in his chamber – in a chamber rendered sacred to him by memories of her who had frequented it. The room is represented as richly furnished – this in mere pursuance of the ideas I have already explained on the subject of Beauty as the sole true poetical thesis.

The locale being thus determined, I had now to introduce the bird – and the thought of introducing him through the window was inevitable. The idea of making the lover suppose, in the first instance, that the flapping of the wings of the bird against the shutter is a "tapping" at the door originated in a wish to increase, by prolonging, the reader's curiosity, and in a desire to admit the incidental effect arising from the lover's throwing open the door, finding all dark and thence adopting the half-fancy that it was the spirit of his mistress that knocked.

I made the night tempestuous, first, to account for the raven's seeking admission, and secondly for the effect of contrast with the (physical) serenity within the chamber.

I made the bird alight on the bust of Pallas also for the effect of contrast between the marble and the plumage – it being understood that the bust was absolutely *suggested* by the bird – the bust of *Pallas* being chosen, first, as most in keeping with the scholarship of the lover, and, secondly, for the sonorousness of the word Pallas itself.

About the middle of the poem, also, I have availed myself of the force of contrast, with a view of deepening the ultimate impression. For example, an air of the fantastic – approaching as nearly to the ludicrous as was admissible – is given to the raven's entrance. He comes in "with many a flirt and flutter".

> Not the *least obeisance made he*, not a moment stopped or stayed he,
> But, *with mien of lord or lady*, perched above my chamber door.

In the two stanzas which follow, the design is more obviously carried out:

> Then this ebony bird beguiling my sad fancy into smiling
> By the *grave and stern decorum of the countenance it wore*,
> "Though thy *crest be shorn and shaven*, thou," I said, "art sure no craven,
> Ghastly grim and ancient raven wandering from the nightly shore –
> Tell me what thy lordly name is on the Night's Plutonian shore!"
>   Quoth the raven, "Nevermore."

> Much I marvelled *this ungainly fowl* to hear discourse so plainly,
> Though its answer little meaning, little relevancy bore,
> For we cannot help agreeing that no living human being
> *Ever yet was blessed with seeing bird above his chamber door –*
> *Bird or beast upon the sculptured bust above his chamber door –*
>   With such name as "Nevermore".

The effect of the denouement being thus provided for, I immediately drop the fantastic for a tone of the most profound seriousness – this tone commencing in the stanza directly following the one last quoted, with the line,

> But the raven, sitting lonely on that placid bust, spoke only, etc.

From this epoch the lover no longer jests – no longer sees anything even of the fantastic in the raven's demeanour. He speaks of him as a "grim, ungainly, ghastly, gaunt and ominous bird of yore", and feels the "fiery eyes" burning into his "bosom's core". This revolution of thought, or fancy, on the lover's part is intended to induce a similar one on the part of the reader – to bring the mind into a proper frame for the denouement, which is now brought about as rapidly and as *directly* as possible.

With the denouement proper – with the raven's reply "nevermore" to the lover's final demand if he shall meet his mistress in another world – the poem, in its obvious phase, that of a simple narrative, may be said to have its completion. So far, everything is within the limits of the accountable – of the real. A raven, having learnt by rote the single word "nevermore" and having escaped from the custody of its owner, is driven at midnight, through the violence of a storm, to seek admission at a window from which a light still gleams – the chamber window of a student occupied half in poring over a volume, half in dreaming of a beloved mistress deceased. The casement being thrown open at the fluttering of the bird's wings, the bird itself perches on the most convenient seat out of the immediate reach of the student, who, amused by the incident and the oddity of the visitor's demeanour, demands of it, in jest and without looking for a reply, its name. The raven, addressed, answers with its customary word, "nevermore" – a word which finds immediate echo in the melancholy heart of the student, who, giving utterance aloud to certain thoughts suggested by the occasion, is again startled by the fowl's repetition of "nevermore". The student now guesses the state of the case, but is impelled, as I have before explained, by the human thirst for self-torture, and in part by superstition, to propound such queries to the bird as will bring him, the lover, the most of the luxury of sorrow through the anticipated answer "Nevermore". With the indulgence, to the utmost extreme, of this self-torture, the narration, in what I have termed its first or obvious phase, has a natural termination, and so far there has been no overstepping of the limits of the real.

But in subjects so handled, however skilfully or with however vivid an array of incident, there is always a certain hardness or nakedness which repels the artistical eye. Two things are invariably required: first, some amount of complexity – or, more properly, adaptation; and, secondly, some amount of suggestiveness – some undercurrent, however indefinite of meaning. It is this latter, in especial, which imparts to a work of art so much of that *richness* (to borrow from colloquy a forcible term) which we are too fond of confounding with *the ideal*. It is the *excess* of the suggested meaning – it is the rendering this the upper- instead of the undercurrent of the theme – which turns into prose (and that of the very flattest kind) the so-called poetry of the so-called Transcendentalists.*

Holding these opinions, I added the two concluding stanzas of the poem – their suggestiveness being thus made to pervade all the narrative which has preceded them. The undercurrent of meaning is rendered first apparent in the lines

> "Take thy beak from out *my heart*, and take thy form from off my door!"
> Quoth the raven, "Nevermore."

It will be observed that the words "from out my heart" involve the first metaphorical expression in the poem. They, with the answer "Nevermore", dispose the mind to seek a moral in all that has been previously narrated. The reader begins now to regard the raven as emblematical – but it is not until the very last line of the very last stanza that the intention of making him emblematical of *mournful and never-ending remembrance* is permitted distinctly to be seen:

And the raven, never flitting, still is sitting, still is sitting,
On the pallid bust of Pallas just above my chamber door.
And his eyes have all the seeming of a demon's that is dreaming,
And the lamplight o'er him streaming throws his shadow on the floor –
And my soul *from out that shadow* that lies floating on the floor
                                        Shall be lifted... nevermore!

THE RATIONALE OF VERSE*

The word "verse" is here used not in its strict or primitive sense, but as the term most convenient for expressing generally and without pedantry all that is involved in the consideration of rhythm, rhyme, metre and versification.

There is, perhaps, no topic in polite literature which has been more pertinaciously discussed, and there is certainly not one about which so much inaccuracy, confusion, misconception, misrepresentation, mystification and downright ignorance on all sides can be fairly said to exist. Were the topic really difficult – or did it lie, even, in the cloudland of metaphysics, where the doubt vapours may be made to assume any and every shape at the will or at the fancy of the gazer – we should have less reason to wonder at all this contradiction and perplexity, but in fact the subject is exceedingly simple: one tenth of it, possibly, may be called ethical – nine tenths, however, appertain to the mathematics, and the whole is included within the limits of the commonest common sense.

"But, if this is the case, how," it will be asked, "can so much misunderstanding have arisen? Is it conceivable that a thousand profound scholars, investigating so very simple a matter for centuries, have not been able to place it in the fullest light, at least, of which it is susceptible?" These queries, I confess, are not easily answered – at all events, a satisfactory reply to them might cost more trouble than would, if properly considered, the whole *vexata quæstio** to which they have reference. Nevertheless, there is little difficulty or danger in suggesting that the "thousand profound scholars" *may* have failed, first because they were scholars, secondly because they were profound, and thirdly because they were a thousand – the impotency of the scholarship and profundity having been thus multiplied a thousandfold. I am serious in these suggestions, for, first again, there is something in "scholarship" which seduces us into blind worship of Bacon's "Idol of the Theatre"* – into irrational deference to antiquity. Secondly, the proper "profundity" is rarely profound: it is the nature of truth in general, as of some ores in particular, to be richest when most superficial. Thirdly, the clearest subject may be overclouded by mere superabundance of talk. In chemistry, the best way of separating two bodies is to add a third; in speculation, fact often agrees with fact and argument with argument, until an additional well-meaning fact or argument sets every thing by the ears.

In one case out of a hundred, a point is excessively discussed because it is obscure; in the ninety-nine remaining it is obscure because excessively discussed. When a topic is thus circumstanced, the readiest mode of investigating it is to forget that any previous investigation has been attempted.

But, in fact, while much has been written on the Greek and Latin rhythms, and even on the Hebrew, little effort has been made at examining that of any of the modern tongues. As regards the English, comparatively nothing has been done. It may be said, indeed, that we are without a treatise on our own verse. In our ordinary grammars and in our works on rhetoric or prosody in general may be found occasional chapters, it is true, which have the heading "Versification", but these are, in all instances, exceedingly meagre. They pretend to no analysis; they propose nothing like system; they make no attempt at even rule; everything depends upon "authority". They are confined, in fact, to mere exemplification of the supposed varieties of English feet and English lines – although in no work with which I am acquainted are these feet correctly given or these lines detailed in anything like their full extent. Yet what has been mentioned is all – if we except the occasional introduction of some pedagogism such as this, borrowed from the Greek prosodies: "When a syllable is wanting, the verse is said to be catalectic; when the measure is exact, the line is acatalectic; when there is a redundant syllable, it forms hypermeter." Now, whether a line be termed catalectic or acatalectic is, perhaps, a point of no vital importance – it is even possible that the student may be able to decide, promptly, when the *a* should be employed and when omitted, yet be incognizant, at the same time, of *all* that is worth knowing in regard to the structure of verse.

A leading defect in each of our treatises (if treatises they can be called) is the confining the subject to mere *versification*, while *verse* in general, with the understanding given to the term in the heading of this paper, is the real question at issue. Nor am I aware of even one of our grammars which so much as properly defines the word "versification" itself. "Versification" – says a work now before me, of which the accuracy is far more than usual, the *English Grammar* of Goold Brown* – "Versification is the art of arranging words into lines of correspondent length so as to produce harmony by the regular alternation of syllables differing in quantity." The commencement of this definition might apply, indeed, to the *art* of versification, but not to versification itself. Versification is not the art of arranging, etc., but the actual arranging – a distinction too obvious to need comment. The error here is identical with one which has been too long permitted to disgrace the initial page of every one of our school grammars. I allude to the definitions of "English grammar" itself. "English grammar," it is

said, "is the art of speaking and writing the English language correctly."
This phraseology, or something essentially similar, is employed, I believe,
by Bacon, Miller, Fisk, Greenleaf, Ingersoll, Kirkham, Cooper, Flint, Pue,
Comley and many others.* These gentlemen, it is presumed, adopted it
without examination from Murray,* who derived it from Lily* (whose
work was "*quam solam Regia Majestas in omnibus scholis docendam
præcipit*")* and who appropriated it without acknowledgement, but with
some unimportant modification, from the Latin grammar of Leonicenus.*
It may be shown, however, that this definition, so complacently received, is
not, and cannot be, a proper definition of "English grammar". A definition
is that which so describes its object as to distinguish it from all others –
it is no definition of any one thing if its terms are applicable to any one
other. But if it be asked "What is the design, the end, the aim of English
grammar?", our obvious answer is: "The art of speaking and writing the
English language correctly" – that is to say, we must use the precise words
employed as the definition of "English grammar" itself. But the object to be
obtained by any means is, assuredly, not the means. "English grammar" and
the end contemplated by "English grammar" are two matters sufficiently
distinct – nor can the one be more reasonably regarded as the other than
a fishing hook as a fish. The definition, therefore, which is applicable in
the latter instance, *cannot*, in the former, be true. Grammar in general is
the analysis of language – English grammar, of the English.

But to return to "versification" as defined in our extract above. "It is the
art," says the extract, "of arranging words into lines *of correspondent
length*." Not so: a correspondence in the length of lines is by no means
essential. Pindaric odes* are, surely, instances of versification, yet these
compositions are noted for extreme diversity in the length of their lines.

The arrangement is moreover said to be for the purpose of producing
"*harmony* by the regular alternation", etc. But *harmony* is not the sole
aim – not even the principal one. In the construction of verse, *melody*
should never be left out of view – yet this is a point which all our prosodies
have most unaccountably forborne to touch. Reasoned rules on this topic
should form a portion of all systems of rhythm.

"So as to produce harmony," says the definition, "by the *regular alter-
nation*", etc. A *regular* alternation, as described, forms no part of any
principle of versification. The arrangement of spondees and dactyls, for
example, in the Greek hexameter, is an arrangement which may be termed
"at random". At least, it is arbitrary. Without interference with the line
as a whole, a dactyl may be substituted for a spondee, or the converse,
at any point other than the ultimate and penultimate feet – of which the

former is always a spondee, the latter nearly always a dactyl. Here, it is clear, we have no "*regular* alternation of syllables differing in quantity".

"So as to produce harmony," proceeds the definition, "by the regular alternation of *syllables differing in quantity*" – in other words, by the alternation of long and short syllables, for in rhythm all syllables are necessarily either short or long. But not only do I deny the necessity of any *regularity* in the succession of feet (and, by consequence, of syllables), but dispute the essentiality of any *alternation*, regular or irregular, of syllables long and short. Our author, observe, is now engaged in a definition of versification in general, not of English versification in particular. But the Greek and Latin metres abound in the spondee and pyrrhic – the former consisting of two long syllables, the latter of two short – and there are innumerable instances of the immediate succession of many spondees and many pyrrhics.

Here is a passage from Silius Italicus:*

> Fallit te, mensas inter quod credis inermem.
> Tot bellis quæsita viro, tot cædibus armat
> Maiestas æterna ducem. Si admoveris ora,
> Cannas et Trebiam ante oculos Trasymennaque busta
> Et Pauli stare ingentem miraberis umbram.

Making the elisions demanded by the classic prosodies, we should scan these hexameters thus:

> Fāllīs | tē mēn | sās īn | tēr qūod | crēdĭs ĭn | ērmēm |
> Tōt bēl | līs qūæ | sītă vĭ | rō tōt | cædĭbŭs | ārmāt |
> Māiēs | tās ē | tērnă dŭ | cēm s'ād | mōvĕrĭs | ōrā |
> Cānnās | ēt Trĕbī | ānt' ŏcŭ | lōs Trăsÿ | mēnnăquĕ | būstā |
> Ēt Pāu | lī stā | r'īngēn | tēm mī | rābĕrĭs | ūmbrām |

It will be seen that, in the first and last of these lines, we have only two short syllables in thirteen, with an uninterrupted succession of no less than *nine* long syllables. But how are we to reconcile all this with a definition of versification which describes it as "the art of arranging words into lines of correspondent length so as to produce harmony by the *regular alternation of syllables differing in quantity*"?

It may be urged, however, that our prosodist's *intention* was to speak of the English metres alone, and that, by omitting all mention of the spondee and pyrrhic, he has virtually avowed their exclusion from our rhythms. A grammarian is never excusable on the ground of good intentions. We demand from him, if from anyone, rigorous precision of style. But grant the design. Let us admit that our author, following the example of all authors on English prosody, has, in defining versification at large, intended a definition merely of the English. All these prosodists, we will say, reject the spondee and pyrrhic. Still all admit the iambus, which consists of a short syllable followed by a long; the trochee, which is the converse of the iambus; the dactyl, formed of one long syllable followed by two short; and the anapaest – two short succeeded by a long. The spondee is improperly rejected, as I shall presently show. The pyrrhic is rightfully dismissed. Its existence in either ancient or modern rhythm is purely chimerical, and the insisting on so perplexing a nonentity as a foot of *two short* syllables, affords, perhaps, the best evidence of the gross irrationality and subservience to authority which characterize our prosody. In the mean time, the acknowledged dactyl and anapaest are enough to sustain my proposition about the "alternation", etc., without reference to feet which are assumed to exist in the Greek and Latin metres alone, for an anapaest and a dactyl may meet in the same line – when of course we shall have an uninterrupted succession of four short syllables. The meeting of these two feet, to be sure, is an accident not contemplated in the definition now discussed, for this definition, in demanding a "regular alternation of syllables differing in quantity", insists on a regular succession of similar *feet*. But here is an example:

Sīng tŏ mĕ | Isăbēlle.

This is the opening line of a little ballad now before me, which proceeds in the same rhythm – a peculiarly beautiful one.* More than all this: English lines are often well composed, entirely, of a regular succession of syllables *all of the same quantity* – the first lines, for instance, of the following quatrain by Arthur C. Coxe:*

> *March! March! March!*
>   Making sounds as they tread –
> Ho! Ho! – how they step,
>   Going down to the dead!

The line italicized is formed of three caesuras. The caesura, of which I have much to say hereafter, is rejected by the English prosodies and grossly misrepresented in the classic. It is a perfect foot – the most important in all verse – and consists of a single *long* syllable... *but the length of this syllable varies.*

It has thus been made evident that there is *not one* point of the definition in question which does not involve an error. And for anything more satisfactory or more intelligible we shall look in vain to any published treatise on the topic.

So general and so total a failure can be referred only to radical misconception. In fact, the English prosodists have blindly followed the pedants. These latter, like *les moutons de Panurge*,* have been occupied in incessant tumbling into ditches, for the excellent reason that their leaders have so tumbled before. The *Iliad*, being taken as a starting point, was made to stand instead of nature and common sense. Upon this poem, in place of facts and deduction from fact or from natural law, were built systems of feet, metres, rhythms, rules – rules that contradict each other every five minutes, and for nearly all of which there may be found twice as many exceptions as examples. If anyone has a fancy to be thoroughly confounded – to see how far the infatuation of what is termed "classical scholarship" can lead a bookworm in the manufacture of darkness out of sunshine – let him turn over, for a few moments, any of the German Greek prosodies. The only thing clearly made out in them is a very magnificent contempt for Leibnitz's principle of "a sufficient reason".*

To divert attention from the real matter in hand by any further reference to these works is unnecessary, and would be weak. I cannot call to mind, at this moment, one essential particular of information that is to be gleaned from them – and I will drop them here with merely this one observation: that, employing from among the numerous "*ancient*" feet the spondee, the trochee, the iambus, the anapaest, the dactyl and the caesura alone, I will engage to scan *correctly* any of the Horatian rhythms,* or any true rhythm that human ingenuity can conceive. And this excess of chimerical feet is, perhaps, the very least of the scholastic supererogations.* *Ex uno disce omnia*.* The fact is that *quantity* is a point in whose investigation the lumber of mere learning may be dispensed with, if ever in any. Its appreciation is universal. It appertains to no region, nor race, nor era in especial. To melody and to harmony the Greeks hearkened with ears precisely similar to those which we employ for similar purposes at present, and I should not be condemned for heresy in asserting that a pendulum at Athens would have vibrated much after the same fashion as does a pendulum in the city of Penn.*

Verse originates in the human enjoyment of equality, fitness. To this enjoyment, also, all the moods of verse – rhythm, metre, stanza, rhyme, alliteration, the *refrain* and other analogous effects – are to be referred. As there are some readers who habitually confound rhythm and metre, it may be as well here to say that the former concerns the *character* of feet (that is, the arrangements of syllables), while the latter has to do with the *number* of these feet. Thus by "a dactylic *rhythm*" we express a sequence of dactyls. By "a dactylic hexa*meter*" we imply a line or measure consisting of six of these dactyls.

To return to *equality*. Its idea embraces those of similarity, proportion, identity, repetition and adaptation or fitness. It might not be very difficult to go even behind the idea of equality and show both how and why it is that the human nature takes pleasure in it, but such an investigation would, for any purpose now in view, be supererogatory. It is sufficient that the *fact* is undeniable – the fact that man derives enjoyment from his perception of equality. Let us examine a crystal. We are at once interested by the equality between the sides and between the angles of one of its faces: the equality of the sides pleases us – that of the angles doubles the pleasure. On bringing to view a second face in all respects similar to the first, this pleasure seems to be squared – on bringing to view a third, it appears to be cubed, and so on. I have no doubt, indeed, that the delight experienced, if measurable, would be found to have exact mathematical relations such as I suggest – that is to say as far as a certain point, beyond which there would be a decrease in similar relations.

The perception of pleasure in the equality of *sounds* is the principle of *music*. Unpractised ears can appreciate only simple equalities, such as are found in ballad airs. While comparing one simple sound with another, they are too much occupied to be capable of comparing the equality subsisting between these two simple sounds, taken conjointly, and two other similar simple sounds taken conjointly. Practised ears, on the other hand, appreciate both equalities at the same instant – although it is absurd to suppose that both are *heard* at the same instant. One is heard and appreciated from itself, the other is heard by the memory, and the instant glides into and is confounded with the secondary appreciation. Highly cultivated musical taste in this manner enjoys not only these double equalities, all appreciated at once, but takes pleasurable cognizance, through memory, of equalities the members of which occur at intervals so great that the uncultivated taste loses them altogether. That this latter can properly estimate or decide on the merits of what is called "scientific music", is of course impossible. But scientific music has no claim to intrinsic excellence: it is fit for scientific ears alone. In its excess it is the triumph of the *physique* over the *morale* of music. The sentiment is overwhelmed by the sense. On the whole, the advocates of the simpler melody and harmony have infinitely the best of the argument – although there has been very little of real argument on the subject.

In *verse*, which cannot be better designated than as an inferior or less capable music, there is, happily, little chance for complexity. Its rigidly simple character not even science – not even pedantry – can greatly pervert.

The rudiment of verse may, possibly, be found in the *spondee*. The very germ of a thought seeking satisfaction in equality of sound would result in the construction of words of two syllables equally accented. In corroboration of this idea we find that spondees most abound in the most ancient tongues. The second step we can easily suppose to be the comparison – that is to say, the collocation of two spondees – of two words composed each of a spondee. The third step would be the juxtaposition of three of these words. By this time the perception of monotone would induce further consideration – and thus arises what Leigh Hunt so flounders in discussing under the title of "The *Principle* of Variety in Uniformity".* Of course there is no principle in the case – nor in maintaining it. The "uniformity" is the principle – the "variety" is but the principle's natural safeguard from self-destruction by excess of self. "Uniformity", besides, is the very worst word that could have been chosen for the expression of the *general* idea at which it aims.

The perception of monotone having given rise to an attempt at its relief, the first thought in this new direction would be that of collating two or more words formed each of two syllables differently accented (that is to say, short and long) but having the same order in each word – in other terms, of collating two or more iambuses, or two or more trochees. And here let me pause to assert that more pitiable nonsense has been written on the topic of *long* and *short* syllables than on any other subject under the sun. In general, a syllable is long or short just as it is difficult or easy of enunciation. The *natural* long syllables are those encumbered – the *natural* short syllables are those *un*encumbered – with consonants: all the rest is mere artificiality and jargon. The Latin prosodies have a rule that "a vowel before two consonants is long". This rule is deduced from "authority" – that is, from the observation that vowels so circumstanced, in the ancient poems, are always in syllables long by the laws of scansion. The philosophy of the rule is untouched, and lies simply in the physical difficulty of giving voice to such syllables – of performing the lingual evolutions necessary for their utterance. Of course, it is not the *vowel* that is long (although the rule says so), but the syllable of which the vowel is a part. It will be seen that the length of a syllable, depending on the facility or difficulty of its enunciation, must have great variation in various syllables, but for the purposes of verse we suppose a long syllable equal to two short ones – and the natural deviation from this relativeness we correct in perusal. The more closely our long syllables approach this relation with our short ones, the better, *ceteris paribus*,* will be our verse, but if the relation does not exist of itself, we force it by emphasis, which can, of course, make any syllable as long as desired – or, by an effort, we can pronounce with unnatural brevity a syllable that is naturally too long. *Accented* syllables are of course always long – but, where *un*encumbered with consonants, must be classed among the *unnaturally* long. Mere custom has declared that we shall accent them – that is to say, dwell upon them – but no inevitable lingual difficulty forces us to do so. In fine, every long syllable must of its own accord occupy in its utterance, or must be *made* to occupy, precisely the time demanded for two short ones. The only exception to this rule is found in the caesura – of which more anon.

The success of the experiment with the trochees or iambuses (the one would have suggested the other) must have led to a trial of dactyls or anapaests (natural dactyls or anapaests) – dactylic or anapaestic *words*. And now some degree of complexity has been attained. There is an appreciation, first, of the equality between the several dactyls, or anapaests, and, secondly, of that between the long syllable and the two short conjointly. But here it may be said that step after step would have been taken, in continuation of this routine, until all the feet of the Greek prosodies became exhausted. Not so: these remaining feet have no existence except in the brains of the scholiasts. It is needless to imagine men inventing these things, and folly to explain how and why they invented them, until it shall be first shown that they are actually invented. All other "feet" than those which I have specified are, if not impossible at first view, merely combinations of the specified – and, although this assertion is rigidly true, I will, to avoid misunderstanding, put it in a somewhat different shape. I will say, then, that at present I am aware of no *rhythm* (nor do I believe that any one can be constructed) which, in its last analysis, will not be found to consist altogether of the feet I have mentioned, either existing in their individual and obvious condition or interwoven with each other in accordance with simple natural laws which I will endeavour to point out hereafter.

We have now gone so far as to suppose men constructing indefinite sequences of spondaic, iambic, trochaic, dactylic or anapaestic words. In *extending* these sequences, they would be again arrested by the sense of monotone. A succession of spondees would *immediately* have displeased; one of iambuses or of trochees, on account of the variety included within the foot itself, would have taken longer to displease; one of dactyls or anapaests, still longer – but even the last, if extended very far, must have become wearisome. The idea, first, of curtailing, and, secondly, of defining the length of a sequence would thus at once have arisen. Here then is the *line* of verse proper.* The principle of equality being constantly at the bottom of the whole process, lines would naturally be made, in the first instance, equal in the number of their feet; in the second instance, there would be variation in the mere number: one line would be twice as long as another; then one would be some less obvious multiple of another; then still less obvious proportions would be adopted. Nevertheless there would be *proportion* – that is to say, a phase of equality, still.

Lines being once introduced, the necessity of distinctly defining these lines *to the ear* (as yet written verse does not exist) would lead to a scrutiny of their capabilities *at their terminations*, and now would spring up the idea of equality in sound between the final syllables – in other words, of *rhyme*. First, it would be used only in the iambic, anapaestic and spondaic rhythms (granting that the latter had not been thrown aside, long since, on account of its tameness), because in these rhythms the concluding syllable, being long, could best sustain the necessary protraction of the voice. No great while could elapse, however, before the effect, found pleasant as well as useful, would be applied to the two remaining rhythms. But as the chief force of rhyme must lie in the accented syllable, the attempt to create rhyme at all in these two remaining rhythms, the trochaic and dactylic, would necessarily result in double and triple rhymes, such as *beauty* with *duty* (trochaic) and *beautiful* with *dutiful* (dactylic).

It must be observed that, in suggesting these processes, I assign them no date – nor do I even insist upon their order. Rhyme is supposed to be of modern origin – and, were this proved, my positions remain untouched. I may say, however, in passing, that several instances of rhyme occur in the *Clouds* of Aristophanes,* and that the Roman poets occasionally employ it. There is an effective species of ancient rhyming which has never descended to the moderns: that in which the ultimate and penultimate syllables rhyme with each other. For example:

> Parturient montes, nascetur ridicu*lus mus*.*

and again –

> Litoreis ingens inventa sub ilici*bus sus*.*

The terminations of Hebrew verse (as far as understood) show no signs of rhyme, but what thinking person can doubt that it did actually exist? That men have so obstinately and blindly insisted, *in general*, even up to the present day, in confining rhyme to the *ends* of lines, when its effect is even better applicable elsewhere, intimates, in my opinion, the sense of some *necessity* in the connection of the end with the rhyme, hints that the origin of rhyme lay in a necessity which connected it with the end, shows that neither mere accident nor mere fancy gave rise to the connection

– points, in a word, at the very necessity which I have suggested (that of some mode of defining lines *to the ear*) as the true origin of rhyme. Admit this, and we throw the origin far back in the night of time – beyond the origin of written verse.

But to resume. The amount of complexity I have now supposed to be attained is very considerable. Various systems of equalization are appreciated at once (or nearly so) in their respective values and in the value of each system with reference to all the others. As our present *ultimatum** of complexity, we have arrived at triple-rhymed, natural-dactylic lines, existing proportionally as well as equally with regard to other triple-rhymed, natural-dactylic lines. For example:

> Virginal Lilian, rigidly, humblily dutiful –
> > Saintlily, lowlily,
> > Thrillingly, holily
> Beautiful!

Here we appreciate, first, the absolute equality between the long syllable of each dactyl and the two short conjointly; secondly, the absolute equality between each dactyl and any other dactyl – in other words, among all the dactyls; thirdly, the absolute equality between the two middle lines; fourthly, the absolute equality between the first line and the three others taken conjointly; fifthly, the absolute equality between the last two syllables of the respective words "dutiful" and "beautiful"; sixthly, the absolute equality between the two last syllables of the respective words "lowlily" and "holily"; seventhly, the proximate equality between the first syllable of "dutiful" and the first syllable of "beautiful"; eighthly, the proximate equality between the first syllable of "lowlily" and that of "holily"; ninthly, the proportional equality (that of five to one) between the first line and each of its members, the dactyls; tenthly, the proportional equality (that of two to one) between each of the middle lines and its members, the dactyls; eleventhly, the proportional equality between the first line and each of the two middle – that of five to two; twelfthly, the proportional equality between the first line and the last – that of five to one; thirteenthly, the proportional equality between each of the middle lines and the last – that of two to one; lastly, the proportional equality, as concerns number, between all the lines, taken collectively and any individual line – that of four to one.

The consideration of this last equality would give birth immediately to the idea of *stanza** – that is to say, the insulation of lines into equal or obviously proportional masses. In its primitive (which was also its best) form, the stanza would most probably have had absolute unity. In other words, the removal of any one of its lines would have rendered it imperfect; as in the case above, where, if the last line, for example, be taken away, there is left no rhyme to the "dutiful" of the first. Modern stanza is excessively loose – and where so, ineffective as a matter of course.

Now, although in the deliberate written statement which I have here given of these various systems of equalities there seems to be an infinity of complexity – so much that it is hard to conceive the mind taking cognizance of them all in the brief period occupied by the perusal or recital of the stanza – yet the difficulty is in fact apparent only when we will it to become so. Anyone fond of mental experiment may satisfy himself, by trial, that, in listening to the lines, he does actually (although with a seeming unconsciousness, on account of the rapid evolutions of sensation) recognize and instantaneously appreciate (more or less intensely as his ear is cultivated) each and all of the equalizations detailed. The pleasure received, or receivable, has very much such progressive increase, and in very nearly such mathematical relations, as those which I have suggested in the case of the crystal.

It will be observed that I speak of merely a proximate equality between the first syllable of "dutiful" and that of "beautiful", and it may be asked why we cannot imagine the earliest rhymes to have had absolute instead of proximate equality of sound. But absolute equality would have involved the use of identical words, and it is the duplicate sameness or monotony – that of sense as well as that of sound – which would have caused these rhymes to be rejected in the very first instance.

The narrowness of the limits within which verse composed of natural feet alone must necessarily have been confined would have led, after a *very* brief interval, to the trial and immediate adoption of artificial feet – that is to say, of feet *not* constituted each of a single word, but two or even three words, or of parts of words. These feet would be intermingled with natural ones. For example:

ă brēath | căn māke | thĕm ās | ă brēath | hăs māde. |

This is an iambic line in which each iambus is formed of two words. Again:

Thĕ ūn | ĭmā | gĭnā | blĕ mīght | ŏf Jōve. |

This is an iambic line in which the first foot is formed of a word and a part of a word; the second and third of parts taken from the body or interior of a word; the fourth of a part and a whole; the fifth of two complete words. There are no *natural* feet in either lines. Again:

Cān ĭt bĕ | fāncĭĕd thăt | Dēĭty | ēvĕr vĭn | dīctĭvely |
Māde ĭn hĭs | īmăge ă | mānnĭkĭn | mĕrely tŏ | māddĕn ĭt? |

These are two dactylic lines in which we find natural feet ("Deity", "man-nikin"), feet composed of two words ("fancied that", "image a", "merely to", "madden it"), feet composed of three words ("can it be", "made in his"), a foot composed of a part of a word ("dictively") and a foot composed of a word and a part of a word ("ever vin").

And now, in our supposititious progress, we have gone so far as to exhaust all the *essentialities* of verse. What follows may, strictly speaking, be regarded as embellishment merely – but even in this embellishment the rudimental sense of *equality* would have been the never-ceasing impulse. It would, for example, be simply in seeking further administration to this sense that men would come, in time, to think of the *refrain*, or burden – where, at the closes of the several stanzas of a poem, one word or phrase is *repeated* – and of alliteration, in whose simplest form a consonant is *repeated* in the commencements of various words. This effect would be extended so as to embrace repetitions both of vowels and of consonants, in the bodies as well as in the beginnings of words, and, at a later period, would be made to infringe on the province of rhyme by the introduction of general similarity of sound between whole feet occurring in the body of a line – all of which modifications I have exemplified in the line above:

Made in his *im*age a *mannikin m*erely to *madden it.*

Further cultivation would improve also the *refrain* by relieving its monotone in slightly varying the phrase at each repetition, or (as I have attempted to do in 'The Raven') in retaining the phrase and varying its application – although this latter point is not strictly a rhythmical effect *alone*. Finally, poets, when fairly wearied with following precedent – following it the more closely the less they perceived it in company with reason – would adventure so far as to indulge in positive rhyme at other points than the ends of lines. First, they would put it in the middle of the line; then at some point where the multiple would be less obvious; then, alarmed at their own audacity, they would undo all their work by cutting these lines in two. And here is the fruitful source of the infinity of "short metre" by which modern poetry, if not distinguished, is at least disgraced. It would require a high degree, indeed, both of cultivation and of courage on the part of any versifier to enable him to place his rhymes – and let them remain – at unquestionably their best position: that of unusual and *unanticipated* intervals.

On account of the stupidity of some people, or (if talent be a more respectable word) on account of their talent for misconception, I think it necessary to add here, first, that I believe the "processes" above detailed to be nearly if not accurately those which *did* occur in the gradual creation of what we now call "verse"; secondly, that, although I so believe, I yet urge neither the assumed fact nor my belief in it as a part of the true proposition of this paper; thirdly, that in regard to the aim of this paper, it is of no consequence whether these processes did occur either in the order I have assigned them or at all – my design being simply, in presenting a general type of what such processes *might* have been and *must* have resembled, to help *them*, the "some people", to an easy understanding of what I have further to say on the topic of verse.

There is one point which, in my summary of the processes, I have purposely forborne to touch, because this point, being the most important of all on account of the immensity of error usually involved in its consideration, would have led me into a series of detail inconsistent with the object of a summary.

Every reader of verse must have observed how seldom it happens that even any one line proceeds uniformly with a succession, such as I have supposed, of absolutely equal feet – that is to say, with a succession of iambuses only, or of trochees only, or of dactyls only, or of anapaests only, or of spondees only. Even in the most musical lines we find the succession interrupted. The iambic pentameters of Pope,* for example, will be found on examination frequently varied by trochees in the beginning or by (what seem to be) anapaests in the body of the line.

> Ŏh thōu | whătē | vĕr tī | tlĕ pleāse | thĭne eār |
> Dĕan Drā | piĕr Bĭck | ĕrstăff | ŏr Gūll | ĭvēr |
> Whēthĕr | thŏu choōse | Cĕrvān | tĕs' sē | rĭoŭs ăir |
> Ŏr laūgh | ănd shāke | ĭn Rāb | ĕlaĭs' eā | sy chaīr |

Were anyone weak enough to refer to the prosodies for the solution of the difficulty here, he would find it *solved* as usual by a *rule*, stating the fact (or what it, the rule, supposes to be the fact), but without the slightest attempt at the *rationale*. "By a *syneresis* of the two short syllables," say the books, "an anapaest may sometimes be employed for an iambus, or a dactyl for a trochee. [...] In the beginning of a line, a trochee is often used for an iambus."

Blending is the plain English for *syneresis*, but there should be *no* blending – neither is an anapaest *ever* employed for an iambus, or a dactyl for a trochee. These feet differ in time, and *no* feet so differing can ever be legitimately used in the same line. An anapaest is equal to four short syllables – an iambus only to three. Dactyls and trochees hold the same relation. The principle of *equality* in verse admits, it is true, of variation at certain points for the relief of monotone, as I have already shown, but the point of *time* is that point which, being the rudimental one, must never be tampered with at all.

To explain. In further efforts for the relief of monotone than those to which I have alluded in the summary, men soon came to see that there was no absolute necessity for adhering to the precise number of syllables, provided the time required for the whole foot was preserved inviolate. They saw, for instance, that in such a line as

Ŏr laūgh | ănd shāke | ĭn Rāb | ĕlaĭs' ēa | sy chāir |

the equalization of the three syllables *elais ea* with the two syllables composing any of the other feet could be readily effected by pronouncing the two syllables *elais* in double-quick time. By pronouncing each of the syllables *e* and *lais* twice as rapidly as the syllable *sy* or the syllable *in*, or any other short syllable, they could bring the two of them, taken together, to the length (that is to say to the time) of any one short syllable. This consideration enabled them to effect the agreeable variation of three syllables in place of the uniform two. And variation was the object – variation to the ear. What sense is there, then, in supposing this object rendered null by the *blending* of the two syllables so as to render them, in absolute effect, one? Of course, there must be *no* blending. Each syllable must be pronounced as distinctly as possible (or the variation is lost), but with twice the rapidity in which the ordinary short syllable is enunciated. That the syllables *elais ea* do not compose an *anapaest* is evident, and the signs (ă ă ā) of their accentuation are erroneous. The foot might be written thus (a̯ a̯ a̯), the inverted crescents expressing double-quick time, and might be called a bastard iambus.

Here is a trochaic line:

Sēe thĕ | dēlĭcăte- | fōotĕd | rēindeĕr. |

The prosodies – that is to say, the most considerate of them – would here decide that "delicate" is a dactyl used in place of a trochee, and would refer to what they call their "rule" for justification. Others, varying the stupidity, would insist upon a Procrustean adjustment* thus ("del'cate") – an adjustment recommended to all such words as *silvery, murmuring*, etc., which, it is said, should be not only pronounced, but written *silv'ry, murm'ring*, and so on, whenever they find themselves in trochaic predicament. I have only to say that "delicate", when circumstanced as above, is neither a dactyl nor a dactyl's equivalent; that I would suggest for it this (a̲a̲a̲) accentuation; that I think it as well to call it a "bastard trochee"; and that all words, at all events, should be written and pronounced *in full*, and as nearly as possible as nature intended them.

About eleven years ago, there appeared in the *American Monthly Magazine* (then edited, I believe, by Messrs Hoffman and Benjamin)* a review of Mr Willis's poems* – the critic putting forth his strength, or his weakness, in an endeavour to show that the poet was either absurdly affected or grossly ignorant of the laws of verse, the accusation being based altogether on the fact that Mr W. made occasional use of this very word "delicate" and other similar words in "the heroic measure, which everyone knew consisted of feet of two syllables". Mr W. has often, for example, such lines as

> That binds him to a woman's *delicate* love…*
> In the gay sunshine, *reverent* in the storm…*
> With its *invisible* fingers, my loose hair…*

Here, of course, the feet *licate love, verent in* and *sible fin* are bastard iambuses, are *not* anapaests and are *not* improperly used. Their employment, on the contrary, by Mr Willis is but one of the innumerable instances he has given of keen sensibility in all those matters of taste which may be classed under the general head of "fanciful embellishment".

It is also about eleven years ago, if I am not mistaken, since Mr Horne (of England), the author of *Orion*,* one of the noblest epics in any language, thought it necessary to preface his *Chaucer Modernized*,* by a very long and evidently a very elaborate essay, of which the greater portion was occupied in a discussion of the seemingly anomalous foot of which we have been speaking. Mr Horne upholds Chaucer in its frequent use; maintains his superiority, *on account* of his so frequently using it, over all English versifiers; and, indignantly repelling the common idea of those who make verse on their fingers (that the superfluous syllable is a roughness and an error), very chivalrously makes battle for it as "a grace". That a grace it *is*, there can be no doubt, and what I complain of is that the author of the most happily versified long poem in existence should have been under the necessity of discussing this grace merely *as* a grace, through forty or fifty vague pages, solely because of his inability to show *how* and *why* it is a grace – by which showing the question would have been settled in an instant.

About the trochee used for an iambus, as we see in the beginning of the line

Whĕthĕr thou choose Cervantes' serious air,

there is little that need be said. It brings me to the general proposition that, in all rhythms, the prevalent or distinctive feet may be varied at will, and nearly at random, by the *occasional* introduction of equivalent feet – that is to say, feet the sum of whose syllabic times is equal to the sum of the syllabic times of the distinctive feet. Thus the trochee *whĕthĕr* is equal, in the sum of the times of its syllables, to the iambus *thŏu choōse* in the sum of the times of *its* syllables, each foot being, in time, equal to three short syllables. Good versifiers who happen to be also good poets contrive to relieve the monotone of a series of feet by the use of equivalent feet only at rare intervals, and at such points of their subject as seem in accordance with the *startling* character of the variation. Nothing of this care is seen in the line quoted above – although Pope has some fine instances of the duplicate effect. Where vehemence is to be strongly expressed, I am not sure that we should be wrong in venturing on *two consecutive* equivalent feet – although I cannot say that I have ever known the adventure made except in the following passage, which occurs in *Al Aaraaf*,* a boyish poem written by myself when a boy. I am referring to the sudden and rapid advent of a star:

> Dim was its little disk, and angel eyes
> Alone could see the phantom in the skies
> Whĕn fīrst thĕ phăntŏm's cōurse wăs fōund tŏ bē
> *Hēadlŏng hīthĕr*ward o'er the starry sea.*

In the "general proposition" above, I speak of the *occasional* introduction of equivalent feet. It sometimes happens that unskilful versifiers, without knowing what they do or why they do it, introduce so many "variations" as to exceed in number the "distinctive" feet – when the ear becomes at once baulked by the *bouleversement** of the rhythm. Too many trochees, for example, inserted in an iambic rhythm, would convert the latter to a trochaic. I may note here that, in all cases, the rhythm designed should be commenced and continued, *without* variation, until the ear has had full time to comprehend what *is* the rhythm. In violation of a rule so obviously founded in common sense, many even of our best poets do not scruple to begin an iambic rhythm with a trochee or the converse – or a dactylic with an anapaest or the converse, and so on.

A somewhat less objectionable error, although still a decided one, is that of commencing a rhythm not with a different equivalent foot, but with a "bastard" foot of the rhythm intended. For example:

Mān̄y ă | thoūght wĭll | cōme tŏ | mĕmŏry. |

Here *many a* is what I have explained to be a "bastard trochee", and, to be understood, should be accented with inverted crescents. It is objectionable solely on account of its position as the *opening* foot of a trochaic rhythm. *Memory*, similarly accented, is also a bastard trochee, but *un*objectionable, although by no means demanded.

The further illustration of this point will enable me to take an important step.

One of our finest poets, Mr Christopher Pearse Cranch, begins a very beautiful poem* thus:

> Many are the thoughts that come to me
>> In my lonely musing,
> And they drift so strange and swift,
>> There's no time for choosing
> Which to follow, for to leave
>> Any seems a losing.

"A losing" to Mr Cranch, of course – but this *en passant*. It will be seen here that the intention is trochaic, although we do *not* see this intention by the opening foot, as we should do – or even by the opening line. Reading the whole stanza, however, we perceive the trochaic rhythm as the general design, and so, after some reflection, we divide the first line thus:

Many are the | thoūghts thăt | cōme tŏ | mē. |

Thus scanned, the line will seem musical. It *is* – highly so. And it is because there is no end to instances of just such lines of apparently incomprehensible music that Coleridge thought proper to invent his nonsensical *system* of what he calls "scanning by accents"* – as if "scanning by accents" were anything more than a phrase. Whenever *Christabel* is really *not rough*, it can be as readily scanned by the true *laws* (not the supposititious *rules*) of verse as can the simplest pentameter of Pope – and where it *is* rough (*passim*), these same laws will enable anyone of common sense to show *why* it is rough and to point out, instantaneously, the remedy for the roughness.

A reads and rereads a certain line, and pronounces it false in rhythm – unmusical. *B*, however, reads it *to A*, and *A* is at once struck with the perfection of the rhythm, and wonders at his dullness in not "catching" it before. Henceforward he admits the line to be musical. *B*, triumphant, asserts that, to be sure, the line is musical – for it is the work of Coleridge – and that it is *A* who is *not*, the fault being in *A*'s false reading. Now here *A* is right and *B* wrong. *That* rhythm is erroneous (at some point or other more or less obvious) which *any* ordinary reader *can*, without design, read improperly. It is the business of the poet so to construct his line that the intention *must* be caught *at once*. Even when these men have precisely the same understanding of a sentence, they differ, and often widely, in their modes of enunciating it. Anyone who has taken the trouble to examine the topic of emphasis (by which I here mean not *accent* of particular syllables, but the dwelling on entire words) must have seen that men emphasize in the most singularly arbitrary manner. There are certain large classes of people, for example, who persist in emphasizing their monosyllables. Little uniformity of emphasis prevails, because the thing itself – the idea, emphasis – is referable to no natural (at least, to no well-comprehended and therefore uniform) law. Beyond a very narrow and vague limit, the whole matter is conventionality. And if we differ in emphasis even when we agree in comprehension, how much more so in the former when in the latter too! Apart, however, from the consideration of natural disagreement, is it not clear that, by tripping here and mouthing there, any sequence of words may be twisted into any species of rhythm? But are we thence to deduce that all sequences of words are rhythmical in a rational understanding of the term? For this is the deduction precisely to which the *reductio ad absurdum** will, in the end, bring all the propositions of Coleridge. Out of a hundred readers of *Christabel*, fifty will be able to make nothing of its rhythm, while forty-nine of the remaining fifty will, with some ado, fancy they comprehend it after the fourth or fifth perusal. The one out of the whole hundred who shall both comprehend and admire it at first sight must be an unaccountably clever person – and I am by far too modest to assume, for a moment, that that very clever person is myself.

In illustration of what is here advanced I cannot do better than quote a poem:

> Pease porridge hot, pease porridge cold –
> Pease porridge in the pot, nine days old.*

Now, those of my readers who have never *heard* this poem pronounced according to the nursery conventionality will find its rhythm as obscure as an explanatory note – while those who *have* heard it will divide it thus, declare it musical, and wonder how there can be any doubt about it.

> Pease | porridge | hot | pease | porridge | cold |
> Pease | porridge | in the | pot | nine | days | old. |

The chief thing in the way of this species of rhythm is the necessity which it imposes upon the poet of travelling in constant company with his compositions, so as to be ready at a moment's notice to avail himself of a well-understood poetical licence – that of reading aloud one's own doggerel.

In Mr Cranch's line,

Many are the | thoughts that | come to | me, |

the general error of which I speak is, of course, very partially exemplified, and the purpose for which, chiefly, I cite it lies yet further on in our topic.

The two divisions ("thoughts that") and ("come to") are ordinary trochees. Of the last division ("me") we will talk hereafter. The first division ("many are the") would be thus accented by the Greek prosodies – mány ăre thĕ – and would be called by them *αστρολογος*. The Latin books would style the foot "*pæon primus*",* and both Greek and Latin would swear that it was composed of a trochee and what they term a pyrrhic, that is to say, a foot of two *short* syllables – a thing that *cannot be*, as I shall presently show.

But now there is an obvious difficulty. The *astrologos*, according to the prosodies' own showing, is equal to *five* short syllables, and the trochee to *three* – yet, in the line quoted, these two feet are equal. They occupy *precisely* the same time. In fact, the whole music of the line depends upon their being *made* to occupy the same time. The prosodies, then, have demonstrated what all mathematicians have stupidly failed in demonstrating: that three and five are one and the same thing.

After what I have already said, however, about the bastard trochee and the bastard iambus, no one can have any trouble in understanding that *many are the* is of similar character. It is merely a bolder variation than usual from the routine of trochees, and introduces to the bastard trochee one additional syllable. But this syllable is not *short*. That is, it is not short in the sense of "*short*" as applied to the final syllable of the ordinary trochee, where the word means merely *the half of long*.

In this case (that of the additional syllable), "short", if used at all, must be used in the sense of *the sixth of long*. And all the three final syllables can be called *short* only with the same understanding of the term. The three together are equal only to the one short syllable (whose place they supply) of the ordinary trochee. It follows that there is no sense in thus (˘) accenting these syllables. We must devise for them some new character which shall denote the sixth of long. Let it be (‹) – the crescent placed with the curve to the left. The whole foot ("mány ăre thĕ") might be called a "quick trochee".

We come now to the final division ("me") of Mr Cranch's line. It is clear that this foot, short as it appears, is fully equal in time to each of the preceding. It is in fact the caesura – the foot which, in the beginning of this paper, I called the most important in all verse. Its chief office is that of pause or termination – and here, at the end of a line, its use is easy, because there is no danger of misapprehending its value. We pause on it, by a seeming necessity, just so long as it has taken us to pronounce the preceding feet, whether iambuses, trochees, dactyls or anapaests. It is thus a *variable foot*, and, with some care, may be well introduced into the body of a line, as in a little poem of great beauty by Mrs Welby:*

> I have | a lit | tle step | s͞o͞n | of on | ly three | years old. |

Here we dwell on the caesura, *son*, just as long as it requires us to pronounce either of the preceding or succeeding iambuses. Its value, therefore, in this line, is that of three short syllables. In the following dactylic line, its value is that of four short syllables.

> Pale as a | lily was | Emily | G͞r͞a͞y͞.* |

I have accented the caesura with a ~~~~ by way of expressing this variability of value.

I observed, just now, that there could be no such foot as one of two short syllables. What we start from in the very beginning of all idea on the topic of verse is quantity, *length*. Thus, when we enunciate an independent syllable, it is long as a matter of course. If we enunciate two, dwelling on both equally, we express equality in the enumeration, or length, and have a right to call them two long syllables. If we dwell on one more than the other, we have also a right to call one short, because it is short in relation to the other. But if we dwell on both equally and with a tripping voice, saying to ourselves: here are two short syllables, the query might well be asked of us: "In relation to what are they short?" Shortness is but the negation of length. To say, then, that two syllables placed independently of any other syllable are short is merely to say that they have no positive length or enunciation – in other words, that they are no syllables, that they do not exist at all. And if, persisting, we add anything about their equality, we are merely floundering in the idea of an identical equation where, x being equal to x, nothing is shown to be equal to zero. In a word, we can form no conception of a pyrrhic as of an independent foot. It is a mere chimera bred in the mad fancy of a pedant.

From what I have said about the equalization of the several feet of a *line*, it must not be deduced that any *necessity* for equality in time exists between the rhythm of *several* lines. A poem, or even a stanza, may begin with iambuses, in the first line, and proceed with anapaests in the second, or even with the less accordant dactyls, as in the opening of quite a pretty specimen of verse by Miss Mary A.S. Aldrich:*

> The wa | ter li | ly sleeps | in pride |
> Dōwn ĭn thĕ | dēpths ŏf thĕ | āzūre | l̃ãke. |

Here *azure* is a spondee, equivalent to a dactyl; *lake* a caesura.

I shall now best proceed in quoting the initial lines of Byron's *Bride of Abydos*:*

> Know ye the land where the cypress and myrtle
>   Are emblems of deeds that are done in their clime –
> Where the rage of the vulture, the love of the turtle,
>   Now melt into softness, now madden to crime?
> Know ye the land of the cedar and vine,
> Where the flowers ever blossom, the beams ever shine,
> And the light wings of Zephyr, oppressed with perfume,
> Wax faint o'er the gardens of Gul* in their bloom –
> Where the citron and olive are fairest of fruit
> And the voice of the nightingale never is mute – [...]
> Where the virgins are soft as the roses they twine,
> And all save the spirit of man is divine?
> 'Tis the land of the East – 'tis the clime of the Sun...
> Can he smile on such deeds as his children have done?
> Oh, wild as the accents of lovers' farewell
> Are the hearts that they bear and the tales that they tell.

Now, the flow of these lines (as times go) is very sweet and musical. They have been often admired, and justly, as times go – that is to say, it is a rare thing to find better versification of its kind. And where verse is pleasant to the ear, it is silly to find fault with it because it refuses to be scanned. Yet I have heard men professing to be scholars who made no scruple of abusing these lines of Byron's on the ground that they were musical in spite of *all law*. Other gentlemen, *not* scholars, abused "all law" for the same reason, and it occurred neither to the one party nor to the other that the law about which they were disputing might possibly be no law at all – an ass of a law in the skin of a lion.

The grammars said something about dactylic lines, and it was easily seen that *these* lines were at least meant for dactylic. The first one was, therefore, thus divided:

Knōw yĕ thĕ | lānd whĕre thĕ | cyprĕss ănd | myrtlĕ. |

The concluding foot was a mystery, but the prosodies said something about the dactylic "measure" calling now and then for a double rhyme – and the court of inquiry were content to rest in the double rhyme without exactly perceiving what a double rhyme had to do with the question of an irregular foot. Quitting the first line, the second was thus scanned:

Arē ĕmblĕms | ōf deĕds thăt | āre dŏne ĭn | thēir clīme. |

It was immediately seen, however, that *this* would not do – it was at war with the whole emphasis of the reading. It could not be supposed that Byron, or anyone in his senses, intended to place stress upon such monosyllables as "are", "of" and "their", nor could "their clime", collated with "to crime" in the corresponding line below, be fairly twisted into anything like a "double rhyme" so as to bring everything within the category of the grammars. But further these grammars spoke not. The inquirers, therefore, in spite of their sense of harmony in the lines when considered without reference to scansion, fell back upon the idea that the "Are" was a blunder – an excess for which the poet should be sent to Coventry – and, striking it out, they scanned the remainder of the line as follows:

— ēmblĕms ŏf | deēds thăt ăre | dōne ĭn thĕir | clīme. |

This answered pretty well, but the grammars admitted no such foot as a foot of one syllable; and besides the rhythm was dactylic. In despair, the books are well searched, however, and at last the investigators are gratified by a full solution of the riddle in the profound "observation" quoted in the beginning of this article: "When a syllable is wanting, the verse is said to be catalectic; when the measure is exact, the line is acatalectic; when there is a redundant syllable, it forms hypermeter." This is enough. The anomalous line is pronounced to be catalectic at the head and to form hypermeter at the tail, and so on, and so on, it being soon discovered that nearly all the remaining lines are in a similar predicament, and that what flows so smoothly to the ear, although so roughly to the eye, is after all a mere jumble of catalecticism, acatalecticism and hypermeter – not to say worse.

Now, had this court of inquiry been in possession of even the shadow of the *philosophy* of verse, they would have had no trouble in reconciling this oil and water of the eye and ear by merely scanning the passage without reference to lines, and, continuously, thus:

Know ye the | land where the | cypress and | myrtle Are | emblems of | deeds
that are | done in their | clime Where the | rage of the | vulture the | love of
the | turtle Now | melt into | softness now | madden to | *crime* | Know ye
the | land of the | cedar and | vine Where the | flowers ever | blossom the |
beams ever | shine And the | light wings of | Zephyr op | pressed by per |
fume Wax | faint o'er the | gardens of | Gul in their | bloom Where the |
citron and | olive are | fairest of | fruit And the | voice of the | nightingale |
never is | mute Where the | virgins are | soft as the | roses they | *twine And* |
all save the | spirit of | man is di | vine. 'Tis the | land of the | East 'tis the |
clime of the | Sun Can he | smile on such | deeds as his | children have |
done Oh | wild as the | accents of | lovers' fare | well Are the | hearts that
they | bear and the | tales that they | *tell.* |

Here "crime" and "tell" (italicized) are caesuras, each having the value of
a dactyl, four short syllables, while "fume Wax", "twine and" and "done
Oh" are spondees which, of course, being composed of two long syllables,
are also equal to four short, and are the dactyl's natural equivalent. The
nicety of Byron's ear has led him into a succession of feet which, with two
trivial exceptions as regards melody, are absolutely accurate – a very rare
occurrence this in dactylic or anapaestic rhythms. The exceptions are found
in the spondee "twine And" and the dactyl "smile on such". Both feet are
false in point of melody. In "twine And", to make out the rhythm, we must
force "And" into a length which it will not naturally bear. We are called
on to sacrifice either the proper length of the syllable as demanded by its
position as a member of a spondee or the customary accentuation of the
word in conversation. There is no hesitation, and should be none. We at
once give up the sound for the sense, and the rhythm is imperfect. In this
instance it is *very* slightly so – not one person in ten thousand could, by
ear, detect the inaccuracy. But the *perfection* of verse, as regards melody,
consists in its *never* demanding any such sacrifice as is here demanded. The
rhythmical must agree *thoroughly* with the reading flow. This perfection
has in no instance been attained – but is unquestionably attainable. "Smile
on such", the dactyl, is incorrect, because "such", from the character of
the two consonants *ch*, cannot *easily* be enunciated in the ordinary time of
a short syllable, which its position declares that it is. Almost every reader
will be able to appreciate the slight difficulty here, and yet the error is by
no means so important as that of the "And" in the spondee. By dexterity
we *may* pronounce "such" in the true time, but the attempt to remedy the
rhythmical deficiency of the *And* by drawing it out merely aggravates the
offence against natural enunciation by directing attention to the offence.

My main object, however, in quoting these lines, is to show that, in spite of the prosodies, the length of a line is entirely an arbitrary matter. We might divide the commencement of Byron's poem thus:

Know ye the | land where the |

Or thus:

Know ye the | land where the | cypress and |

Or thus:

Know ye the | land where the | cypress and | myrtle are |

Or thus:

Know ye the | land where the | cypress and | myrtle are | emblems of |

In short, we may give it any division we please, and the lines will be good – provided we have at least *two* feet in a line. As in mathematics two units are required to form number, so rhythm (from the Greek αριθμος, number)* demands for its formation at least two feet. Beyond doubt, we often see such lines as

> Know ye the...
> Land where the...

lines of one foot – and our prosodies admit such, but with impropriety, for common sense would dictate that every so obvious division of a poem as is made by a line should include within itself all that is necessary for its own comprehension, but in a line of one foot we can have no appreciation of *rhythm*, which depends upon the equality between *two* or more pulsations. The false lines, consisting sometimes of a single caesura, which are seen in mock Pindaric odes, are of course "rhythmical" only in connection with some other line – and it is this want of independent rhythm which adapts them to the purposes of burlesque alone. Their effect is that of incongruity (the principle of mirth), for they include the blankness of prose amid the harmony of verse.

My second object in quoting Byron's lines was that of showing how absurd it often is to cite a single line from amid the body of a poem for the purpose of instancing the perfection or imperfection of the line's rhythm. Were we to see by itself

> Know ye the land where the cypress and myrtle,

we might justly condemn it as defective in the final foot, which is equal to only three, instead of being equal to four, short syllables.

In the foot "flowers ever" we shall find a further exemplification of the principle of the bastard iambus, bastard trochee and quick trochee, as I have been at some pains in describing these feet above. All the prosodies on English verse would insist upon making an elision in "flowers", thus "flow'rs" – but this is nonsense. In the quick trochee "mānỹ ăre thĕ" occurring in Mr Cranch's *trochaic* line, we had to equalize the time of the three syllables (*ny, are, the*) to that of the one *short* syllable whose position they usurp. Accordingly, each of these syllables is equal to the third of a short syllable, that is to say, the *sixth of a long*. But in Byron's *dactylic* rhythm, we have to equalize the time of the three syllables (*ers, ev, er*) to that of the one *long* syllable whose position they usurp or, (which is the same thing) of the *two short*. Therefore the value of each of the syllables (*ers, ev* and *er*) is the *third of a long*. We enunciate them with only half the rapidity we employ in enunciating the three final syllables of the quick trochee – which latter is a rare foot. The "flowers ever", on the contrary, is as common in the dactylic rhythm as is the *bastard* trochee in the trochaic or the bastard iambus in the iambic. We may as well accent it with the curve of the crescent to the right and call it a *bastard dactyl*. A *bastard anapaest*, whose nature I now need be at no trouble in explaining, will of course occur, now and then, in an anapaestic rhythm.

In order to avoid any chance of that confusion which is apt to be introduced in an essay of this kind by too sudden and radical an alteration of the conventionalities to which the reader has been accustomed, I have thought it right to suggest for the accent marks of the bastard trochee, bastard iambus, etc., etc., certain characters which, in merely varying the direction of the ordinary short accent (˘), should imply – what is the fact – that the feet themselves are not *new* feet in any proper sense, but simply modifications of the feet, respectively, from which they derive their names. Thus a bastard iambus is, in its essentiality (that is to say, in its time) an iambus. The variation lies only in the *distribution* of this time. The time, for example, occupied by the one short (or *half of long*) syllable in the ordinary iambus is, in the bastard, spread equally over two syllables, which are accordingly the *fourth of long*.

But this fact, the fact of the essentiality, or whole time, of the foot being unchanged, is now so fully before the reader that I may venture to propose, finally, an accentuation which shall answer the real purpose – that is to say, what should be the real purpose of all accentuation: the purpose of expressing to the eye the exact relative value of every syllable employed in verse.

I have already shown that enunciation, or *length*, is the point from which we start. In other words, we begin with a *long syllable*. This then is our unit, and there will be no need of accenting it at all. An unaccented syllable, in a system of accentuation, is to be regarded always as a long syllable. Thus a spondee would be without accent. In an iambus, the first syllable, being "short", or the *half* of long, should be accented with a small 2, placed *beneath* the syllable; the last syllable, being long, should be unaccented; the whole would be thus: "control". In a trochee, these accents would be merely conversed, thus "manly". In a dactyl, each of the two final syllables, being the half of long, should also be accented with a small 2 beneath the syllable – and, the first syllable left unaccented, the whole would be thus: "happiness". In an anapaest, we should converse the dactyl thus: "in the land". In the bastard dactyl, each of the three concluding syllables being the *third* of long should be accented with a small 3 beneath the syllable, and the whole foot would stand thus: "flowers ever". In the bastard anapaest, we should converse the bastard dactyl thus: "in the rebound". In the bastard iambus, each of the two initial syllables, being the fourth of long, should be accented, below, with a small 4; the whole foot would be thus: "in the rain". In the bastard trochee, we should converse the bastard iambus thus: "many a". In the quick trochee, each of the three concluding syllables, being the *sixth* of long, should be accented below with a small 6; the whole foot would be thus: "many are the". The quick iambus is not yet created, and most probably never will be, for it will be excessively useless, awkward and liable to misconception, as I have already shown that even the quick trochee is – but, should it appear, we must accent it by conversing the quick trochee. The caesura, being variable in length, but always *longer than* "long", should be accented *above* with a number expressing the length, or value, of the distinctive foot of the rhythm in which it occurs. Thus a caesura, occurring in a spondaic rhythm, would be accented with a small 2 above the syllable (or, rather, foot). Occurring in a dactylic or anapaestic rhythm, we also accent it with the 2 above the foot. Occurring in an iambic rhythm, however, it must be accented, above, with 1½, for this is the relative value of the iambus. Occurring in the trochaic rhythm, we give it, of course, the same accentuation. For the complex 1½, however, it would be advisable to substitute the simpler expression ¾, which amounts to the same thing.

In this system of accentuation, Mr Cranch's lines quoted above would thus be written:

Many are the | thoughts that | come to | me | ³⁄₂
In my | lonely | musing |
And they | drift so | strange and | swift | ³⁄₂
There's no | time for | choosing | ³⁄₂
Which to | follow | for to | leave |
Any | seems a | losing. |

In the ordinary system, the accentuation would be thus:

Māny arĕ thĕ | thōughts thăt | cōme tŏ | mē |
In my | lōnely | mūsing |
Ānd thĕy | drīft sŏ | strānge ănd | swīft |
Thēre's nŏ | time fŏr | choōsing |
Whīch tŏ | fōllŏw, | fōr tŏ | lēave |
Āny | seēms ă | lōsĭng. |

It must be observed, here, that I do not grant this to be the "ordinary" *scansion*. On the contrary, I never yet met the man who had the faintest comprehension of the true scanning of these lines, or of such as these. But granting this to be the mode in which our prosodies would divide the feet, they would accentuate the syllables as just above.

Now, let any reasonable person compare the two modes. The first advantage seen in my mode is that of simplicity – of time, labour and ink saved. Counting the fractions as *two* accents, even, there will be found only *twenty-six* accents to the stanza. In the common accentuation there are *forty-one*. But admit that all this is a trifle, which it is *not*, and let us proceed to points of importance. Does the common accentuation express the truth, in particular, in general, or in any regard? Is it consistent with itself? Does it convey either to the ignorant or to the scholar a just conception of the rhythm of the lines? Each of these questions must be answered in the negative. The crescents, being precisely similar, must be understood as expressing, all of them, one and the same thing, and so all prosodies have always understood them and wished them to be understood. They express, indeed, "short" – but this word has all kinds of meanings. It serves to represent (the reader is left to guess *when*) sometimes the half, sometimes the third, sometimes the fourth and sometimes the sixth of "long" – while "long" itself, in the books, is left undefined and undescribed. On the other hand, the horizontal accent, it may be said, expresses sufficiently well, and unvaryingly, the syllables which are meant to be long. It does nothing of the kind. This horizontal accent is placed over the caesura (wherever, as in the Latin prosodies, the caesura is recognized) as well as over the ordinary long syllable, and implies anything and everything, just as the crescent. But grant that it does express the ordinary long syllables (leaving the caesura out of question), have I not given the identical expression by not employing any expression at all? In a word, while the prosodies, with a certain number of accents, express *precisely nothing whatever*, I, with scarcely half the number, have expressed everything which, in a system of accentuation, demands expression. In glancing at my mode in the lines of Mr Cranch, it will be seen that it conveys not only the exact relation of the syllables and feet among themselves in those particular lines, but their precise value in relation to any other existing or conceivable feet or syllables in any existing or conceivable system of rhythm.

The object of what we call *scansion* is the distinct marking of the rhythmical flow. Scansion without accents or perpendicular lines between the feet – that is to say scansion *by* the voice only – is scansion *to* the ear only, and all very good in its way. The written scansion addresses the ear through the eye. In either case the object is the distinct marking of the rhythmical, musical or reading flow. There *can* be no other object, and there is none. Of course, then, the scansion and the reading flow should go hand in hand. The former must agree with the latter. The former represents and expresses the latter, and is good or bad as it truly or falsely represents and expresses it. If by the written scansion of a line we are not enabled to perceive any rhythm or music in the line, then either the line is unrhythmical or the scansion false. Apply all this to the English lines which we have quoted, at various points, in the course of this article. It will be found that the scansion exactly conveys the rhythm, and thus thoroughly fulfils the only purpose for which scansion is required.

But let the scansion *of the schools* be applied to the Greek and Latin verse, and what result do we find? That the verse is one thing and the scansion quite another. The ancient verse, *read* aloud, is in general musical, and occasionally *very* musical. *Scanned* by the prosodial rules we can, for the most part, make nothing of it whatever. In the case of the English verse, the more emphatically we dwell on the divisions between the feet, the more distinct is our perception of the kind of rhythm intended. In the case of the Greek and Latin, the more we dwell, the *less* distinct is this perception. To make this clear by an example:

> Mæcenas, atavis edite regibus,
> O et præsidium et dulce decus meum:
> Sunt quos curriculo pulverem Olympicum
> Collegisse iuvat, metaque fervidis
> Evitata rotis palmaque nobilis
> Terrarum dominos evehit ad deos.*

Now, in *reading* these lines, there is scarcely one person in a thousand who, if even ignorant of Latin, will not immediately feel and appreciate their flow – their music. A prosodist, however, informs the public that the *scansion* runs thus:

> Mæce | nas ata | vis | edite | regibus |
> O et | præsidi' | et | dulce de | cus meum |
> Sunt quos | curricu | lo | pulver' O | lympicum |
> Colle | gisse iu | vat | metaque | fervidis |
> Evi | tata ro | tis | palmaque | nobilis |
> Terra | rum domi | nos | evehit | ad deos. |

Now, I do not deny that we get a *certain sort* of music from the lines if we read them according to this scansion, but I wish to call attention to the fact that this scansion and the certain sort of music which grows out of it are entirely at war not only with the reading flow which any ordinary person would naturally give the lines, but with the reading flow universally given them, and never denied them, by even the most obstinate and stolid of scholars.

And now these questions are forced upon us: "Why exists this discrepancy between the modern verse with its scansion and the ancient verse with its scansion? Why, in the former case, are there agreement and representation, while in the latter there is neither the one nor the other?" Or, to come to the point: "How are we to reconcile the ancient verse with the scholastic scansion of it?" This absolutely necessary conciliation, shall we bring it about by supposing the scholastic scansion wrong because the ancient verse is right, or by maintaining that the ancient verse is wrong because the scholastic scansion is not to be gainsaid?

Were we to adopt the latter mode of arranging the difficulty, we might, in some measure at least, simplify the expression of the arrangement by putting it thus: because the pedants have no eyes, therefore the old poets had no ears.

"But," say the gentlemen without the eyes, "the scholastic scansion, although certainly not handed down to us in form from the old poets themselves (the gentlemen without the ears), is nevertheless deduced from certain facts which are supplied us by careful observation of the old poems."

And let us illustrate this strong position by an example from an American poet – who must be a poet of some eminence, or he will not answer the purpose. Let us take Mr Alfred B. Street.* I remember these two lines of his:

> His sinuous path, by blazes, wound
> Among trunks grouped in myriads round.

With the *sense* of these lines I have nothing to do. When a poet is in a "fine frenzy", he may as well imagine a large forest as a small one – and "by blazes" is *not* intended for an oath. My concern is with the rhythm, which is iambic.

Now, let us suppose that, a thousand years hence, when the "American language" is dead, a learned prosodist should be deducing from "careful observation" of our best poets a system of scansion for our poetry. And let us suppose that this prosodist had so little dependence in the generality and immutability of the laws of nature as to assume in the outset that, because we lived a thousand years before his time and made use of steam engines instead of mesmeric balloons,* we must therefore have had a *very* singular fashion of mouthing our vowels, and altogether of hudsonizing* our verse. And let us suppose that with these and other fundamental propositions carefully put away in his brain he should arrive at the line

> Among | trunks grouped | in my | riads round. |

Finding it in an obviously iambic rhythm, he would divide it as above – and observing that "trunks" made the first member of an iambus, he would call it short, as Mr Street intended it to be. Now further: if instead of admitting the possibility that Mr Street – who by that time would be called Street simply, just as we say Homer – that Mr Street might have been in the habit of writing carelessly, as the poets of the prosodist's own era did, and as all poets will do (on account of being geniuses) – instead of admitting this, suppose the learned scholar should make a "rule" and put it in a book, to the effect that, in the American verse, the vowel *u*, *when found embedded among nine consonants*, was *short*. What, under such circumstances, would the sensible people of the scholar's day have a right not only to think, but to say of that scholar? Why, that he was "a fool – by blazes!"

I have put an extreme case, but it strikes at the root of the error. The "rules" are grounded in "authority" – and this "authority", can anyone tell us what it means? Or can anyone suggest anything that it may *not* mean? Is it not clear that the "scholar" above referred to might as readily have deduced from authority a totally false system as a partially true one? To deduce from authority a consistent prosody of the ancient metres would indeed have been within the limits of the barest possibility – and the task has *not* been accomplished, for the reason that it demands a species of ratiocination altogether out of keeping with the brain of a bookworm. A rigid scrutiny will show that the very few "rules" which have not as many exceptions as examples are those which have, by accident, their true bases not in authority, but in the omniprevalent laws of syllabification – such, for example, as the rule which declares a vowel before two consonants to be long.

In a word, the gross confusion and antagonism of the scholastic prosody, as well as its marked inapplicability to the reading flow of the rhythms it pretends to illustrate, are attributable first to the utter absence of natural principle as a guide in the investigations which have been undertaken by inadequate men, and secondly to the neglect of the obvious consideration that the ancient poems, which have been the *criteria* throughout, were the work of men who must have written as loosely and with as little definitive system as ourselves.

Were Horace alive today, he would divide for us his first ode thus, and "make great eyes" when assured by the prosodists that he had no business to make any such division:

> Mæcenas | atavis | edite | regibus |
> O et præ | sidium et | dulce de | cus meum |
> Sunt quos cur | riculo | pulverem O | lympicum |
> Collegisse | iuvat | metaque | fervidis |
> Evitata | rotis | palmaque | nobilis |
> Terrarum | dominos | evehit | ad deos. |

Read by this scansion, the flow is preserved – and the more we dwell on the divisions, the more the intended rhythm becomes apparent. Moreover, the feet have all the same time, while in the scholastic scansion trochees – admitted trochees – are absurdly employed as equivalents to spondees and dactyls. The books declare, for instance, that *Colle*, which begins the fourth line, is a trochee, and seem to be gloriously unconscious that to put a trochee in apposition with a longer foot is to violate the inviolable principle of all music: *time*.

It will be said, however, by "some people" that I have no business to make a dactyl out of such obviously long syllables as *sunt*, *quos*, *cur*. Certainly I have no business to do so. I *never* do so. And Horace should not have done so. But he did. Mr Bryant and Mr Longfellow do the same thing every day. And merely because these gentlemen, now and then, forget themselves in this way, it would be hard if some future prosodist should insist upon twisting the 'Thanatopsis' or the 'Spanish Student'* into a jumble of trochees, spondees and dactyls.

It may be said, also, by some other people, that in the word *decus* I have succeeded no better than the books in making the scansional agree with the reading flow, and that *decus* was not pronounced de*cus*. I reply that there can be no doubt of the word having been pronounced, in this case, de*cus*. It must be observed that the Latin inflection, or variation of a word in its terminating syllables, caused the Romans – *must* have caused them – to pay greater attention to the termination of a word than to its commencement, or than we do to the terminations of our words. The end of the Latin word established that relation of the word with other words which we establish by prepositions or auxiliary verbs. Therefore, it would seem infinitely less odd to them than it does to us to dwell at any time, for any slight purpose, abnormally on a terminating syllable. In verse, this licence – scarcely a licence – would be frequently admitted. These ideas unlock the secret of such lines as the

> Litoreis ingens inventa sub ilici*bus sus*

and the

> Parturient montes et nascetur ridicu*lus mus*

which I quoted, some time ago, while speaking of rhyme.

As regards the prosodial elisions, such as that of *rem* before O in *pulverem Olympicum*, it is really difficult to understand how so dismally silly a notion could have entered the brain even of a pedant. Were it demanded of me why the books cut off one *vowel* before another, I might say: "It is, perhaps, because the books think that, since a bad reader is so apt to slide the one vowel into the other at any rate, it is just as well to print them *ready-slided*." But in the case of the terminating *m*, which is the most readily pronounced of all consonants (as the infantile *mamma* will testify) and the most impossible to cheat the ear of by any system of sliding – in the case of the *m*, I should be driven to reply that, to the best of my belief, the prosodists did the thing because they had a fancy for doing it and wished to see how funny it would look after it was done. The thinking reader will perceive that, from the great facility with which *em* may be enunciated, it is admirably suited to form one of the rapid short syllables in the bastard dactyl "pulverem O", but because the books had no conception of a bastard dactyl, they knocked it in the head at once – by cutting off its tail!

Let me now give a specimen of the true scansion of another Horatian measure* – embodying an instance of proper elision.

Integer | vitæ | scelerisque | purus |
Non eget | Mauris | iaculis ne | que arcu |
Nec vene | natis | gravida sa | gittis |
Fusce pha | retra. |

Here the regular recurrence of the bastard dactyl gives great animation to the rhythm. The *e* before the *a* in *que arcu* is, almost of sheer necessity, cut off – that is to say, run into the *a* so as to preserve the spondee. But even this licence it would have been better not to take.

Had I space, nothing would afford me greater pleasure than to proceed with the scansion of *all* the ancient rhythms, and to show how easily, by the help of common sense, the intended music of each and all can be rendered instantaneously apparent. But I have already overstepped my limits, and must bring this paper to an end.

It will never do, however, to omit all mention of the heroic hexameter.

I began the "processes" by a suggestion of the spondee as the first step towards verse. But the innate monotony of the spondee has caused its disappearance, as the basis of rhythm, from all modern poetry. We *may* say, indeed, that the French heroic – the most wretchedly monotonous verse in existence – is, to all intents and purposes, spondaic.* But it is not designedly spondaic – and if the French were ever to examine it at all, they would no doubt pronounce it iambic. It must be observed that the French language is strangely peculiar in this point: *that it is without accentuation and, consequently, without verse*. The genius of the people, rather than the structure of the tongue, declares that their words are, for the most part, enunciated with an uniform dwelling on each syllable. For example, *we* say "syl*lab*ification." A Frenchman would say "syl-la-bi-fi-ca-ti-on", dwelling on no one of the syllables with any noticeable particularity. Here again I put an extreme case in order to be well understood, but the general fact is as I give it – that, comparatively, the French have *no* accentuation. And there can be nothing worth the name of verse without. Therefore, the French have no verse worth the name – which is the fact, put in sufficiently plain terms. Their iambic rhythm so superabounds in absolute spondees as to warrant me in calling its basis spondaic, but French is the *only* modern tongue which has any rhythm with such basis – and even in the French it is, as I have said, unintentional.

Admitting, however, the validity of my suggestion, that the spondee was the first approach to verse, we should expect to find, first, natural spondees (words each forming just a spondee) most abundant in the most ancient languages, and, secondly, we should expect to find spondees forming the basis of the most ancient rhythms. These expectations are in both cases confirmed.

Of the Greek hexameter, the intentional basis is spondaic. The dactyls are the *variation* of the theme. It will be observed that there is no absolute certainty about *their* points of interposition. The penultimate foot, it is true, is usually a dactyl, but not uniformly so, while the ultimate, on which the ear *lingers*, is always a spondee. Even that the penultimate is usually a dactyl may be clearly referred to the necessity of winding up with the *distinctive* spondee. In corroboration of this idea, again, we should look to find the penultimate spondee most usual in the most ancient verse – and, accordingly, we find it more frequent in the Greek than in the Latin hexameter.

But besides all this, spondees are not only more prevalent in the heroic hexameter than dactyls, but occur to such an extent as is even unpleasant to modern ears, on account of monotony. What the modern chiefly appreciates and admires in the Greek hexameter is the *melody of the abundant vowel sounds*. The Latin hexameters *really* please very few moderns – although so many pretend to fall into ecstasies about them. In the hexameters quoted several pages ago, from Silius Italicus, the preponderance of the spondee is strikingly manifest. Besides the natural spondees of the Greek and Latin, numerous artificial ones arise in the verse of these tongues on account of the tendency which inflection has to throw full accentuation on terminal syllables – and the preponderance of the spondee is further ensured by the comparative infrequency of the small prepositions which *we* have to serve us *instead* of case, and also the absence of the diminutive auxiliary verbs with which *we* have to eke out the expression of our primary ones. These are the monosyllables whose abundance serve to stamp the poetic genius of a language as tripping or dactylic.

Now, paying no attention to these facts, Sir Philip Sidney,* Professor Longfellow and innumerable other persons more or less modern have busied themselves in constructing what they supposed to be "English hexameters on the model of the Greek". The only difficulty was that (even leaving out of question the melodious masses of vowel) these gentlemen never could get their English hexameters to *sound* Greek. Did they *look* Greek? That should have been the query – and the reply might have led to a solution of the riddle. In placing a copy of ancient hexameters side by side with a copy (in similar type) of such hexameters as Professor Longfellow* or Professor Felton* or the Frogpondian* professors collectively are in the shameful practice of composing "on the model of the Greek", it will be seen that the latter (hexameters, not professors) are about one third longer *to the eye*, on an average, than the former. The more abundant dactyls make the difference. And it is the greater number of spondees in the Greek than in the English (in the ancient than in the modern tongue) which has caused it to fall out that while these eminent scholars were groping about in the dark for a Greek hexameter, which is a spondaic rhythm varied now and then by dactyls, they merely stumbled, to the lasting scandal of scholarship, over something which, on account of its long-leggedness, we may as well term a "Feltonian hexameter", and which is a dactylic rhythm interrupted, rarely, by artificial spondees which are no spondees at all, and which are curiously thrown in by the heels at all kinds of improper and impertinent points.

Here is a specimen of the Longfellow hexameter:*

Also the | church with | in was a | dorned for | this was the | season |
In which the|young their | parents' | hope and the | loved ones of | Heaven |
Should at the | foot of the | altar re | new the | vows of their | baptism |
Therefore each|nook and|corner was|swept and|cleaned and the|dust was|
Blown from the | walls and | ceiling and | from the | oil-painted | benches. |

Mr Longfellow is a man of imagination – but *can* he imagine that any individual with a proper understanding of the danger of lockjaw would make the attempt of twisting his mouth into the shape necessary for the emission of such spondees as "par*ents*" and "from the" or such dactyls as "cleaned and the" and "loved ones of"? "Baptism" is by no means a bad spondee – perhaps because it happens to be a dactyl. Of all the rest, however, I am dreadfully ashamed.

But these feet – dactyls and spondees, all together – should thus be put at once into their proper position:

Also, the church within was adorned, for this was the season in which the young, their parents' hope, and the loved ones of Heaven, should, at the foot of the altar, renew the vows of their baptism. Therefore, each nook and corner was swept and cleaned, and the dust was blown from the walls and ceiling, and from the oil-painted benches.

There! That is respectable prose – and it will incur no danger of ever getting its character ruined by anybody's mistaking it for verse.

But even when we let these modern hexameters go, as Greek, and merely hold them fast in their proper character of Longfellownian, or Feltonian, or Frogpondian, we must still condemn them as having been committed in a radical misconception of the philosophy of verse. The spondee, as I observed, is the *theme* of the Greek line. Most of the ancient hexameters *begin* with spondees, for the reason that the spondee *is* the theme, and the ear is filled with it as with a burden. Now, the Feltonian dactylics have, in the same way, dactyls for the theme, and most of them begin with dactyls, which is all very proper if not very Greek – but, unhappily, the one point at which they *are* very Greek is that point, precisely, at which they should be nothing but Feltonian. They always *close* with what is meant for a spondee. To be consistently silly, they should die off in a dactyl.

That a truly Greek hexameter *cannot*, however, be readily composed in English is a proposition which I am by no means inclined to admit. I think I could manage the point myself. For example:

Do tell! | When may we | hope to make | men of sense | out of the | pundits |
Born and brought|up with their|snouts deep|down in the|mud of the|Frog Pond?|
Why ask? | Who ever | yet saw | money made | out of a | fat old |
Jew or | downright | upright | nutmegs | out of a | pine knot? |

The proper spondee predominance is here preserved. Some of the dactyls are not so good as I could wish, but, upon the whole, the rhythm is very decent – to say nothing of its excellent sense.

Abbreviations

AAR: Edgar Allan Poe, *Al Aaraaf, Tamerlane and Minor Poems* (Baltimore: Hatch and Dunning, 1829), reprinted by the Facsimile Text Society (New York: Columbia University Press, 1933), with a bibliographical note by Thomas Ollive Mabbott

COLL1: *The Collected Works of Edgar Allan Poe*, ed. Thomas Ollive Mabbott, Vol. 1, *Poems* (Cambridge, MA: Belknap Press of Harvard University Press, 1969)

COM: *The Complete Poems of Edgar Allan Poe*, ed. J.H. Whitty (Boston and New York: Houghton Mifflin Company, 1911)

ISR: Hervey Allen, *Israfel: The Life and Times of Edgar Allan Poe* (New York: George H. Doran, 1926)

PMS: Edgar Allan Poe, *Poems* (New York: Elam Bliss, 1831)

QUI: Arthur Hobson Quinn, *Edgar Allan Poe: A Critical Biography* (New York: D. Appleton-Century Company, Inc., 1941)

RAV: Edgar Allan Poe, *The Raven and Other Poems* (New York: Wiley and Putnam, 1845)

TAM: Edgar Allan Poe, *Tamerlane and Other Poems* (Boston: Calvin F.S. Thomas, 1827)

WOR: *The Works of the Late Edgar Allan Poe*, ed. N.P. Willis, J.R. Lowell and R.W. Griswold (New York: J.S. Redfield, 1850), Vol. 2

Note on the Texts

Edgar Allan Poe was an obsessive reviser. Most of his poems were heavily revised from manuscript to print and between editions. The texts in the present volume are taken from the first editions of the collections in which they originally appeared, if published during the author's lifetime (please refer to the notes to the relevant collections for details). For the poems that were uncollected at the time of Poe's death, we have generally followed the text of their first publication, with some exceptions (see relevant notes for details). The most significant variants between published versions have been indicated in the notes. Wherever a poem is sufficiently different from the original version, we have reprinted the entire alternative text. The punctuation has been regularized, and the spelling has been standardized and modernized throughout.

Notes

p. 3, *Tamerlane and Other Poems*: A volume of poems published in 1827 (see Abbreviations, "TAM", for details). Only one hundred copies of the book were printed. The epigraph is from *Tirocinium, or A Review of Schools* (ll. 444–45), a 1784 poem by William Cowper (1731–1800). We follow the text and most of the suggested emendations provided by Richard Herne Shepherd in his edition of the work (London: George Redway, 1884).

p. 5, *Tamerlane*: Of the history of Tamerlane little is known, and with that little I have taken the full liberty of a poet. That he was descended from the family of Zinghis Khan [Genghis Khan] is more than probable – but he is vulgarly supposed to have been the son of a shepherd, and to have raised himself to the throne by his own address. He died in the year 1405, in the time of Pope Innocent VII.

How I shall account for giving him "a friar" as a deathbed confessor, I cannot exactly determine. He wanted someone to listen to his tale – and why not a friar? It does not pass the bounds of possibility – quite sufficient for my purposes – and I have at least good authority on my side for such innovations [POE'S NOTE]. Poe reworked the poem completely in 1828 (a fragmentary copy of the manuscript has survived, and it was reprinted in COLL1, pp. 40–45) and again in 1829 for the publication of AAR (see pp. 53–60 for this version, which is the one the author followed – with some revisions – when he published PMS and RAV). Tamerlane is the name by which the Turko-Mongol conqueror Timur (1336–1405), Emir of the Timurid Empire, was known to Europeans.

p. 7, *Nos hæc novimus esse nihil*: "We knew that these things amount to nothing" (Latin), a quotation from Martial's *Epigrams* (XIII, 2, l. 8) – also used by John Gay (1685–1732) as the epigraph to *The Beggar's Opera*.

p. 10, *The mists of the Taglay have shed*: The mountains of Belur Taglay are a branch of the Imaus, in the southern part of Independent Tartary. They are celebrated for the singular wildness and beauty of their valleys [POE'S NOTE]. Imaus (or Mount Imeon) is the ancient name of a complex of mountain ranges comprising the present Hindu Kush, Pamir and Tian Shan.

p. 13, *no purer... than thine*: I must beg the reader's pardon for making Tamerlane, a Tartar of the fourteenth century, speak in the same language as a Boston gentleman of the nineteenth, but of the Tartar mythology we have little information [POE'S NOTE].

p. 13, *Which blazes upon Edis' shrine*: A deity presiding over virtuous love, upon whose imaginary altar a sacred fire was continually blazing [POE'S NOTE].

p. 16, *who hardly... their own sphere*: Although Tamerlane speaks this, it is not the less true. It is a matter of the greatest difficulty to make the generality of mankind believe that one with whom they are upon terms of intimacy shall be called, in the world, a "great man". The reason is evident. There are few great men. Their actions are consequently viewed by the mass of the people through the medium of distance. The prominent parts of their character are alone noted – and those properties which are minute and common to everyone, not being observed, seem to have no connection with a great character.

Whoever read the private memorials, correspondence, etc., which have become so common in our time, without wondering that "great men" should act and think "so abominably"? [POE'S NOTE].

p. 16, *Her own Alexis, who should plight*: That Tamerlane acquired his renown under a feigned name is not entirely a fiction [POE'S NOTE].

p. 18, *Look round thee now on Samarcand*: I believe it was after the Battle of Angora that Tamerlane made Samarcand his residence. It became for a time the seat of learning and the arts [POE'S NOTE]. The Battle of Ankara (or Angora) was fought on 20th July 1402 between the forces of the Ottoman Sultan Bayezid I (*c.*1360–1403) and those of Timur, which secured a resounding victory.

p. 18, *Timur, he*: He was called Timur Bek as well as Tamerlane [POE'S NOTE].

p. 18, *The Zinghis' yet re-echoing fame*: The conquests of Tamerlane far exceeded those of Zinghis Khan. He boasted to have two thirds of the world at his command [POE'S NOTE]. The reference is to Genghis Khan (*c.*1162–1227), the founder and first Great Khan of the Mongol Empire.

p. 19, *the sound... hearken*: I have often fancied that I could distinctly hear the sound of the darkness as it steals over the horizon – a foolish fancy, perhaps, but not more unintelligible than to see music: "The mind, the music breathing from her face" [POE'S NOTE]. The quotation is from Lord Byron's *The Bride of Abydos* (see second note to p. 218) 1, 6, l. 22.

p. 19, *Let life, then, as the day flower fall*: There is a flower (I have never known its botanic name) vulgarly called the "day flower". It blooms beautifully in the daylight, but withers towards evening, and by night its leaves appear totally shrivelled and dead. I have forgotten, however, to mention in the text that it lives again in the morning. If it will not flourish in Tartary, I must be forgiven for carrying it thither [POE'S NOTE].

p. 23, *Of young passion free*: RAV: "(Whatever it might be)".

p. 23, *chainèd*: RAV: "aching".

p. 23, *might*: RAV: "could".

p. 23, *I ween*: RAV: "perhaps".

p. 24, *Alone... are near*: AAR: "Mid dark thoughts of the grey tombstone – / Not one of all the crowd".

p. 24, *For the night*: AAR: "The night".

p. 25, *From their thrones in the dark heaven*: AAR: "From their high thrones in the heaven".

p. 25, *withering heart*: AAR: "weariness".

p. 25, *But 'twill leave thee... in thee*: AAR: "Now are thoughts thou shalt not banish – / Now are visions ne'er to vanish: / From thy spirit shall they pass / No more – like dewdrop from the grass. // The breeze – the breath of God – is still, / And the mist upon the hill – / Shadowy, shadowy, yet unbroken – / Is a symbol and a token... / How it hangs upon the trees, / A mystery of mysteries!"

p. 28, *A wilder'd… my soul?*: Omitted from the AAR and RAV versions.

p. 28, *through misty night… afar*: AAR: "through storm and night / So trembled from afar".

p. 29, *In youth's spring*: RAV: "In spring of youth".

p. 29, *world*: RAV: "earth".

p. 29, *And the wind… lake*: AAR: "And the black wind murmur'd by, / In a dirge of melody – / My infant spirit would awake / To the terror of the lone lake." RAV: "And the mystic wind went by / Murmuring in melody – / Then, ah, then I would awake / To the terror of the lone lake."

p. 29, *And a feeling… darken'd mind*: AAR: "A feeling not the jewell'd mine / Should ever bribe me to define – / Nor love, although the love be thine." RAV: "A feeling not the jewell'd mine / Could teach or bribe me to define – / Nor love, although the love were thine."

p. 29, *dark*: AAR and RAV: "lone".

p. 29, *wildering thought could even make*: AAR and RAV: "solitary soul could make".

p. 31, *Al Aaraaf, Tamerlane and Minor Poems*: A collection published in 1829 (see Abbreviations, "AAR", for details).

p. 33, *Entiendes… Mientes, Fabio*: "'Do you understand what I am telling you, Fabio?' 'How can I not understand it?' 'You are lying, Fabio.'" The quotation is from a satirical sonnet ('Cediendo a mi descrédito anhelante', ll. 12–13) by the Spanish playwright and poet Lope de Vega (1562–1635). After launching into an unintelligible outburst, filled with bookish and cerebral expressions, the sonnet's narrator asks his interlocutor, Fabio, whether he understands what he was saying. When Fabio replies in the affirmative, the narrator accuses him of lying, and rounds off the sonnet with: "Because I who said these words don't understand them myself." The humorous epigraph warns any reader baffled by the obscurity of the poem that he, the author, can't make much sense of it either. We have corrected the Spanish of the original epigraph, which contained several misprints.

p. 33, *What has… sleep?*: From *Comus* (l. 122), a 1634 poem by Milton

p. 35, *Who drinks the deepest?… Here's to him*: From 'A Song of Sack' (l. 36), a poem attributed to John Cleveland (1613–58).

p. 37, *Tycho Brahe*: The Danish astronomer Tycho Brahe (1546–1601). The extracts from the poem published in the *Baltimore Gazette* of 18th May 1829 are prefaced by the following Introductory Note: "Al Aaraaf, among the Arabians a medium between Heaven and Hell, is supposed to be located in the celebrated star discovered by Tycho Brahe, which burst forth in one night upon the eyes of the world, and disappeared as suddenly. Michelangelo is represented as transferred to this star, and speaking to the 'lady of his unearthly love' of the regions he had left." The version of the poem published in PMS (1831) has the following alternative beginning, replacing the first fifteen lines of AAR:

> Mysterious star!
> Thou wert my dream
> All a long summer night –
> Be now my theme!
> By this clear stream
> Of thee will I write –
> Meantime from afar
> Bathe me in light!
>
> Thy world has not the dross of ours,
> Yet all the beauty – all the flowers
> That list our love, or deck our bowers
> In dreamy gardens, where do lie
> Dreamy maidens all the day,
> While the silver winds of Circassy
> On violet couches faint away.
>
> Little, oh, little dwells in thee
> Like unto what on earth we see:
> Beauty's eye is here the bluest
> In the falsest and untruest –
> On the sweetest air doth float
> The most sad and solemn note.
> If with thee be broken hearts,
> Joy so peacefully departs
> That its echo still doth dwell
> Like the murmur in the shell.
> Thou! Thy truest type of grief
> Is the gentle falling leaf...
> Thou! Thy framing is so holy,
> Sorrow is not melancholy.

The version published in RAV substantially follows that in AAR.

p. 39, *Meet*: RAV: "True".

p. 39, *soar*: RAV: "soared".

p. 39, *hamadryad… naiad*: Hamadryads and naiads are wood and river (or spring) nymphs, respectively.

p. 39, *The gentle naiad from her fountain flood*: RAV: "Hast thou not torn the Naiad from her flood".

p. 39, *shrubbery*: RAV: "tamarind tree".

p. 41, *With nothing*: RAV: "Oh, nothing".

p. 41, *A garden spot*: RAV: "An oasis".

p. 42, *Achaian*: Amended from "Archaian", based on RAV.

p. 42, *rear'd*: Amended from "rear", based on RAV.

p. 42, *On the fair Capo Ducato*: On Santa Maura – olim Leucadia [POE'S NOTE]. Capo Ducato is the old Italian name of Cape Doukato (Leucadian Cape) on the Greek island of Lefkada, or Leucadia (called Santa Maura in the Middle Ages by its Italian rulers). It was also known as "Sappho's Leap" as, according to legend, the Greek poet Sappho killed herself by jumping off the Leucadian cliffs.

p. 42, *Of her who lov'd a mortal*: Sappho [POE'S NOTE].

p. 42, *of Trebizond misnam'd*: This flower is much noticed by Lewenhoeck and Tournefort. The bee, feeding upon its blossom, becomes intoxicated [POE'S NOTE]. The names of the sephalica and the Trebizond flower are taken from the notes to *Lalla Rookh*, an oriental romance by Thomas Moore (1779–1852), first published in 1817, in which the author quotes the authorities of the English philologist Sir William Jones (1746–94) and the French botanist Joseph Pitton de Tournefort (1656–1708), respectively, to illustrate the intoxicating powers of these flowers. Lewenhoeck is probably the Dutch microbiologist and microscopist Antonie van Leeuwenhoek (1632–1723).

p. 42, *Nyctanthes*: Another flower taken from Moore's notes to *Lalla Rookh*.

p. 42, *clytia*: "The Chrysanthemum Peruvianum (or, to employ a better-known term, the turnsole), which turns continually towards the sun, covers itself, like Peru, the country from which it comes, with dewy clouds which cool and refresh its flowers during the most violent heat of the day." B. de St Pierre [POE'S NOTE]. The quotation is taken from *Études de la nature* (*Studies of Nature*), a 1784 work by the French novelist and botanist Bernardin de Saint-Pierre (1737–1814).

p. 43, *that aspiring flower*: "There is cultivated in the king's garden at Paris a species of serpentine aloe without prickles, whose large and beautiful flower exhales a strong odour of the vanilla during the time of its expansion, which is very short. It does not blow till towards the month of July – you then perceive it gradually open its petals, expand them, fade and die." St. Pierre [POE'S NOTE]. Another quotation from Saint-Pierre's *Studies of Nature*.

p. 43, *Vallisnerian lotus*: There is found, in the Rhône, a beautiful lily of the Vallisnerian kind. Its stem will stretch to the length of three or four feet – thus preserving its head above water in the swellings of the river [POE'S NOTE].

p. 43, *thy most lovely... Fior di Levante!*: The hyacinth [POE'S NOTE]. The Greek island of Zakynthos (called Zante by the Venetians, who ruled over it between 1484 and 1797) is said to derive its name from the wild hyacinth. "Isola d'oro" ("Golden island") and "Fior di Levante" ("Flower of the Levant") are appellations given to Zakynthos by the Venetians, which Poe borrowed from *Travels in Greece, Palestine, Egypt and Barbary* by François-René de Chateaubriand (1768–1848).

p. 43, *the nelumbo... holy river*: It is a fiction of the Indians that Cupid was first seen floating in one of these down the river Ganges, and that he still loves the cradle of his childhood [POE'S NOTE]. The name of the nelumbo and its association with Cupid are taken from a note in Moore's *Lalla Rookh*.

p. 43, *To bear... up to heaven*: "And golden vials full of odours, which are the prayers of the saints." Rev. St John [POE'S NOTE]. The quotation is from Revelation 5:8, a book traditionally attributed to John the Apostle.

p. 43, *the beings... a model of their own*: "The Humanitarians held that God was to be understood as having really a human form. Vide Clarke's *Sermons*, Vol. 1, p. 26, fol. edit. The drift of Milton's argument leads him to employ language which would appear, at first sight, to verge upon their doctrine, but it will be seen immediately that he guards himself against the charge of having adopted one of the most ignorant errors of the dark ages of the Church." Dr Sumner's *Notes on Milton's Christian Doctrine*.

This opinion, in spite of many testimonies to the contrary, could never have been very general. Audaeus, a Syrian of Mesopotamia, was condemned for the opinion as heretical. He lived in the beginning of the fourth century. His disciples were called Anthropomorphites. Vide du Pin.

Among Milton's minor poems are these lines:

> *Dicite sacrorum præsides nemorum Deæ*, etc.,
> *Quis ille primus cujus ex imagine*
> *Natura solers finxit humanum genus,*
> *Æternus, incorruptus, æquævus polo,*
> *Unusque et universus, exemplar Dei?*

And afterwards,

> *Non cui profundum cæcitas lumen dedit*
> *Dircæus augur vidit hunc alto sinu*, etc.
>
> [POE'S NOTE].

The quotation about the Humanitarians (people who believe that Christ's nature is only human and not divine) is taken from a footnote to the English translation of Milton's unfinished religious work *De doctrina christiana* by the Church of England prelate Charles R. Sumner (1790–1874), first published as *A Treatise on Christian Doctrine* in 1825. Sumner's reference is to the first volume of the folio edition (1738) of the *Sermons* of the English philosopher and Anglican cleric Samuel Clarke (1675–1729). The French historian Louis Ellies du Pin (or Dupin, 1657–1719) is the author of a 58-volume *Nouvelle bibliothèque des auteurs ecclésiastiques* ("New Library of Ecclesiastical Authors"), the first volume of which appeared in 1686. Audaeus (or Audius) was the founder of Audianism, a sect whose belief was that God created humans to resemble His physical form. The Milton quotations are from his poem 'De Idea Platonica, quemadmodum Aristoteles intellexit' ('On the Platonic Idea as Understood by Aristotle'), and translate: "Say, O Goddesses, guardians of the sacred grove, […] / Who the first was after whose image / Ingenious Nature moulded mankind – / The eternal, incorruptible, heaven-coeval, / Singular and universal exemplar of God? […] Not even the Theban prophet [Tiresias], who was given keener sight / By his blindness, ever beheld him in the depth of vision" (ll. 1, 7–10, 25–26).

p. 44, *By wingèd Fantasy*:

> *Seltsamen Tochter Jovis,*
> *Seinem Schoßkinde,*
> *Der Phantasie.*
>
> Goethe
> [POE'S NOTE].

The quotation is from the poem 'Meine Göttin' ("My Goddess") by the German poet Johann Wolfgang von Goethe (1749–1832), which translates:

> Wondrous daughter of Jove,
> His best-beloved offspring,
> Fantasy (ll. 7–9).

p. 44, *embassy*: Message.

p. 44, *Here*: RAV: "All".

p. 44, *sightless*: Too small to be seen. Legge [POE'S NOTE]. The obscure reference is probably to an unidentified sermon by Edward Legge (1767–1827), Bishop of Oxford.

p. 44, *like fireflies in Sicilian night*: I have often noticed a peculiar movement of the fireflies: they will collect in a body and fly off, from a common centre, into innumerable radii [POE'S NOTE].

p. 45, *her Therasaean reign*: Therasaea, or Therasea, the island mentioned by Seneca which, in a moment, arose from the sea to the eyes of astonished mariners [POE'S NOTE]. According to Seneca's account in his *Naturales quæstiones* ("Natural Questions", VI, 21, 1), the island emerged from the sea near the Greek islands of Thera (Santorini) and Therasia.

p. 45, *What time*: When.

p. 45, *quadrated*: The moon is "quadrated" when one half of the disk is illuminated.

p. 45, *nursled*: Nursed, fostered.

p. 45, *molten stars... such as fall*:

> "Some star which from the ruin'd roof
> Of shak'd Olympus by mischance did fall." Milton
> [POE'S NOTE].

The quotation is from Milton's ode 'On the Death of a Fair Infant Dying of a Cough' (ll. 43–44).

p. 45, *ebon*: Black (like ebony).

p. 46, *ventur'd*: RAV: "peerèd".

p. 46, *Achaian*: Amended from "Archaian", based on RAV.

p. 46, *Tadmor... Balbec*: Voltaire, in speaking of Persepolis, says, "*Je connais bien l'admiration qu'inspirent ces ruines – mais un palais érigé au pied d'une chaîne de rochers steriles, peut-il être un chef d'œuvre des arts?*" [POE'S NOTE]. The quotation from Voltaire (François-Marie Arouet, 1694–1778) – which translates: "I know well what admiration these ruins inspire – but can a palace built at the foot of a chain of barren rocks be called a masterpiece of art?" – is adapted from a passage in the fifth chapter of his *Essai sur les mœurs et l'esprit des nations* ("Essay on the Customs and the Spirit of the Nations", 1756). Tadmor is the Arabic name of the ancient city of Palmyra, in present-day Syria. Persepolis, located in modern-day Iran, was the capital of the Achaemenid Empire (*c*.550–330 BC).

Balbec, or Baalbek, known in antiquity as Heliopolis, was an ancient city situated in present-day Lebanon. The three cities are famed archaeological sites.

p. 46, *the stilly, clear abyss... too late to save*: Ula Degnisi is the Turkish appellation, but on its own shores it is called Bahar Loth, or Almontanah. There were undoubtedly more than two cities engulfed in the "dead sea". In the valley of Siddim were five – Admah, Zeboim, Zoar, Sodom and Gomorrah. Stephen of Byzantium mentions eight, and Strabo thirteen (engulfed) – but the last is out of all reason.

It is said (Tacitus, Strabo, Josephus, Daniel of St Saba, Nau, Maundrell, Troilo, D'Arvieux) that after an excessive drought the vestiges of columns, walls, etc., are seen above the surface. At *any* season, such remains may be discovered by looking down into the transparent lake, and at such distance as would argue the existence of many settlements in the space now usurped by the "Asphaltites" [POE'S NOTE]. The Turkish name for the Dead Sea, Ula Degnisi (*Ölüdeniz*), is taken from Chateaubriand's *Travels* (see third note to p. 43). Bahar Loth and Almontanah (Al-Muntinah) are Arabic names for the Dead Sea. Stephanus of Byzantium (fl. sixth century AD) in fact talks of ten cities in the entry "Sodoma" of his geographical dictionary *Ethnica*. Strabo does mention that "thirteen cities once existed there, the capital of which was Sodom" (*Geographica* XVI, 2). The references for the authorities mentioned by Poe in the second paragraph, which perhaps he borrowed from other sources, are (apart from the already-mentioned Strabo): Tacitus (*c.*56–*c.*120 AD), *Historiæ* V, 7; Josephus (*c.*37–*c.*100 AD), *De bello judaico* V, 5; the Jesuit priest Michel Nau (1623–83), *Voyage nouveau de la Terre-Sainte* ("New Journey through the Holy Land", 1679) IV, 8, in which he quotes information given to him by Daniel, Abbot of St Saba, a monastery near the Dead Sea; the clergyman Henry Maundrell (1665–1701), *Journey from Aleppo to Jerusalem at Easter A.D. 1697* (1703), under date "Tuesday, Mar. 30"; Franz Ferdinand von Troilo (*c.*1635–*c.*1700), *Orientalische Reise* (Dresden: Melchior Bergens, 1676), 'Das Tode Meer', pp. 344–47; Laurent d'Arvieux (1635–1702), *Mémoires* (1735), Vol. 2, Chapter 16. Asphaltites (Lacus Asphaltites) is the Latin name for the Dead Sea.

p. 46, *near*: RAV: "in".

p. 46, *Eyraco*: Chaldea [POE'S NOTE]. Chaldea was an ancient state and region of lower Mesopotamia. The Chaldeans were renowned astrologers. Eyraco probably refers to Iraq, a term used in medieval times to denote lower Mesopotamia.

p. 46, *Is it not its form... loud*: I have often thought I could distinctly hear the sound of the darkness as it stole over the horizon [POE'S NOTE].

p. 46, *zone*: A girdle, an encircling band.

p. 46, *Young flowers... melody*: "Fairies use flowers for their charactery." *Merry Wives of Windsor* [POE'S NOTE]. The quotation is from *The Merry Wives of Windsor*, Act v, Sc. 5, l. 72.

p. 47, *That keeps... The moonbeam away*: In Scripture is this passage: "The sun shall not harm thee by day, nor the moon by night." It is, perhaps, not generally known that the moon, in Egypt, has the effect of producing blindness to those who sleep with the face exposed to its rays, to which circumstances the passage evidently alludes [POE'S NOTE]. Poe's allusion is to Psalm 121:6.

p. 47, *hang*: RAV: "lead".

p. 48, *Ligeia... to melody run*: The name Ligeia derives from the Greek for "canorous". A woman called Ligeia appears in an eponymous story by Poe, in which he describes "the almost magical melody, modulation, distinctness, and placidity of her very low voice".

p. 48, *Like the lone albatross*: The albatross is said to sleep on the wing [POE'S NOTE]. Poe found this detail in a note in Moore's *Lalla Rookh* (see fifth note to p. 42): "These birds sleep in the air."

p. 48, *The murmur that springs*: I met with this idea in an old English tale, which I am now unable to obtain and quote from memory: "The verie essence and, as it were, springe heade and origine of all musiche is the verie pleasaunte sounde which the trees of the forest do make when they growe" [POE'S NOTE]. The quotation is probably Poe's own invention.

p. 49, *Some... have slept with the bee*: The wild bee will not sleep in the shade if there be moonlight.

The rhyme in the verse, as in one about sixty lines before [see l. 234 above], has an appearance of affectation. It is, however, imitated from Sir W. Scott – or, rather, from Claud Halcro, in whose mouth I admired its effect:

> Oh, were there an island,
>   Though ever so wild,
> Where woman might smile and
>   No man be beguil'd, etc.
>   [POE'S NOTE].

The quotation is the beginning of the fourth stanza of a Claud Halcro's song ('Mary') from *The Pirate* (Chapter 12) by Walter Scott (1771–1832).

p. 49, *simoom*: A hot, dust-laden wind blowing in the desert.

p. 49, *"to be"*: Perhaps an allusion to Hamlet's famous soliloquy, which begins: "To be or not to be…"

p. 49, *Apart from Heaven's… far from Hell*: With the Arabians there is a medium between Heaven and Hell where men suffer no punishment, but yet do not attain that tranquil and even happiness which they suppose to be characteristic of heavenly enjoyment.

> *Un no rompido sueño,*
> *Un día puro, alegre, libre quiero –* […]
> *Libre de amor, de celo,*
> *De odio, de esperanzas, de recelo.*
>   Luis Ponce de Leon

Sorrow is not excluded from "Al Aaraaf", but it is that sorrow which the living love to cherish for the dead, and which, in some minds, resembles the delirium of opium. The passionate excitement of love and the buoyancy of spirit attendant upon intoxication are its less holy pleasures – the price of which, to those souls who make choice of "Al Aaraaf" as their residence after life, is final death and annihilation [POE'S NOTE]. The quotation is from the ode 'A la vida retirada' ("On Retired Life"), ll. 26–27, 39–40, by the Spanish lyric poet and Augustinian friar Luis Ponce de Léon (1527–91), and translates: "What I seek is an uninterrupted sleep, / A pure, happy, free day – […] / Free from love, zeal, / Hatred, hope and apprehension."

p. 50, *"tears of perfect moan"*:

> There be tears of perfect moan
> Wept for thee in Helicon.
>   Milton
>   [POE'S NOTE].

The quotation (with "Here" replacing "There" in the original) is from Milton's poem 'An Epitaph on the Marchioness of Winchester', ll. 55–56.

p. 50, *young Angelo*: The spirit of Michelangelo (see note to p. 37).

p. 50, *one constant star*: RAV: "the orb of earth".

p. 50, *Lemnos*: A Greek island, in the northern Aegean Sea, sacred to the god of metalworking, Hephaestus. According to Greek mythology, when Zeus hurled Hephaestus out of Olympus, he landed on Lemnos.

p. 50, *Persian Saadi in his Gulistan*: The reference is to the Persian poet and writer Saadi (1210–*c*.1291) – author, among other works, of the *Gulistan* ("Rose Garden"), a collection of stories and personal anecdotes, mainly in prose.

p. 50, *it*: RAV: "he".

p. 50, *the Parthenon*: It was entire in 1687 – the most elevated spot in Athens [POE'S NOTE]. The Parthenon, a Greek temple on the Athenian Acropolis, was partially destroyed by the Venetians during their siege of September 1687.

p. 50, *More beauty… beats withal*:

> Shadowing more beauty in their airy brows
> Than have the white breasts of the Queen of Love.
>> Marlowe
>> [POE'S NOTE].

The quotation is from *Doctor Faustus* (ll. 127–28) by Christopher Marlowe (1564–93).

p. 51, *pennon'd*: "Pennon" for "pinion". Milton [POE'S NOTE]. See *Paradise Lost* II, l. 933: "Fluttering his pennons vain, plumb down he drops."

p. 51, *Daedalion*: In Greek mythology, one of the two sons of Hesperus. According to the myth, heartbroken at the death of his daughter Chione, Daedalion tried to throw himself off Mount Parnassus, but was transformed into a hawk by Apollo.

p. 53, *Tamerlane [1829 version]*: For the 1827 version of 'Tamerlane' see pp. 5–20. See also note to p. 5. The 1829 version of 'Tamerlane' includes an 'Advertisement' – "This poem was printed for publication in Boston, in the year 1827, but suppressed through circumstances of a private nature" – as well as the following dedication: "TO / JOHN NEAL / THIS POEM / IS / RESPECTFULLY DEDICATED". John Neal (1793–1876) was an American author and poet.

p. 53, *a knell*: PMS has four additional lines at the end of this stanza: "Despair, the fabled vampire bat, / Hath long upon my bosom sat, / And I would rave but that he flings / A calm from his unearthly wings."

p. 54, *The mists of the Taglay have shed*: See note to p. 10.

p. 54, *Have*: Amended from "Hath", based on RAV.

p. 54, *Was giant-like – so thou, my mind!*: RAV: "Rendered me mad and deaf and blind."

p. 55, *Ev'n then… had a part*: PMS: "Ev'n then who knew that as infinite / My soul, so was the weakness in it."

p. 55, *I have no words… with none*: In PMS this stanza is replaced by the following two stanzas, numbered VIII and IX:

For in those days it was my lot
To haunt of the wide world a spot
The which I could not love the less.
So lovely was the loneliness
Of a wild lake with black rock bound,
And the sultan-like pines that tower'd around!
But when the night had thrown her pall
Upon that spot as upon all,
And the black wind murmur'd by
In a dirge of melody,
My infant spirit would awake
To the terror of that lone lake.
Yet that terror was not fright,
But a tremulous delight –
A feeling not the jewell'd mine
Could ever bribe me to define,
Nor love, Ada, though it were thine!
How could I from that water bring
Solace to my imagining –
My solitary soul, how make
An Eden of that dim lake?

But then a gentler, calmer spell
like moonlight on my spirit fell,
And oh, I have no words to tell
The loveliness of loving well!
I will not now attempt to trace
The more than beauty of a face
Whose lineaments upon my mind
Are shadows on the unstable wind.
I well remember having dwelt
Pages of early lore upon
With loitering eye, till I have felt
The letters, with their meaning, melt
To fantasies – with none.

p. 55, *Oh, she was worthy of all love!*: PMS: "Was she not worthy of all love?"
p. 56, *I'd throw me on her throbbing breast*: PMS: "I'd lean upon her gentle breast".
p. 56, *her*: PMS: "hers".

p. 56, *Yet more… a new tone*: Lines omitted in PMS.

p. 56, *Its joy… the ideal*: PMS: "Of pleasure or of pain – / The good, the bad, the ideal".

p. 57, *had passed*: Would have passed.

p. 57, *I was ambitious… loveliness*: Stanza omitted in PMS.

p. 57, *begirt*: Girdled.

p. 58, *rabble men*: Amended from "rabble – men", based on PMS.

p. 58, *Look round thee now on Samarcand*: See first note to p. 18.

p. 58, *Timur, he*: See note to p. 5.

p. 58, *Look round… outlaw!*: In PMS this stanza is replaced by the following stanza, also numbered XVII:

> Say, holy father, breathes there yet
> A rebel or a Bajazet?
> How now! Why tremble, man of gloom,
> As if my words were the simoom!
> Why do the people bow the knee,
> To the young Tamerlane — to me!

Bajazet (Bayezid I) was the Turkish sultan captured by Tamerlane (see first note to p. 18). For "simoom", see second note to p. 49.

p. 58, *siroc-wither'd plain*: Siroc is another name for the hot wind sirocco.

p. 59, *And boyhood… which is all*: Lines omitted in PMS.

p. 60, *I reach'd my home… a deeper woe*: In PMS this stanza is replaced by the following stanza, also numbered XXII:

> I reach'd my home – what home? Above
> My home, my hope, my early love,
> Lonely, like me, the desert rose,
> Bow'd down with its own glory, grows.

p. 60, *Eblis*: In Islamic religion, Eblis (or Iblis) is the Devil.

p. 60, *unpolluted*: PMS: "undefiled".

p. 60, *very hair*: PMS ends with the following additional stanza, numbered XXIV:

> If my peace hath flown away
> In a night, or in a day –
> In a vision, or in none –
> Is it, therefore, the less gone?
> I was standing mid the roar

> Of a wind-beaten shore,
> And I held within my hand
> Some particles of sand –
> How bright... and yet to creep
> Through my fingers to the deep!
> My early hopes? No, they
> Went gloriously away,
> Like lightning from the sky –
> Why in the battle did not I?

These lines appear, with some changes, in 'To –', ll. 13–26 (see p. 65).

p. 61, *Miscellaneous Poems*: The following poems have been omitted from this section, since already published (in a slightly different form) in TAM: 'To —' (see p. 23); 'The Lake — To —' ('The Lake' – see p. 29); 'Spirits of the Dead' ('Visit of the Dead' – see pp. 24–25); 'A Dream' ('A Wilder'd Being from My Birth' – see p. 28).

p. 61, *My nothingness... Southey's Pers.*: The last two lines of 'Imitation from the Persian', a poem by Robert Southey (1774–1843) which was included in *The Bijou* annual for 1828. The original on which Southey based his imitation is a poem by the Persian poet Suzani (d. 1166). "SOUTHEY'S PERS." is a conjectural reading of the original "SOUTHEY E PERSIS", an obvious misprint (some critics have proposed "SOUTHEY'S POEMS"; others "SOUTHEY'S PERSIS").

p. 61, *And some flowers... Milton*: An adapted quotation from Milton's poem 'An Epitaph on the Marchioness of Winchester', l. 57. The original reads: "And some flowers, and some bays."

p. 63, *paroquet*: Parakeet.

p. 63, *condor years*: Condors are noted for their voracity. There may be an allusion to Shakespeare's "cormorant devouring Time" of *Love's Labour's Lost* (Act I, Sc. I, l. 4).

p. 63, *I hardly have had time for cares*: RAV: "I have no time for idle cares".

p. 66, *Shade of Zeno*: Zeno of Citium (*c.*334–*c.*262 BC) was the founder of the Stoic school of philosophy.

p. 66, *trifles*: RAV: "baubles".

p. 67, *To the River —*: The poem is probably addressed to the River Po, a pun on the author's name.

p. 67, *Of labyrinth-like water*: RAV: "Of crystal, wandering water".

p. 67, *old Alberto's daughter*: Possibly a reference to the city of Mantua, famed for its architectural and artistic treasures, and to Alberto Pitentino (*c*.1100–*c*.1200), the hydraulic engineer who altered the course of the River Mincio, an affluent of the Po, in order to create protective artificial lakes around the city.

p. 67, *The scrutiny of her eyes*: RAV: "Of her soul-searching eyes".

p. 68, *sort*: RAV: "kind".

p. 69, *Over hamlets and rich halls*: RAV: "Over hamlets, over halls".

p. 69, *Like... almost any thing*: Plagiarism – see the works of Thomas Moore, *passim*. Ed. [POE'S NOTE]. For Thomas Moore, see fifth note to p. 42.

p. 69, *(The unbelieving things!)*: RAV: "(Never-contented things!)"

p. 71, *Poems*: A volume of poems published in 1831 (see Abbreviations, "PMS", for details). *Al Aaraaf* and *Tamerlane*, which were reprinted by Poe at the end of this collection, have been omitted here, since already published (in a slightly different form) in AAR and TAM. For *Al Aaraaf*, see pp. 33–52 (and note to p. 37 for the alternative introductory lines that appear only in the 1831 version); for *Tamerlane*, see pp. 5–20 (1827 version), pp. 53–60 (1829 version).

p. 71, *Title-page epigraph*: "Everybody is right" (French). The quotation cannot be traced back to François de La Rochefoucauld (1613–80), but appears to have been taken from the 1747 play *La Gouvernante* ("The Governess"), Act 1, Sc. 3, l. 64, by Pierre-Claude Nivelle de La Chaussée (1692–1754). The full quotation runs: "When everybody is wrong, everybody is right."

p. 73, *Dedication*: Poe dedicated this volume to his former fellow cadets at the West Point academy, New York, many of whom subscribed to the book.

p. 75, *Epigraph*: A slightly adapted quotation from 'The Lie' (ll. 43–46), a poem attributed to Sir Walter Raleigh (*c*.1552–1618).

p. 77, *B—*: Probably Poe's publisher, Elam Bliss (1779–1848).

p. 77, *Shakespeare*: Spelt "Shakspeare" throughout by Poe.

p. 78, *Paradise Regained*: Milton's poem of 1671 (four years after the first publication of his epic poem *Paradise Lost*), dealing with the Temptation of Christ.

p. 78, *Comus*: See second note to p. 33.

p. 78, *the "Lake School"*: The "Lake School" of poetry, whose main exponents were William Wordsworth (1770–1850), Samuel Taylor Coleridge (1772–1834) and Robert Southey (see second note to p. 61).

p. 79, *a work of supererogation*: A superfluous act.

p. 79, *the most philosophical of all writings*: *Spoudiotaton kai philosophikotaton genos* [POE'S NOTE]. The correct quotation, from

Aristotle's *Poetics* IX, 6–7, reads: "*Dio kai filosofōteron kai spoudai-oteron poiēsis historias estin*" ("For this reason poetry is both a more philosophical and a more earnest thing than history").

p. 79, *ceteris paribus*: "All other things being equal" (Latin).

p. 79, *Melmoth*: *Melmoth the Wanderer*, an 1820 Gothic novel by the Irish clergyman and writer Charles Maturin (1780–1824).

p. 79, *Trifles... dive below*: From the Prologue (ll. 25–26) of *All for Love*, a 1677 heroic drama by John Dryden (1631–1700), with "Errors" replacing "Trifles" in the original.

p. 80, *Bacon*: The English philosopher Francis Bacon (1561–1626).

p. 80, *confusion worse confounded*: *Paradise Lost* II, l. 996.

p. 80, *Biographia Literaria*: An autobiographical work by Coleridge, first published in 1817.

p. 80, *de omni scibili et quibusdam aliis*: "About everything that can be known, and all kinds of other things too" (Latin). The expression (more correctly "*De omni re scibili et quibusdam aliis*"), often used to berate pedantry or pomposity in learning, is attributed to Voltaire.

p. 80, *Of genius... never done before*: From Wordsworth's 'Essay, Supplementary to the Preface' appended to the first volume of his 1815 *Poems* (p. 371).

p. 81, *Barrington, the pickpocket*: George Barrington (1755–1804) was a famous convict who was transported to Australia, where he rose to a high position.

p. 81, *whether they be Ossian's or M'Pherson's*: In the 1760s the Scottish writer James Macpherson (1736–96) published a collection of what he claimed were translations (into loosely rhythmical English prose) of Gaelic poetry he had transcribed in the Highlands from traditional ballad singers and storytellers. He presented the collection as fragments of long-lost epic poems by the legendary bard Ossian, dating back to the early centuries of the modern era. The apparent antiquity of the poems and their distinctive Celtic background caused a sensation in Britain and across literary Europe, exerting a major influence on the Romantic movement. Not many years later, however, Macpherson was denounced as a literary fraud. Nonetheless, the Ossianic poems continued to influence European culture into the nineteenth century.

p. 81, *Tantæne animis?*: A reference to a famous line in Virgil's *Aeneid* (I, l. 11): "*Tantæne animis cælestibus iræ?*" ("Can such fury inhabit heavenly minds?").

p. 81, *Temora*: *Temora: An Ancient Epic Poem* (1763), one of Macpherson's Ossianic works.

p. 81, *Peter Bell*: A narrative poem by William Wordsworth, written in 1798 and first published in 1819.

p. 81, *And now... the doctor*: A slightly inaccurate quotation from Wordsworth's 'The Idiot Boy', ll. 392–96, 402–3 and 407.

p. 81, *The dew... to a stone*: The first six lines of Wordsworth's pastoral poem 'The Pet Lamb'.

p. 82, *Stamboul*: Istanbul.

p. 82, *he has given immortality to a wagon*: An allusion to Wordsworth's poem *The Waggoner* (1805).

p. 82, *the bee Sophocles... chorus of turkeys*: In ancient Greece, poets were called "bees", as they gathered nectar. In Sophocles's tragedy *Philoctetes*, the hero is wounded in the foot. According to Pliny (see *Natural History* XXXVII, 11 and X, 38), in Sophocles's lost tragedy *Meleager*, a chorus of birds ("a kind of turkeycocks, or African hens") laments the hero's death.

p. 82, *J'ay trouvé... qu'elles nient*: The quotation is from a letter from Gottfried Wilhelm Leibniz (1646–1716) to Nicolas Rémond (*c.*1676–1725), chief counsellor of the Duke of Orléans and brother of the mathematician Pierre Rémond de Montmort (1678–1719). It is cited by Coleridge in Chapter 12 of *Biographia Literaria*. It translates: "I have often found that most sects are largely right in what they propose, but not so much in what they deny."

p. 82, *"imprisoned his own conceptions"*: Taken from the same passage in *Biographia Literaria*.

p. 82, *Nyctanthes*: See sixth note to p. 42.

p. 82, *Corcyra*: The Greek island of Corfu (Kerkyra) was referred to in antiquity under several different names, including "Corcyra".

p. 82, *"Très volontiers"*: "Most gladly" (French).

p. 82, *a Dr Johnson*: That is, a "Dr Johnson" dictionary. The English writer Samuel Johnson (1709–84) first published his influential *Dictionary of the English Language* in 1755, in which he defines poetry as "metrical composition".

p. 82, *Ursa Major*: The name of a constellation – but, in its literal sense, "Great Bear" (Latin).

p. 82, *Tempest... Titania*: Prospero is the protagonist of *The Tempest*, and Oberon and Titania are the king and the queen of the fairies in *A Midsummer Night's Dream*.

p. 83, *the invective against him who had no music in his soul?*: Probably an allusion to *The Merchant of Venice*, Act V, Sc. 1, ll. 83–88: "The man that hath no music in himself, / Nor is not moved with concord of sweet sounds, / Is fit for treasons, stratagems and spoils. / The motions of his spirit are dull as night, / And his affections dark as Erebus. / Let not such man be trusted."

p. 83, *No Indian prince… to the gallows*: From *Hudibras* (II, I, ll. 273–74) by Samuel Butler (1613–80).

p. 85, *Introduction*: For a previous version of this poem, see 'Preface', p. 63.

p. 85, *paroquet*: See first note to p. 63.

p. 85, *lang syne*: "Long since" (Scottish).

p. 85, *Anacreon*: A Greek lyric poet (*c*.582–*c*.485 BC) famous for his drinking songs.

p. 86, *Hymen*: The god of marriage ceremonies.

p. 86, *condor years*: See second note to p. 63.

p. 87, *Nicean barks… native shore*: Many interpretations of this obscure passage have been proposed. Among the most plausible are the following: the "weary, way-worn wanderer" is Ulysses, and the "Nicean barks" are those of the Phaeacians, which took him back to Ithaca; the "Nicean barks" are the ships of Alexander the Great; "Nicean" is a misspelling for "Nyseian", alluding to the island of Nysa and the Greek god Dionysus; Poe intended "Nicaean", and to allude to the poet Catullus, who returned home after a sojourn in the Roman province of Bithynia (whose main city was Nicaea), on the shores of the Black Sea, as narrated in his Carmen XLVI.

p. 87, *Israfel*: "And the angel Israfel who has the sweetest voice of all God's creatures." Koran [POE'S NOTE]. The quotation is not from the Koran, but from the 'Preliminary Discourse' (Section IV) to the English translation (1734) of the Koran by George Sale (1697–1736), which Poe derived from Moore's notes to *Lalla Rookh* ("melodious" replaces "sweetest" in the original and in Moore). Israfel (or Israfil) is the angel who blows the trumpet to announce the Qiyamah (Day of Judgement) in Islam.

p. 87, *levin*: Lightning.

p. 90, *Fairy Land*: For a previous version of this poem, see pp. 68–69.

p. 91, *Dog Star*: Sirius, the brightest star in the night sky.

p. 92, *in panoply*: In full armour.

p. 92, *Lethe*: In Greek mythology, a river whose waters, when drunk, are said to cause forgetfulness.

p. 93, *Destinies*: The Fates, the three goddesses of destiny in Greek mythology.

p. 96, *The Valley Nis*: One of the possible interpretations of this poem is that it alludes to the world after the Fall as the Valley of "Sin" (an anagram of "Nis").

p. 97, *asphodel*: A flower sacred to Proserpine, the Latin goddess of the underworld (corresponding to the Greek goddess Persephone), and a symbol of death.

p. 99, *The Raven and Other Poems*: A volume published in 1845 (see Abbreviations, "RAV", for details). Several of the poems in this collection, reprinted in a section entitled 'Poems Written in Youth' – which included, besides *Al Aaraaf* and *Tamerlane*, 'A Dream' ('A Wilder'd Being from My Birth', see p. 28), 'Romance' ('Preface', see p. 63), 'Fairy Land' (see pp. 68–69), 'To —' (see p. 66), 'To the River —' (see p. 67), 'The Lake – To —' ('The Lake', see p. 29), 'Song' ('To –', see p. 23) and 'To Helen' (see p. 87), already published (often in a slightly different form) in TAM, AAR or PMS – have been here omitted. We have also omitted 'Scenes from *Politian*', an unfinished verse drama which concludes the first part of the collection, before the section entitled 'Poems Written in Youth'.

p. 101, *Dedication*: The volume is dedicated to Elizabeth Barrett Browning (1806–61), whose *Poems* (1844) – published in the United States as *A Drama of Exile and Other Poems* – appeared under her maiden name, Elizabeth Barrett Barrett ("Barrett" being both the poet's middle name and an abbreviation of her maiden name, Moulton-Barrett).

p. 105, *The Raven*: For Poe's essay on the writing of 'The Raven', see 'The Philosophy of Composition', pp. 181–93.

p. 106, *Pallas*: Pallas Athena, the Greek goddess of wisdom.

p. 106, *the Night's Plutonian shore*: In Roman mythology, Pluto was the ruler of the underworld.

p. 107, *nepenthe*: In Greek myth, a drink which is supposed to bring forgetfulness of pain or sorrow.

p. 107, *is there balm in Gilead?*: See Jeremiah 8:22: "Is there no balm in Gilead – is there no physician there? Why then is not the health of the daughter of my people recovered?" Gilead is a region in modern-day Jordan, east of the river that gives the country its name.

p. 107, *Aidenn*: Eden.

p. 108, *The Valley of Unrest*: For a previous version of this poem, see 'The Valley Nis', pp. 96–97.

p. 110, *The Sleeper*: For a previous version of this poem, see 'Irene', pp. 92–94.

p. 110, *Lethe*: See second note to p. 92.

p. 110, *Destinies*: See note to p. 93.

p. 110, *rout*: Crowd.

p. 111, *Type*: Symbol, emblem.

p. 111, *Eld*: Antiquity.

p. 112, *Judaean king... gardens of Gethsemane*: An allusion to Jesus Christ, the "King of the Jews" (see John 19:19), who experienced great anguish and prayed to God in the garden of Gethsemane (see Matthew 26:36–43 and Mark 14:32–40) before being arrested and crucified.

p. 112, *Chaldee... stars*: See sixth note to p. 46.

p. 112, *As melody from Memnon to the Sun*: A reference to a colossal statue (there are in fact two, still standing, in the Theban necropolis) erected to Memnon, the son of Eos (Aurora, the dawn), near Thebes (Luxor) in Upper Egypt. It was said that this statue (the northern one, known as the "Colossus of Memnon"), as a salute to his mother, produced a melodious sound each morning when touched by the first rays of light, and a mournful one when the sun was setting.

p. 113, *Lenore*: For a previous version of this poem, see 'A Paean', pp. 94–96.

p. 113, *Peccavimus*: "We have sinned" (Latin). From Psalm 106:6 (Vulgate).

p. 113, *"gone before"*: See Ben Jonson (1572–1637), Epigram XXXIII (ll. 2–3): "thou art but gone before / Whither the world must follow."

p. 114, *Israfel*: "And the angel Israfel, whose heartstrings are a lute, and who has the sweetest voice of all God's creatures." Koran [POE'S NOTE]. For a previous version of this poem, see pp. 87–89. See also second note to p. 87. "Whose heartstrings are a lute" is Poe's interpolation, probably derived from the last two lines of the poem 'Le Refus' ("The Refusal", ll. 41–42) by Pierre-Jean de Béranger (1780–1857), which translate: "My heart is a pendant lute / Which resounds as soon as it's touched."

p. 114, *levin*: See third note to p. 87.

p. 114, *the rapid Pleiads... seven*: The Pleiades (also known as the "Seven Sisters"), a cluster of stars located in the constellation Taurus.

p. 115, *an eidolon*: A spectre, a phantom.

p. 115, *ultimate... Thule*: The "ultima Thule" ("farthest Thule", an island north of Britain) of the Romans (and, earlier, of the Greeks): the extreme limit of the earth.

p. 115, *Titan woods*: Gigantic woods. In Greek mythology, the Titans were a gigantic breed born of Gaia (the Earth) who fought with the giants against Zeus.

p. 116, *With forms... all over*: See 'Fairy Land', p. 68, ll. 3–4.

p. 116, *tarns*: Small mountain lakes.

p. 117, *Zante*: See third note to p. 43.

p. 117, *The City in the Sea*: For a previous version of this poem, see 'The Doomed City', pp. 89–90.

p. 120, *Astarte within the sky*: Astarte was a Phoenician goddess of fertility and sexual love, sometimes associated with the moon.

p. 120, *To F—s S. O—d*: The poem (originally written by Poe sometime before 1834 for his cousin Elizabeth Rebecca Herring) is addressed to the American poet Frances Sargent Osgood (1811–50), with whom the author was romantically associated at the time.

p. 121, *To F—*: The poem was originally entitled 'To Mary' (possibly Mary Winfree of Chesterfield, Virginia) and written before the summer of 1835. It is here addressed to Frances Sargent Osgood (see previous note).

p. 121, *incorporate*: Incorporeal.

p. 121, *type*: See first note to p. 111.

p. 121, *corporate*: Corporeal.

p. 122, *condor*: See second note to p. 63.

p. 122, *rout*: See fourth note to p. 110.

p. 123, *Porphyrogene*: From the Greek for "born in the purple", an epithet given to Constantine VII (905–59), emperor of the Eastern Roman Empire, and referring to the Purple Chamber of the imperial palace, where legitimate children of reigning emperors were normally born.

p. 124, *morrow*: Amended from "sorrow", based on a manuscript copy of part of the poem.

p. 127, *Poetry*: These two lines, the earliest known verse written by Poe, date from 1824. First published in ISR.

p. 127, *Oh, Tempora! Oh, Mores!*: Written around 1825, and first published in the *Southern Opinion* of 7th March 1868. Text from the *No Name Magazine* of October 1889. We follow the emendations proposed by Mabbott in COLL1. The Latin phrase of the title ("Oh, what times! Oh, what customs!") is usually attributed to Cicero, who used it in four of his speeches.

p. 127, *Heraclitus... Democritus of Thrace*: Heraclitus of Ephesus (fl. 500 BC) was known as the "weeping philosopher", since he suffered from bouts of melancholy. Democritus of Abdera (*c*.460–*c*.370 BC), a city in Thrace, on the other hand, was known as the "laughing philosopher", as he regarded good humour as essential for human happiness.

p. 128, *counter-hopper*: A male shop assistant.

p. 128, *with a Vestris air*: A reference to the French dancer Auguste Vestris (1760–1842).

p. 129, *To be grave exceeds the power of face*: A quotation from Pope's 'Epistle to Doctor Arbuthnot', l. 36.

p. 129, *Tom and Jerry brim*: A "Tom and Jerry hat" was a silk top hat in the style of those worn by the protagonists of *Life in London, or The Day and Night Scenes of Jerry Hawthorn, Esq., and his elegant friend, Corinthian Tom*, a book by the English journalist Pierce Egan (1772–1849), first published in 1821 and adapted the same year into a popular play, *Tom and Jerry, or Life in London*.

p. 129, *beau idéal*: "The highest type of beauty" (French).

p. 129, *Pitts*: A clerk in the leading fashionable dry-goods store of Richmond, Virginia.

p. 130, *To Margaret*: A parodic cento (with lines deliberately misquoted) written at the beginning of 1827. First published in *Notes and Queries* of 28th November 1931.

p. 130, *Who hath seduced... to write divine*: The sources are as follows. Line 1: "Who first seduced them to that foul revolt?" (*Paradise Lost* I, l. 33); line 2: "Dan Chaucer, well of English undefiled" (Edmund Spenser, *Faerie Queene* IV, 2, l. 32); lines 3–4: "Self-banished from society, prefer / Such squalid sloth to honourable toil" (William Cowper, *The Task* I, ll. 578–79); line 5: "To die... to sleep... / To sleep... perchance to dream" (*Hamlet*, Act III, Sc. 1, ll. 65–66); line 6: "I cannot fight upon this argument" (*Troilus and Cressida*, Act I, Sc. 1, l. 95); line 7: "To err is human – to forgive divine" (Alexander Pope, *Essay on Criticism* II, l. 525).

p. 130, *'When Wit and Wine and Friends Have Met'*: Lines written on 1st May 1827 in the album of Octavia Walton (1810–77), daughter of the politician George Walton (1789–1863).

p. 130, *'From Childhood's Hour I Have Not Been'*: Written around 1829, and first published in *Scribner's Magazine* of September 1875, where it is entitled 'Alone'.

p. 131, *'It Was My Choice or Chance or Curse'*: Included in a letter to the publisher Isaac Lea (1792–1886) written not long before 27th May 1829, and first published in QUI.

p. 131, *'Elizabeth – It Surely Is Most Fit'*: An acrostic written by Poe in around 1829 in the album of his cousin, Elizabeth Rebecca Harding. First published in COM.

p. 131, *Zeno*: Zeno of Citium (see first note to p. 66), who believed that one's own name should not appear in one's own book.

p. 132, *'Elizabeth, It Is in Vain You Say'*: Another acrostic written by Poe, perhaps in 1829, in the album of his cousin Elizabeth Rebecca Harding. First published in COM.

p. 132, *L.E.L.*: Letitia Elizabeth Landon (better known by her initials "L.E.L.", 1802–38), an English poet Poe admired.

p. 132, *Zantippe's talents*: Xanthippe was Socrates's wife, depicted by some ancient sources as a jealous shrew.

p. 132, *Endymion... for he died*: A muddled allusion to the story of Endymion and the Moon ("Luna" in Latin). In Greek mythology, Selene (Diana for the Romans), the goddess of the moon, fell in love with the beautiful shepherd Endymion and visited him each night as he lay asleep on Mount Latmos.

p. 132, *'As For Locke, He Is All in My Eye'*: Humorous verses written by Poe at the West Point military academy in 1830–31, and first published in the Philadelphia *Saturday Museum* of 4th March 1843. The target of his satire is Lieutenant Joseph Locke (1808–64), instructor of military tactics and inspector at the academy. In his role as inspector, he reported infractions of the rules by the cadets.

p. 132, *John Locke*: The English philosopher John Locke (1632–1704).

p. 132, *Serenade*: Written in 1833 and first published in the *Baltimore Saturday Visiter* of 20th April 1833.

p. 132, *Seven Pleiades*: See third note to p. 114.

p. 132, *a second love*: That is, the reflection of the moon. For Endymion, see fourth note to p. 132.

p. 133, *To —*: Written in 1833 and first published (under the pseudonym "Tamerlane") in the *Baltimore Saturday Visiter* of 11th May 1833.

p. 134, *Fanny*: Written in 1833 and first published (under the pseudonym "Tamerlane") in the *Baltimore Saturday Visiter* of 18th May 1833.

p. 134, *sunburst*: A burst of light.

p. 134, *Epigram for Wall Street*: Written in 1845 and first published in the New York *Evening Mirror* of 23rd January 1845.

p. 134, *Impromptu – To Kate Carol*: Written in 1845 and first published in the *Broadway Journal* of 26th April 1845. Kate Carol was a pseudonym used by Frances Sargent Osgood (see second note to p. 120).

p. 135, *To —*: Written in 1845 and first published in the *Broadway Journal* of 24th May 1845. Violet Vane was another pseudonym used by Frances Sargent Osgood.

p. 135, *The Divine Right of Kings*: Written in 1845 and first published in the *Graham Magazine* for October 1845. "Ellen" appears to have been another pseudonym used by Frances Sargent Osgood.

p. 136, *Stanzas*: Written in 1845 and first published in the *Graham Magazine* for December 1845. These lines are also addressed to Frances Sargent Osgood.

p. 137, *'For Her These Lines Are Penned…'*: Written on 13th February 1846, and first published in the New York *Evening Mirror* of 21st February 1846. The poem contains, hidden among its lines, the name of Frances Sargent Osgood. To find it, one should read the first letter in the first line, the second in the second line, and so on. Osgood's middle name is misspelt "Sargeant" in the hidden acrostic. Poe later reworked the poem to correct the mistake. The later version's final eight lines read as follows:

> Enwritten upon the leaf where now are peering
> Eyes scintillating soul, there lie *perdus*
> Three eloquent words oft uttered in the hearing
> Of poets by poets – as the name is a poet's, too.
> Its letters, although naturally lying
> Like the knight Pinto – Mendez Ferdinando –
> Still form a synonym for truth. Cease trying!
> You will not read the riddle, though you do the best you *can* do.

The Portuguese explorer Ferdinand Mendez Pinto (Fernão Mendes Pinto, *c.*1509–83) was the author of a book of travels (*Pilgrimage*, 1614) which was widely doubted for its accuracy and earned him the punning nickname of "Ferdinand Mendez Minto" ("Ferdinand, are you lying?" – "I am").

p. 137, *the stars of Leda*: The stars Castor and Pollux of the constellation Gemini. According to Greek myth, Castor and Pollux were twin half-brothers mothered by Leda from different fathers: Castor from Tyndareus, and Pollux by Zeus (who raped Leda under the guise of a swan).

p. 137, *Gordian knot*: The legendary, intricate knot tied by King Gordius, which was eventually cut through by Alexander the Great.

p. 137, *perdu*: Concealed (from the French for "lost").

p. 137, *'Deep in Earth My Love Is Lying'*: Written soon after the funeral of Poe's wife Virginia on 2nd February 1847 and first published in the *Bulletin of the New York Public Library*, December 1914.

p. 137, *To Miss Louise Olivia Hunter*: The recipient of this Valentine poem, written on 14th February 1847 and first published in the *New York Times* of 14th February 1932, was a student at Rutgers Female Institute and the winner of a prize composition. Poe had served as chairman of the prize committee and read Louise Olivia Hunter's poem at the award ceremony.

p. 138, *To M.L. S—*: Written soon after the death of Poe's wife Virginia (see fifth note to p. 137) and before Valentine's day 1847. First published in the *Home Journal* of 13th March 1847. The poem is addressed to Marie Louise Shew, the daughter of a physician, who nursed Virginia Poe during her last illness and later the poet, who became desperately ill after his wife's death.

p. 139, *To —*: Probably written between December 1847 and January 1848, and first published in the *Columbian Lady's and Gentleman's Magazine* for March 1848. The addressee is again Marie Louise Shew (see previous note).

p. 139, *Maintained the "power of words"*: In "Marginalia", No. 149, published in *Graham's Magazine* for March 1846, Poe had written: "Now, so entire is my faith in the *power of words* that, at times, I have believed it possible to embody even the evanescence of fancies such as I have attempted to describe."

p. 139, *two foreign, soft disyllables*: Shew's French-sounding name: Marie Louise. The "Italian tones" of the following line are Poe's attempt at mystification. In a manuscript copy of the poem these are replaced by "Two gentle sounds".

p. 139, *"dew... on Hermon Hill"*: A quotation from the play *David and Bethsabe* (ll. 46–47) by George Peele (1556–96).

p. 139, *that are... diviner visions*: MS copy: "scarcely the shades of thought, / Bewildering fantasies, far richer visions".

p. 139, *Israfel... God's creatures*: See second note to p. 87.

p. 139, *Could hope... are broken*: MS copy: "Would hope to utter. Ah, Marie Louise! / In deep humility I own that now / All pride, all thought of power, all hope of fame, / All wish for heaven, is merged for evermore / Beneath the palpitating tide of passion / Heaped o'er my soul by thee. Its spells are broken."

p. 139, *though bidden... or think*: MS copy: "I *cannot* write, / I cannot speak, I cannot even think."

p. 139, *gate of dreams*: An allusion to Virgil's *Aeneid* VI, l. 893.

p. 139, *empurpled vapours*: MS copy: "the clouds of glory" – a quotation from 'Intimations of Immortality' (l. 64) by William Wordsworth.

p. 139, *Ulalume – A Ballad*: Written towards the end of 1847 and first published in the *American Review* for December 1847.

p. 140, *tarn*: See second note to p. 116.

p. 140, *titanic*: See third note to p. 115.

p. 140, *scoriac*: Lava-like.

p. 140, *night of all nights in the year*: Hallowe'en.

p. 140, *senescent*: Growing old.

p. 140, *Astarte's bediamonded crescent*: See first note to p. 120.

p. 140, *Dian*: Diana.

p. 140, *the stars of the Lion*: The constellation Leo.

p. 141, *Lethean*: See second note to p. 92.

p. 141, *Sibyllic*: Sibylline; mysterious.

p. 141, *legended*: Bearing an inscription.

p. 142, *woodland of Weir*: A MS copy of the poem, written by Poe in a letter to Susan Ingram on 10th September 1849, ends with the following additional stanza:

> Said we, then – the two, then: "All, can it
>   Have been that the woodlandish ghouls,
>   The pitiful, the merciful ghouls,
> To bar up our way and to ban it
>   From the secret that lies in these wolds –
>   From the thing that lies hidden in these wolds –
> Have drawn up the spectre of a planet
>   From the limbo of lunary souls –
> This sinfully scintillant planet
>   From the hell of the planetary souls?"

p. 142, *An Enigma*: Probably written in November 1847 and first published in the *Union Magazine of Literature and Art* for March 1848. The present text is from WOR. The poem is addressed to Poe's friend Sarah Anna Lewis, whose name can be worked out by taking the first letter of the first line, the second letter of the second line, and so on.

p. 142, *Solomon Don Dunce*: Probably a humorous reference to himself by the poet.

p. 142, *Petrarchan stuff*: The Italian poet Petrarch was famous for his love poetry, as well as being a master sonneteer.

p. 142, *tuckermanities*: Henry Theodore Tuckerman (1813–71) was an American poet and critic, and the writer of sonnets. The word was replaced by "Petrarchanities" in the first published version of the poem.

p. 143, *The Bells*: Initially written around May 1848; revised, expanded and completed on 6th February 1849. First published in *Sartain's Union Magazine* for November 1849.

p. 143, *Runic rhyme*: A verse with a mysterious or magical significance.

p. 146, *To Helen*: Written shortly before June 1848 and first published in the *Union Magazine* for November 1848. The present text is based on WOR, which includes two lines (ll. 26–27) omitted in the first published version. The addressee is the poet Sarah Helen Whitman (1803–78), a romantic interest of Poe at the time, who published some of her poetry under the name "Helen". Poe's poem is in response to a Valentine addressed to him by Whitman.

p. 147, *Dian*: See seventh note to p. 140.

p. 147, *A Dream within a Dream*: Written in 1849 and first published in the Boston *Flag of Our Union* of 31st March 1849. A reworking of part of the 1829 poem 'To —' (ll. 13–22 – see p. 65), which in turn is indebted to the 1827 poem 'Imitation' (see p. 26).

p. 148, *For Annie*: Written sometime before 23rd March 1849 and first published in the Boston *Flag of Our Union* of 28th April 1849. The present text is from WOR. The addressee of the poem is Nancy Locke ("Annie") Richmond (née Heywood, 1820–98), to whom Poe developed a platonic attachment at the time.

p. 151, *Eldorado*: Written sometime before April 1849 and first published in the Boston *Flag of Our Union* of 21st April 1849. The present text is from WOR.

p. 152, *To My Mother*: Written sometime before mid-May 1849 and first published in the Boston *Flag of Our Union* of 7th July 1849. The present text is from WOR. The addressee of this poem is Poe's mother-in-law, Maria Poe Clemm (1790–1871).

p. 152, *Annabel Lee*: Written in May 1849 and first published in the *New-York Tribune* of 9th October 1849 (morning edition). The present text is from WOR.

p. 153, *night-tide*: Night-time.

p. 157, *The Poetic Principle*: Written, for a series of lectures in Virginia, before 17th August 1849 and first published in WOR.

p. 160, *ceteris paribus*: See third note to p. 79.

p. 160, *The Columbiad*: An epic poem by Joel Barlow (1754–1812), first published in 1807.

p. 160, *Lamartine*: The French poet Alphonse de Lamartine (1790–1869), author, among other things, of the long poem *Jocelyn* (1836) and the vast metaphysical poem *La Chute d'un ange* ("The Fall of an Angel", partially published in 1838).

p. 160, *Pollok*: The Scottish poet Robert Pollok (1799–1827), author of the ten-book religious poem *The Course of Time* (1827).

p. 160, *De Béranger*: The French poet Pierre-Jean de Béranger (see first note to p. 114).

p. 161, *faint*: Become faint.

p. 161, *champak*: "The Indian tree *Michelia Champaca*, a species of magnolia bearing orange-coloured highly fragrant flowers" (*OED*).

p. 161, *I arise... break at last*: 'Lines to an Indian Air' (1819) by Percy Bysshe Shelley (1792–1822), also known as 'The Indian Serenade'. The text of the poem is taken from its first publication in Leigh Hunt's *The Liberal* (1822).

p. 161, *Willis*: The American poet and editor Nathaniel Parker Willis (1806–67).

p. 162, *twilight-tide*: Twilight time.

p. 164, *the desire of the moth for the star*: A quotation from 'To —' ("One word is too often profaned", l. 13) by Percy Bysshe Shelley.

p. 164, *Abate Gravina... through excess of pleasure*: A reference to the Italian jurist and man of letters Gian Vincenzo Gravina (1664–1718), who in his *Della ragion poetica* ("On the Foundations of Poetry", 1708) wrote: "Any feeling of emotion, even a painful one, is always mingled with pleasure" (I, 11).

p. 165, *Thomas Moore*: See fifth note to p. 42.

p. 165, *Mr Longfellow's Waif*: *The Waif* (1845) was the title of a poetical anthology edited and with a proem by Henry Wadsworth Longfellow (1807–82).

p. 167, *the North American Review*: A literary magazine founded in Boston in 1815.

p. 167, *a Cockney exquisite*: A London dandy.

p. 167, *Bryant*: The American poet William Cullen Bryant (1794–1878).

p. 167, *only a portion of it*: From l. 19 to the end.

p. 167, *oriole*: A melodious songbird.

p. 169, *Edward Coote Pinkney*: The American poet Edward Coote Pinkney (1802–28).

p. 170, *It was the misfortune... too far south*: Pinkney was in fact born in London. He returned with his family to Baltimore, Maryland, when he was eight years old.

p. 170, *Boccalini... for his reward*: The story of the critic and Apollo is in Traiano Boccalini's (1556–1613) *Ragguagli di Parnaso* ("News from Parnassus", 1612–15), Vol. I, 100, which Poe derived from *The Club* (chapter entitled 'Critic'), a 1713 work by the English inventor and writer James Puckle (1667–1724). The name of the Greek grammarian and Cynic philosopher Zoilus (*c*.400–320 BC) has become synonymous with that of a bitter and carping critic.

p. 170, *Melodies*: *Irish Melodies* (1808–34).

p. 171, *"I would I were by that dim lake"*: The correct first line of Moore's poem is "I wish I was by that dim lake".

p. 171, *Thomas Hood*: The English poet Thomas Hood (1799–1845).

p. 173, *cerements*: Wax wrappings for the dead.

p. 177, *Though the day... spirit of thee*: 'Stanzas to Augusta' (1816).

p. 177, *Alfred Tennyson*: The English poet Alfred, Lord Tennyson (1809–92).

p. 178, *Tears, idle tears... that are no more*: *The Princess* (1847) IV, ll. 21–40.

p. 178, *the Uranian... the Dionaean Venus*: According to Plato (*Symposium*, 180), there were two Aphrodites (Venuses): one had no mother (Aphrodite Urania, "Heavenly", representing spiritual love); the other (Aphrodite Pandemos, "Common", representing lust and sexual love) was the daughter of Zeus and Dione.

p. 178, *harp of Aeolus*: Aeolian harp.

p. 179, *Motherwell*: The Scottish poet William Motherwell (1797–1835).

p. 179, *Heart-whole*: Unafraid, undismayed.

p. 181, *The Philosophy of Composition*: First published in *Graham's Magazine* for April 1846.

p. 183, *an examination... Barnaby Rudge*: While *Barnaby Rudge* was still being serialized, Poe wrote an article in the Philadelphia *Saturday Evening Post* (1st May 1841) in which he correctly identified the murderer in Dickens's mystery novel.

p. 183, *Godwin wrote his Caleb Williams backwards*: In his preface to the 1832 edition of his novel *Caleb Williams* (1794), William Godwin (1756–1836) wrote: "I formed a conception of a book of fictitious adventure, that should in some way be distinguished by a very powerful interest. Pursuing this idea, I invented first the third volume of my tale, then the second, and last of all the first."

p. 184, *histrio*: A derogatory term for an actor.

p. 185, *ceteris paribus*: See third note to p. 79.

p. 185, *Robinson Crusoe*: A novel (1719) by Daniel Defoe (1660–1731).

p. 189, *acatalectic... catalectic*: As Poe explains in 'The Rationale of Verse' (see below, p. 198): "When a syllable is wanting, the verse is said to be catalectic; when the measure is exact, the line is acatalectic."

p. 192, *the so-called poetry of the so-called Transcendentalists*: Transcendentalism was a philosophical movement that developed in New England in the late 1820s and 1830s, advocating self-reliance and the use of insight over logic. Its main exponents were Henry David Thoreau (1817–62) and Ralph Waldo Emerson (1803–82), who both wrote poetry.

p. 195, *The Rationale of Verse*: Some few passages of this article appeared, about four years ago, in *The Pioneer*, a monthly magazine published by J.R. Lowell and R. Carter. Although an excellent work, it had a *very* limited circulation [POE'S NOTE]. Part of this essay was published as 'Notes on English Verse' in *The Pioneer* (March 1843). It was published in its final form, under the present title, in the *Southern Literary Messenger* (October and November 1848). James Russell Lowell (1819–91) was an American poet and editor. Robert Carter (1819–79) was an American historian and editor.

p. 197, *vexata quæstio*: "Thorny question" (Latin).

p. 197, *Bacon's "Idol of the Theatre"*: See Francis Bacon's *Novum Organum* (1620) X, 44: "There are idols which have crept into men's minds from the various dogmas of peculiar systems of philosophy, and also from the perverted rules of demonstration – and these we denominate idols of the theatre: for we regard all the systems of philosophy hitherto received or imagined as so many plays brought out and performed, creating fictitious and theatrical worlds."

p. 198, *the English Grammar of Goold Brown*: *The Institutes of English Grammar* (1823), by the American grammarian Goold Brown (1791–1857).

p. 199, *Bacon... and many others*: Not all the authors mentioned by Poe can be identified with certainty. The following identifications have been proposed: Caleb Bacon, Tobias Ham Miller (*c*.1802–70), Allen Fisk, Jeremiah Greenleaf (1791–1864), Charles M. Ingersoll, Samuel Kirkham (spelt Kirkland in Poe's essay), Joab Goldsmith Cooper (1777–1832), Abel Flint, Hugh A. Pue and John Comley.

p. 199, *Murray*: The American lawyer and grammarian Lindley Murray (1745–1826).

p. 199, *Lily*: The English grammarian William Lily (1468–1522).

p. 199, *quam solam... præcipit*: "Which alone His Royal Majesty commands to be taught in all schools" (Latin) – words that appeared on the title page of *Lily's Grammar*, a Latin grammar that Henry VIII ordered to be used in all English grammar schools.

p. 199, *Leonicenus*: The Italian grammarian Ognibene Bonisoli da Lonigo (Omnibonus Leonicenus, 1412–74), author of *De arte metrica* ("On Versification") and the grammar book *De octo partibus orationis* ("On the Eight Parts of Rhetoric").

p. 199, *Pindaric odes*: A reference to the odes of the Greek lyric poet Pindar (*c*.518–*c*.438 BC).

p. 200, *Silius Italicus*: The Roman senator and poet Silius Italicus (*c*.26–*c*.101 AD), author of a long epic poem about the Second Punic War (218–201 BC), *Punica*, the source of Poe's following quotation (II, ll. 342–46), which translates:

You are wrong if you think that while feasting he is not armed.
He is armed with immortal glory won
By endless war and slaughter. If you face him,
Cannae, Trebia, the dead of Lake Trasimene
And the mighty shade of Paulus will rise up before your eyes.

p. 201, *a little ballad… beautiful one*: The ballad has not been traced.

p. 201, *Arthur C. Coxe*: The American prelate Arthur Cleveland Coxe (1818–96). The following quotation is from his poem 'March', ll. 1–4.

p. 202, *les moutons de Panurge*: "Panurge's sheep" (French). The reference is to Rabelais's *Gargantua and Pantagruel* IV, 4, where Panurge throws a ram into the sea, and all the other sheep in his ship leap into the waters, one after another.

p. 202, *Leibnitz's principle of "a sufficient reason"*: The principle of sufficient reason, which states that everything must have a cause or a reason, is at the heart of the philosophy of Gottfried Wilhelm Leibniz (1646–1716).

p. 202, *Horatian rhythms*: A reference to the poetry of the Roman poet Horace (65–8 BC).

p. 202, *supererogations*: Superfluities.

p. 202, *Ex uno disce omnia*: "From one person learn everything" (Latin). The common Latin phrase is "*Ex uno disce omnes*": "From one person learn all persons."

p. 202, *the city of Penn*: Philadelphia, which was founded in 1682 by the English Quaker William Penn (1644–1718).

p. 204, *Leigh Hunt… "The Principle of Variety in Uniformity"*: The English poet Leigh Hunt (1784–1859) uses this phrase (the italics are Poe's) in 'An Answer to the Question "What Is Poetry?"', the introductory essay to his poetry anthology *Imagination and Fancy* (1844), in which he argues that in great poetry there is both variety and oneness: "Everything is diversified according to the demand of the moment, of the sounds, the sights, the emotions; […] and yet […] *the whole is one and of the same character*."

p. 204, *ceteris paribus*: See third note to p. 79.

p. 205, *Here then is the line of verse proper*: Verse, from the Latin *vertere*, to turn, is so called on account of the turning or recommencement of the series of feet. Thus a verse, strictly speaking, is a line. In this sense, however, I have preferred using the latter word alone, employing the former in the general acceptation given it in the heading of this paper [POE'S NOTE].

p. 206, *Aristophanes*: The Greek comediographer Aristophanes (*c.*448–*c.*385 BC), whose works include *The Clouds* and *The Birds*.

p. 206, *Parturient montes, nascetur ridiculus mus*: A quotation from Horace's *Ars Poetica*, l. 139: "The mountains are in labour; a ridiculous mouse will be born."

p. 206, *Litoreis ingens inventa sub ilicibus sus*: A quotation from *Aeneid* III, l. 390: "A large sow will be found lying under the oaks by the shore."

p. 207, *ultimatum*: Extreme limit.

p. 207, *stanza*: A stanza is often vulgarly, and with gross impropriety, called a *verse* [POE'S NOTE].

p. 210, *Pope*: Alexander Pope (1688–1746). The quotation that follows is from *The Dunciad* (1729 Edn) I, ll. 19–22.

p. 211, *a Procrustean adjustment*: A shortening. In Greek mythology, Procrustes was a smith who cut off (or stretched) the legs of people in order to make them fit the dimensions of a particular iron bed.

p. 212, *Messrs Hoffman and Benjamin*: Charles Fenno Hoffman (1806–84) and Park Benjamin (1809–64).

p. 212, *a review of Mr Willis's poems*: The review, which appeared in the *American Monthly Magazine* of September 1836, was of Willis's *Melanie and Other Poems* (1835). For Nathaniel Parker Willis, see fourth note to p. 161.

p. 212, *That binds... delicate love*: From Willis's poem 'Hagar in the Wilderness' (l. 47). Here and in the following two lines the italics are Poe's.

p. 212, *In the gay... in the storm*: From 'Extract from a Poem Delivered at the Departure of the Senior Class of Yale College In 1826' (l. 72), not included in *Melanie and Other Poems*.

p. 212, *With its invisible fingers, my loose hair*: From 'Dawn' (l. 8).

p. 212, *Mr Horne... Orion*: The English poet Richard Henry ("Hengist") Horne (1802–84), author of the mythological poem *Orion* (1843).

p. 212, *Chaucer Modernized*: Horne was the editor of *The Poems of Geoffrey Chaucer, Modernized* (1841), containing updated versions of Chaucer by, among others, William Wordsworth, Leigh Hunt, Elizabeth Barrett Barrett (see note to p. 101) and Horne himself.

p. 213, *Al Aaraaf*: See pp. 33–52.

p. 213, *Dim was... starry sea*: Lines 411–14 (see p. 51). Poe changes the third line from "When first Al Aaraaf knew her course to be".

p. 213, *bouleversement*: "Subversion" (French).

p. 214, *Mr Christopher Pearse Cranch... beautiful poem*: The Transcendental poet Christopher Pearse Cranch (1813–92). In his essay, Poe misspells, perhaps intentionally (see the short nursery rhyme "Pease porridge pot" a few paragraphs below), the poet's middle name "Pease". The following quotation is from his poem 'My Thoughts'.

p. 214, *Coleridge... "scanning by accents"*: In his preface to *Christabel* (1816), Coleridge says: "I have only to add that the metre of the *Christabel* is not, properly speaking, irregular, though it may seem so from its being founded on a new principle: namely, that of counting in each line the accents, not the syllables."

p. 215, *reductio ad absurdum*: "Reduction to absurdity" (Latin), the carrying through of a premise to its logical extreme.

p. 215, *Pease porridge... nine days old*: The opening lines of 'Pease Porridge Hot', a well-known nursery rhyme and singing game.

p. 216, *αστρολογος... pæon primus*: In fact the word *αστρολογος* ("astrologos", that is, "astrologer") was used in some Greek prosody books as an example to illustrate the *παιών* (*pæon primus* in Latin), a rhythmic unit scanned ⁻ˇˇˇ.

p. 217, *a little poem... by Mrs Welby*: The American poet Amelia Welby (1819–52). The following line is adapted or misquoted from her poem 'The Little Stepson' (see ll. 1 and 24).

p. 217, *Pale... Gray*: Probably adapted from the last stanza of 'Everard Grey' by Henry Beck Hirst (1813–74):

> Time... it has passed, and the lady is pale –
> Pale as the lily that lolls on the gale;
> Weary and worn she hath waited for years,
> Keeping her grief ever green with her tears –
> Years will she tarry, for cold is the clay
> Fettering the form of her Everard Grey.

p. 218, *a pretty specimen of verse... Miss Mary A.S. Aldrich*: The opening lines of 'The Water Lily', ascribed to a Miss Mary A.S. Aldrich in *Godey's Lady's Book* of December 1846 (p. 271).

p. 218, *Byron's Bride of Abydos*: *The Bride of Abydos, A Turkish Tale* (1813), a narrative poem by Lord Byron. The following quotation is from 1, ll. 1–10, 14–19. In the original, line 16 reads: "'Tis the clime of the East – 'tis the land of the Sun", and "which" replaces "that" twice in the last line.

p. 218, *the gardens of Gul*: See fifth note to p. 50.

p. 221, *rhythm... number*: Poe's etymology is incorrect: the word "rhythm" derives from the Greek *ῥυθμός*, "regular movement".

p. 225, *Mæcenas… ad deos*: Horace, *Odes* I, 1, ll. 1–6:

> O Maecenas, born of kingly ancestors,
> The shield and the sweet ornament of my life!
> There are those who like to collect
> The dust of Olympia with their chariot,
> And who exalt the goal shunned by hot wheels
> And the palm of glory to the gods that rule mankind.

p. 226, *Alfred B. Street*: The American poet Alfred Billings Street (1811–81). The following quotation is from his poem 'The Lost Hunter' (ll. 1–2).

p. 227, *mesmeric balloons*: That is, balloons moved by mesmeric (magnetic) power.

p. 227, *hudsonizing*: That is, "Americanizing" – but the word is also a punning allusion to the American scholar Henry Norman Hudson (1814–86), whose work Poe criticized.

p. 228, *'Thanatopsis'… 'Spanish Student'*: Poems by William Cullen Bryant and Henry Wadsworth Longfellow, respectively.

p. 229, *a specimen… Horatian measure*: The quoted excerpt is from *Odes* I, 22, ll. 1–4:

> The man who is righteous and pure from all guilt
> Does not need, O Fuscus, Mauretanian javelins,
> Or a bow or a quiver full
>   Of poisoned arrows.

p. 230, *the French heroic… spondaic*: The alexandrine, which in fact is not spondaic (or iambic), as French verse is not based on feet or stress, but on syllables.

p. 231, *Sir Philip Sidney*: The English courtier, soldier and poet Sir Philip Sidney (1554–86).

p. 231, *such hexameters as Professor Longfellow*: Longfellow had used an English version of the hexameter in *The Children of the Lord's Supper*, a translation of a poem (*Nattvardsbarnen*) by the Swedish prelate and professor of Greek Esaias Tegnér (1782–1846) included in his 1842 collection *Ballads and Other Poems*. In the preface to the book, Longfellow wrote: "I have preserved even the measure – that inexorable hexameter in which, it must be confessed, the motions of the English Muse are not unlike those of a prisoner dancing to the music of his chains. And perhaps, as Dr Johnson said of the dancing dog, 'the wonder is not that she should do it so well, but that she should do it at all'."

p. 231, *Professor Felton*: The American educator Cornelius Conway Felton (1807–62), who reviewed Longfellow's *Ballads and Other Poems* in the *North American Review* (No. 116, July 1842), discussing at length the use of the hexameter in ancient and modern poetry. Felton was professor of Greek literature at Harvard University at the time.

p. 231, *Frogpondian*: Bostonian. The allusion is to the Frog Pond in the Boston Common. Boston scholars are compared to frogs living in a stagnating pond and imitating their peers' and predecessors' sounds.

p. 232, *a specimen of the Longfellow hexameter*: From *The Children of the Lord's Supper*, ll. 20–24.

Extra Material

on

Edgar Allan Poe's

*The Raven
and Other Poems*

Edgar Allan Poe's Life

Edgar Allan Poe was born in a lodging house in Boston, Massachusetts, on 19th January 1809. His mother, Eliza (née Arnold, 1787–1811), an actress and a celebrated beauty, had arrived in the United States from England in 1796, going on to play more than two hundred parts in the theatre over the course of her brief career. On 14th March 1806 she had married an aspiring actor, David Poe, Jr (1784–c.1811), in Richmond, Virginia – her first husband, Charles Hopkins, another thespian, having died the previous year. Her new husband failed to match Eliza's success on the stage, however, and was a heavy drinker. Their first child, Henry, was born in January 1807. Due to his parents' itinerant lifestyle, at the age of two the young boy was sent to be cared for by his paternal grandparents, Elizabeth (1756–1835) and "General" David Poe (1743–1816), in Baltimore, Maryland. (The senior David Poe was not in fact a general, although he had served as deputy quartermaster general for the city of Baltimore during the War of American Independence.) After his own birth, Edgar too was cared for by his paternal grandparents for several months, returning to his parents in Richmond in the summer of 1809. A third child, Rosalie, was born in December 1810. By this time, both of Edgar's parents were suffering from tuberculosis, and the family's financial situation was dire.

In spring 1811 David Poe abandoned his family. The reason for his disappearance is unclear, although there was speculation that Rosalie was not his. Then, in November, Eliza died. Later in his life, Poe reported in a letter that his father passed away only a few weeks after his mother

Early Life and Family

– whether this is true or not, the three children were now in effect orphans. "I have many occasional dealings with adversity," he wrote, "but the want of parental affection has been the heaviest of my trials."

After their mother's death, the children were separated: Rosalie was thereafter raised by a family named the Mackenzies, while Edgar was taken in by the twenty-five-year-old Frances ("Fanny") Allan (1784–1829), who had visited the dying Eliza in response to a plea for help that had appeared in the *Richmond Enquirer* during her final illness, and had taken an interest in the young boy. She was the wife of John Allan (1779–1834), a Scottish-born merchant, who resided above the premises of Ellis & Allan on the corner of Thirteenth Street and Main Street in Richmond. The Allans proved to be kindly foster parents – Fanny, in particular, pampered her new charge. The change in Edgar's circumstances was reflected in the name he was christened with on 7th January 1812: Edgar Allan Poe.

London   In June 1815, in a move made necessary by a decline in John Allan's fortunes, the family left for Liverpool aboard the *Lothair*, arriving in England on 29th July. After a tour of Scotland, they reached London in October, taking lodgings on Southampton Row. In April 1816, Edgar began attending a boarding school in Sloane Street, where he proved an able learner: "Edgar is a fine boy and reads Latin pretty sharply," wrote John Allan in June 1818. In July of the same year, he was moved to the Manor House School in Stoke Newington, then a rural village north-east of the capital, whose headmaster, the Reverend John Bransby, later described Edgar as "quick and clever", claiming that he "would have been a very good boy if he had not been spoilt by his parents" – evidence of the doting affection that Fanny Allan had for her foster son. Edgar's time at the Manor House School – which he subsequently described as "sad, lonely and unhappy" – later inspired the short story 'William Wilson' (1839).

Return to   Due to a drop in tobacco prices in London, the Allans
Richmond   returned to Richmond in the summer of 1820, lodging initially with John Allan's business partner, Charles Ellis,

who was perhaps instrumental in persuading him to remain in his post and not to abandon trade in favour of a career in farming, as he had planned to do. Edgar was sent to a local school, Richmond Academy, where, as well as acquitting himself capably in both his academic work and as a sportsman, he proved himself, in the words of one teacher, to be a "born poet", whose verses were written "*con amore* and not as mere tasks". According to one contemporary, however, he was "self-willed, capricious, inclined to be imperious, and though of generous impulses, not steadily kind, or even amiable"; another remarked that he was "retiring in disposition and singularly unsociable in manner". During this period Edgar began to form his first romantic attachments: first to the mother of a school friend, the thirty-year-old Jane Stanard, who inspired the poem 'To Helen' ("Helen, thy beauty is to me"), which appeared in the 1831 collection *Poems*, and whose death in spring 1824 affected him profoundly, and then to the fifteen-year-old Elmira Royster, who lived opposite his school. Meanwhile, Edgar had to contend with new-found domestic difficulties, as Fanny's health deteriorated and relations with his foster father began to show signs of strain. John Allan complained that Edgar "possesses not a spark of affection for us, not a particle of gratitude for all my care and kindness towards him", while Edgar later described his surrogate parent as "a man of gross and brutal temperament".

In February 1826, Edgar began attending the schools of Ancient Languages and Modern Languages at the newly founded University of Virginia in Charlottesville. Though he excelled in his scholarly endeavours, he once again showed himself to be somewhat aloof, forming no close friendships with his fellow students, one of whom remembered him as having "a sad, melancholy face always – and even a smile... seemed to be forced". The same student also referred to Edgar's tendency to "put himself under the influence" of alcohol as a means of medicating the "nervous excitability" that plagued him, while another described his "passion" for gambling.

University; First Book of Poems

Increasingly resentful of his errant charge, who had by now amassed debts of $2,000, at the end of 1826 John Allan announced that he would no longer subsidize Edgar's university career, as a consequence of which relations between foster father and son reached a new low. In the following March, the disgruntled and penniless young man – his mood worsened by the revelation that Elmira Royster was engaged to be married to another man – left the home of the Allans and travelled to Boston. It was here that, with the help of a young printer, Calvin Frederick Stephen Thomas, he published fifty copies of his first book of verse, *Tamerlane and Other Poems*.

The Army Failing to secure any stable employment in Boston, in May 1826 Poe elected to enlist in the US Army, which he did under the pseudonym "Edgar A. Perry". Over the next two years he served first in an artillery battery off Boston Harbor, then at Fort Moultrie on Sullivan's island off the coast of South Carolina, and finally at Fortress Monroe on the Virginia Peninsula, where, in early 1829, he was made regimental sergeant major, the highest non-commissioned rank. By this time tiring of life as a common soldier, however, he sought his foster father's consent in securing a discharge, in order that he might then apply to West Point, the officers' academy on the west bank of the Hudson River in New York State. His request coincided with the final illness of Fanny Allan, however – Poe learnt of her death on 1st March and returned to Richmond the following day, only to find that the funeral had already taken place. He later wrote to Allan: "*Your* love I never valued – but she I believed loved me as her own child." His resolve perhaps weakened by his loss, John Allan acceded to Poe's entreaty, and in April the young man left the army, submitting his application to West Point soon afterwards.

Meeting with Virginia Clemm; Second Book of Poems In May 1829 Poe travelled to Baltimore to visit his elder brother, Henry, in order to become more closely acquainted with his paternal grandfather's family. "General" Poe was now dead; his widow, along with Henry, Poe's aunt Maria Clemm (1790–1871) and her six-year-old daughter

Virginia (1822–47), were living in poverty. Henry, according to Poe's account a drunkard, was dying of consumption; both his grandmother and Maria Clemm were also in poor health. Nevertheless, Poe formed a profound attachment to both Maria and Virginia. From Baltimore Poe travelled by steamer to Philadelphia, where he presented the manuscript of a new collection of poems to Isaac Lea of the publishing house Carey, Lea & Carey, only to receive a standard rejection letter a few weeks later. He therefore offered it instead to the Baltimore firm of Hatch & Dunning, who published *Al Aaraaf, Tamerlane and Minor Poems*, by "Edgar A. Poe", in December 1829.

The parlous state of Poe's finances compelled him to *West Point* return to Richmond in early 1830. Then, in May, he left for West Point, where he lodged with three fellow cadets at 28 South Barracks. A contemporary remembered him as "shy, proud, sensitive and unsociable… He spent more time in reading than in study." Another, Cadet Gibson, stated: "Very early in his brief career at the Point he established a high reputation for genius, and poems and squibs of local interest were daily issued from Number 28." Characteristically, however, Poe quickly grew weary of life as an officer cadet – but his efforts to resign were thwarted by John Allan, whose parental permission was required if his wayward foster son was to receive an honourable discharge. Newly remarried, and eager to free himself of the burden that Edgar had become, Allan went so far as to attempt to sever relations with him – something that, in a letter to his surrogate parent, Poe responded to with predictable self-pity: "It was my crime to have no one on earth who cared for me or loved me." In the absence of Allan's blessing, therefore, from early 1831 Poe set about deliberately attempting to provoke his superiors into expelling him from the academy. His persistent heavy drinking, combined with his failure to attend to his duties, led to a court martial at the end of January, as a result of which he was charged with "gross neglect of duty" and "disobedience of orders", and dismissed.

Third Book of Poems; Early Fiction

On 19th February he left for New York, where – miserable, impecunious and plagued by ill health – he stayed for three months. It was here, in April, that his third book of poetry, entitled simply *Poems* – financed in part by some of his West Point colleagues, each of whom contributed seventy-five cents towards the cost – was published, by the printer Elam Bliss. In May, Poe returned to Baltimore, where his brother Henry died in August. During this time he became increasingly dependent on his aunt, Maria Clemm, nicknamed "Muddy", who shouldered the burden of keeping the household together (she was later described as the "ever-vigilant guardian of the home" by a neighbour), and deepened his attachment to the eight-year-old Virginia, whom he called "Sis" or "Sissie". Unable to find work, and receiving no answer to the begging letters he sent to his erstwhile guardian, John Allan, he now turned his hand to fiction as a means of earning a living – Poe always believed that his true vocation was as a poet – with the result that 'Metzengerstein', a Gothic tale "in imitation of the German" appeared in Philadelphia's *Saturday Courier* in January 1832. Despite this, and the four further sensational or supernatural tales that appeared in the same publication over the course of the year, plus an unknown quantity of journalistic hack work, Poe was forced to turn to his foster father for help one final time, in April 1833. "For God's sake pity me," he wrote, "and save me from destruction." Allan did not reply, and communication between the two ceased for ever.

In autumn 1833 Poe won a competition in the weekly periodical the *Baltimore Saturday Visiter* for his story 'MS Found in a Bottle', a nautical tale with a supernatural flavour, and was awarded fifty dollars. It was published in the magazine in October. As a result, he made the acquaintance of John P. Kennedy, one of the *Visiter*'s editorial committee, who became his de facto patron. In the month in which this story was printed, it was announced in the *Visiter* that a collection entitled *Tales of the Folio Club*, containing seventeen pieces by Poe – satires on various literary styles – was to be published by subscription. The proposed volume never in fact materialized, however, due to the unwillingness of American publishers to take on work by one of their compatriots – the lack of copyright legislation ensuring that it was more profitable to produce pirated editions of works by British authors. Nevertheless, the individual tales – including 'The Duc de L'Omelette', 'Lionizing' and 'King Pest' – appeared in the *Philadelphia Saturday Courier* and the *Southern Literary Messenger* between 1832 and 1836.

In March 1834 John Allan died, leaving nothing to Poe in his will, provoking a typically resentful and self-indulgent response from his former charge in which he bemoaned his poverty and friendlessness. Penniless as ever, Poe turned for help to Kennedy, who, in the spring of 1835, recommended him to Thomas Willis White, the editor of the new monthly *Southern Literary Messenger*, based in Richmond, who agreed to publish a characteristically macabre new story, 'Berenice'. In correspondence Poe told White that he believed that the best stories contained "the ludicrous heightened into the grotesque, the fearful coloured into the horrible, the witty exaggerated into the burlesque, the singular wrought out into the strange and mystical", as well as offering him a great deal of unsolicited editorial advice. As a consequence, in June White offered Poe a job as a staff writer and critic on the magazine – his first ever secure employment – at sixty dollars per month. After some prevarication, Poe accepted and returned to Richmond. However, White was soon complaining about his "rather dissipated" and unreliable new employee. Meanwhile, Poe's stories continued to appear – including 'Morella' (April 1835) and 'Hans Phaall – A Tale' (June 1835).

Poe abandoned his new post in September on learning to his horror that his beloved Virginia, now thirteen, was to be taken in by his cousin, Neilson Poe. Fearful of losing his "darling little wifey" – who was half his age – he returned to Baltimore, where it is conjectured that he married her in secret. Either way, Virginia's proposed

Death of John Allan; the Southern Literary Messenger

relocation to the home of her relative did not take place. He then requested of White that he be allowed to return to his job on the *Messenger*. White agreed so long as Poe promised to abstain from alcohol. "No man is safe who drinks before breakfast," he warned him.

Marriage to Virginia

Poe returned to Richmond in October, bringing with him Maria and Virginia, the trio presenting themselves as a mother and daughter accompanied by their unmarried cousin. No longer tormented by the prospect of losing Virginia, Poe temporarily gave up drinking, and was made editor of the *Messenger* by White. In the spring of 1836, in a service performed by the Presbyterian minister Amasa Converse, Poe married Virginia formally, lying about her age – one witness stated on oath that she was twenty-one. By September, Poe had fallen back into the habit of immoderate drinking, and was given notice by White, but was able to persuade the editor to reconsider. White imposed certain conditions, but Poe proved unable to keep them, and so was finally dismissed in January 1837 – the same month in which the first instalment of a novel, *The Narrative of Arthur Gordon Pym of Nantucket*, appeared in the *Messenger*. "I am as sick of his writings as I am of him," White wrote.

Philadelphia; the Burton's Gentleman's Magazine

At the end of February 1837, Poe and his family left for New York, where they stayed for an unhappy year, during which Poe succeeded in publishing only two stories. Furthermore, serialization of *Arthur Gordon Pym* in the *Messenger* ceased after only two instalments. At the beginning of 1838, therefore, Poe, accompanied as ever by his wife and Maria, relocated to Philadelphia, at the time the largest city in the United States as well as the hub of the country's publishing industry. The family were now desperately poor. That summer, *Arthur Gordon Pym* was published in volume form by Harper & Brothers, but received mixed reviews and made no money – Poe himself dismissed it as "a very silly book". 'Ligeia', a story inspired by a dream, was published in September in the *American Museum of Literature and the Arts* – Poe later called it "my *best* tale".

Still in straitened circumstances, in the spring of 1839 Poe offered his services as assistant to William E. Burton, a comic actor from England who was editor of the eponymously named and Philadelphia-based *Burton's Gentleman's Magazine*. Burton accepted, proposing to pay him ten dollars a day for two hours' work. He was formally employed in June, and quickly gained a reputation for the vicious, scathing reviews he wrote of the work of other writers. "I intend to put up with nothing that I can *put down*," he wrote to a correspondent in August. Many of his finest stories appeared in the *Burton's Gentleman's Magazine* in this period, including 'The Fall of the House of Usher' (September 1839) and 'William Wilson' (October 1839). At the end of the year, twenty-five of Poe's tales, including these two, were collected as *Tales of the Grotesque and Arabesque*, published in two volumes by Lea & Blanchard (the successor firm of Carey, Lea & Carey, who had previously rejected Poe's second book of poetry). The two volumes did not sell well, however, and Poe received no payment.

The perennial problem of Poe's heavy drinking continued to interfere with his working life, however, resulting in the breakdown in his relationship with Burton and his dismissal in May 1840. In response Poe hatched a plan to establish his own journal, the *Penn Magazine*, which he said would inhabit "the loftiest regions of literature", and thus began to contact editors, publishers and journalists in order to build up a subscription list. The first edition was planned for early 1841; however, in late 1840 Poe was bedridden for a month with what he described as a "severe illness", and so publication was pushed back to March – but then a financial crisis in February forced him to abandon the project altogether.

Plans for the Penn Magazine

Poe once again offered his services to the *Burton's Gentleman's Magazine*, now under the ownership of George Rex Graham, a Philadelphia lawyer with little journalistic experience, and retitled *Graham's Lady's and Gentleman's Magazine*. He consequently became editor of the book reviews in spring 1841 at a salary of eight hundred dollars per year. Over the next two years nine more of his stories appeared in the magazine, including the pioneering detective tale 'The Murders in the Rue Morgue' (April 1841) and 'A Descent into the Maelstrom' (May 1841). Despite now enjoying the highest income he had ever received, he considered the appointment a temporary one, and after a few months tried – with the help of the writer Frederick W. Thomas, one of his few close friends – to secure a position with the Department of the Treasury in Washington DC. This plan foundered, however, and in autumn 1841 he agreed to stay in his role with *Graham's* – whose circulation had increased from five to twenty-five thousand, due in no small part to the presence in its pages of Poe's fiction and journalism – for a further year. At this time he proposed to Lea & Blanchard another collection of his short fiction, which would comprise the contents of *Tales of the Grotesque and Arabesque* plus eight newer stories, and was to be called *Phantasy Pieces*. Lea & Blanchard, however, declined, on the basis that they were still burdened with unsold copies of the former work.

Resignation from Graham's Magazine

In January 1842 Virginia began to cough up blood, a sign of the tuberculosis that would eventually claim her life. "Mrs Poe is again dangerously ill with haemorrhage from the lungs. It is folly to hope," Poe despaired. He later wrote that "at each accession of the disorder I loved her more dearly and clung to her life with more desperate pertinacity". In his misery he turned to drink once more, and, in the spring, resigned from *Graham's*, claiming to be disgusted with the "namby-pamby character" of the magazine – although in reality he was forced to leave because of the irregularity of his own behaviour. In the summer he went to New York, ostensibly to look for journalistic work. The expedition, however, degenerated into a drinking "spree" (his own term for such binges), during which he went missing. In the words of Mary Devereaux, an old flame he had decided in his inebriation to visit, Poe was eventually found "in the woods on the outskirts of Jersey City, wandering about like a crazy man". Despite his misfortunes, he produced some of his greatest stories during this year: 'The Masque of the Red Death' (published in May 1842), 'The Mystery of Marie Rogêt' (published in November 1842) and 'The Tell-Tale Heart' (published in January 1843).

In the next year, 1843, with his drinking now the gossip of Philadelphia and his family once again in dire financial straits, Poe sought to secure a clerkship at the Philadelphia Custom House, something that he hoped would give him the security he needed to launch his journal, now to be called *The Stylus* – which, he claimed, would "far surpass all American journals of its kind". The attempt to secure an administrative position came to nothing, although at this time Poe was fortunate enough to make the acquaintance of Thomas C. Clarke, editor of the Philadelphia *Saturday Museum*, who agreed to finance the proposed magazine. Poe travelled to Washington to look for subscribers – while there, he also entertained the fanciful notion of securing an audience with the US president, John Tyler, as part of his ongoing efforts to obtain an administrative position with the federal government. As before, however, in practice the trip was nothing more than another humiliating alcoholic "spree".

Back in Philadelphia, Poe began writing 'The Raven'. Meanwhile, his adventure yarn 'The Gold Bug' won a prize of one hundred dollars in the city's *Dollar Newspaper*, and was published in two instalments on 21st and 28th June. The story was described in the *Saturday Museum* as "the most remarkable piece of American fiction that has been published within the last fifteen years". Other major stories were written at this time but published later, including 'The Premature Burial' (published in July 1844) and 'The Purloined Letter' (published in December 1844). In November Poe began a series of lectures, the first of which was held at the Julianna Street Church in Philadelphia on the subject of "American poetry". He was typically acerbic in his pronouncements, singling out the poet Rufus Wilmot Griswold, his successor at *Graham's* and already a literary rival, whose anthology *Poets and*

Poetry of America (1842) was, he said, the best of those available, but still showed a "miserable want of judgement – the worst specimens being chosen instead of the best". This contributed to a literary feud that continued to rage even after Poe's death.

New York;
'The Raven'

In April 1844, Poe and Virginia moved again to New York, staying at a boarding house on Greenwich Street, where they were joined a short while later by Maria. Almost immediately on arrival, Poe sold a story to the *New York Sun* about a man, Monck Mason – the name of a real-life balloonist – who had apparently crossed the Atlantic in three days aboard a hot-air balloon. The story, a hoax, appeared on 13th April, but was retracted two days later. In June the family moved to a farmhouse five miles outside the city, where it was hoped that the country air might improve Virginia's health. With the family as indigent as ever, Maria Clemm took it upon herself to find work for Poe, travelling into the city and calling on Nathaniel P. Willis, editor of the new *Evening Mirror*. As a result, Poe became a "mechanical paragraphist" on the newspaper, a relatively lowly copy-writing position. In the winter, the family moved back to Greenwich Street in order that Poe might be closer to his place of work.

'The Raven' was published in the *Evening Mirror* on 29th January 1845, and quickly became a sensation. The *New York Express* claimed that it transcended "anything that has been done even by the best poets of the age". It earned Poe the acclaim he had craved all his life. He began to appear at New York literary salons, and for the time being succeeded in remaining sober. Poe himself became known as "the Raven" – not least because of his custom of dressing entirely in black. For its author, the poem was calculated to achieve commercial success: "'The Raven' has had a great 'run'," he wrote to Frederick W. Thomas, "but I wrote it for the express purpose of running." He also wrote an essay, 'The Philosophy of Composition', published in April 1846, in which he elucidated in great technical detail the poetic processes involved in bringing the poem into existence.

Buoyed by this success, Poe left his job on the *Evening Mirror* and joined the *Broadway Journal* as editor soon afterwards (February 1845). In its pages he repeatedly attacked the eminent American poet Henry Wadsworth Longfellow, accusing him, not for the first time, of plagiarism, calling him a "determined imitator and a dextrous adapter of the ideas of other people" (specifically Tennyson). Although Longfellow did not respond, and while such diatribes may have been merely a publicity stunt designed to draw attention to the *Broadway Journal*, Poe's repeated assaults on his literary contemporary came to be known as "the Longfellow War", one of the most notorious literary feuds in American history. Poe levelled the accusation of plagiarism at other poets during this period, including James Russell Lowell and Richard Henry Stoddard.

Soon, however, Poe – complaining of being "dreadfully unwell" – expressed a desire to give up his post on the *Broadway Journal*, where, once again, his drinking had made him unreliable. Although his partner, Charles Frederick Briggs – who had come to regard Poe as a liability, describing him as "a drunken sot" and the "most purely selfish of human beings" – was more than happy to see him go, Poe quickly changed his mind, desiring instead to be given "entire control" of the magazine in order to turn it into "the great literary journal of the future". Thus in October he bought Briggs out and became proprietor, with full editorial authority. Only six weeks later, however, he sold half his interest to a man named Thomas H. Lane, and, after another month, went on one of his debauched "sprees". Lane closed the magazine in January 1846. Appropriately enough, Poe's story 'The Imp of the Perverse' – about the impulse to perform self-destructive actions "merely because we feel we should not" – was published during this period (in the July 1845 issue of *Graham's*).

Meanwhile, in March 1845, Poe made the acquaintance of the poet Frances Sargent Osgood, whom he had praised in his lecture on American poetry, and with whom he

The Broadway Journal; the "Longfellow War"

Frances Sargent Osgood and Elizabeth F. Ellet

embarked on what seemed to be a romantic dalliance. Poe printed several of her poems in the *Broadway Journal*, responding with some of his own, including 'To F—s S. O—d' and 'To F—', both of which had originally been written for other women. 'For Her These Lines Are Penned…' – which appeared in the *Evening Mirror* on 21st February 1846 – even contained within it the name "Frances Sargent Osgood", obtained by taking the first letter of the first line, the second of the second line, and so on. The admiration was clearly mutual – one writer remembered how Osgood had been put under Poe's "wizard spell" – although it is unlikely that the relationship was sexual: indeed, it may even have been purely platonic, not least because it was conducted with the knowledge of Virginia, who seemed in fact to approve of the association on the basis that it kept her husband sober, as well as of Osgood's spouse, the painter Samuel Stillman Osgood.

Scandal ensued in early 1846, however, when Elizabeth F. Ellet, another poet and perhaps Osgood's rival for Poe's attentions, claimed that Virginia had shown her an indiscreet letter from Osgood to Poe, and advised Ellet to retrieve her correspondence from him. When two other literary women, Margaret Fuller and Anne Lynch, subsequently demanded that Poe return Osgood's letters, Poe retaliated by suggesting that Ellet "look after her *own* letters". Poe was then threatened by Ellet's brother, Colonel William Lummis, who did not believe the former's claim to have already returned his sister's letters. In response Poe attempted to borrow a pistol – to use in self-defence – from the writer Thomas Dunn English, but the conversation devolved into a fist fight when English stated that he did not believe that Poe had ever possessed any correspondence from Ellet. Poe subsequently persuaded his doctor to write an apologetic letter to Ellet in which he attributed his behaviour to temporary insanity. In July, under threat of legal action from Osgood's husband, Ellet sent a letter of apology to Osgood, in which she said that the note she had seen must have been a forgery created by Poe himself. The scandal abated, although the flirtation between Poe and Osgood – as well as between Poe and Ellet – was at an end.

1845 also saw the publication first of *Tales* (June) and then of *The Raven and Other Poems* (November), the first poetry collection published by Poe since 1831. Then, in the spring of 1846, Poe began to publish a series of critical articles under the title 'The Literati of New York City' for the magazine *Godey's Lady's Book*, in which he attacked many of the prominent literary figures of the day with typical brutality. Some of his targets were minded to reciprocate, including Thomas Dunn English, who responded with a piece in the *New York Mirror* in which he accused Poe of, among other things, forgery and plagiarism. In turn, Poe set about suing the newspaper for libel. At this time he and his family moved to a cottage in the village of Fordham, thirteen miles north of New York, where their poverty was acute enough to compel Maria to dig up and cook the turnips that were intended as fodder for the cattle. Meanwhile, Poe's claim of temporary insanity during the Ellet affair had become the subject of gossip, leading to much speculation in the press, with the Baltimore *Saturday Visiter* claiming that he was suffering from "mental derangement" and had been consigned to an asylum in Utica. Poe's physical well-being also became the focus of attention, with New York's *Morning Express* stating on 15th December that the writer and his wife were both "dangerously ill with the consumption" and so poor as to be "barely able to obtain the necessaries of life". Several papers – including the *Mirror*, the publication being sued by Poe – appealed for financial contributions on his family's behalf. Such publicity brought Poe's plight to the attention of a woman named Marie Louise Shew, who became Virginia's nurse during her final days.

Virginia Poe died on 30th January 1847. Several weeks later Poe wrote: "I was overwhelmed by a sorrow so poignant as to deprive me for several weeks of all power of thought or action." Shew, believing Poe to be suffering from madness produced by a lesion on the brain, nursed

Move to Fordham

Death of Virginia

him back to health. The day before Virginia's funeral, Poe's libel case against the *Mirror* was heard before the New York Superior Court. During the hearing English called Poe "a notorious liar" and "a common drunkard" – nevertheless, the court found in Poe's favour, and he was awarded $225.06 in damages and $101.42 in costs. Thereafter, with Shew's help, his health slowly recovered from the blow dealt by his wife's death, to the extent that by the summer he was able to visit Washington and Philadelphia in yet another attempt to launch *The Stylus*. As so often, however, he resorted to the bottle when separated from the restraining influences of home.

Eureka On 3rd February 1848, Poe gave a lecture on the subject of "The Cosmography of the Universe" at the Society Library on Leonard Street and Broadway, in which he expounded on his theories about the origins and nature of the cosmos to sixty somewhat bemused audience members (inclement weather having ensured only sparse attendance). The lecture put a strain on Poe's relationship with Shew, who, considering the ideas it described to be heretical, left him in the early summer. Poe subsequently adapted the lecture into *Eureka: A Prose Poem*, published in March 1848 by George P. Putnam. Around this time Poe also composed 'Ulalume' and 'The Bells', two of his best-known poems.

Annie Richmond and Sarah Helen Whitman Poe's behaviour became increasingly erratic in the period following Virginia's death, as demonstrated by his somewhat hysterical and simultaneous pursuit of two unobtainable women. In summer 1848, while visiting a married friend named Jane E. Locke (yet another woman to whom he had written passionate letters) in Lowell, Massachusetts, he was introduced to, and immediately smitten with, a married woman named Nancy Locke ("Annie") Richmond. Very soon afterwards, in September, he proposed marriage to a widow named Sarah Helen Whitman, a poet and spiritualist from Providence, Rhode Island, who had come to his attention by writing him a Valentine's poem earlier in the year. Whitman declined – on the basis that she was responsible for the care of her elderly mother – but Poe persisted, only to be met with further refusal, or at any rate prevarication. When Richmond, aware of Poe's relationship with the other woman, recommended that he marry Whitman, he was grief-stricken by her apparent willingness to countenance his romantic attachment to another – thus, in November, in an apparent bid to end his life, Poe purchased two ounces of laudanum before boarding a train from Lowell to Boston. The suicide attempt succeeded only in making Poe severely ill, and two days later he travelled to Providence to visit Whitman, apparently in a state of mental disorder. After he had recuperated, Whitman finally agreed to marry him – on the condition that he stop drinking. However, when, during a visit made by the couple to a Providence library, an anonymous note was handed to Whitman notifying her that Poe had reneged on his promise to stay sober, she broke off the engagement.

In early 1849 Poe completed the poem 'The Bells' and began writing 'Annabel Lee', but by April had become unwell and depressed once more: "My life seems wasted – the future looks a dreary blank," he wrote. On 29th June he set off on a steamboat to Philadelphia, en route to Richmond, where he was to deliver a series of lectures, but relapsed into dipsomaniacal ways on the journey. The events of the following two or three days in the former city – where he mislaid the suitcase containing his lecture notes – are obscured by an alcoholic miasma. For instance, he told Mária Clemm that he had been arrested for drunkenness, although there is no record of this having taken place. Meanwhile George Lippard, a Philadelphia journalist, reported that a penniless Poe had visited him wearing only one shoe. Poe attributed his erratic behaviour on this occasion to "*mania a potu*" – that is, delirium tremens. He eventually made it to Richmond, where he recovered somewhat, as well as reacquainting himself with his sister Rosalie. He also called on his boyhood sweetheart Elmira Royster, now Elmira Shelton and a widow. Rumours began to circulate that they were engaged, although Shelton later denied

Richmond; Engagement to Elmira Shelton

that this was the case. As is often the case with Poe, it is difficult to determine the truth of what happened.

Last Days and
Mysterious
Death

In September, Poe, still in Richmond, was invited to travel to Philadelphia to edit a volume of poems by the wife of a piano manufacturer, an uncongenial job he accepted for the money, with the intention of then travelling on to New York, where he planned to make further preparations for the launch of *The Stylus*. He expected to be away from Richmond for a total of two weeks. The day before his departure he visited Shelton, who judged that he was too ill to travel. Nevertheless, early the next morning, 27th September, he boarded the steamboat for Baltimore – forgetting to take his luggage with him. The next six days are shrouded in mystery. As his cousin, Neilson Poe, subsequently wrote to Maria Clemm: "At what time he arrived in [Baltimore], where he spent the time he was here, or under what circumstances, I have been unable to ascertain." Poe was found insensible in a Baltimore inn called Gunner's Hall, clad in a straw hat and strange clothes (not those he had been wearing on leaving Richmond) on 3rd October. The inn was at that time doubling as a polling station for congressional elections that were taking place in Maryland on that day. One popular theory is that Poe, in his inebriated state, had somehow become involved in electoral fraud by being persuaded to don a different set of garments in order to vote more than once for a particular candidate. Whatever the explanation, Poe – after his cousin, Henry Herring, who coincidentally arrived on the scene, had refused to take responsibility for him – was removed from the tavern to the city's Washington College Hospital, where, delirious and full of self-reproach, he died four days later. The official cause of death was given as "phrenitis" – inflammation of the brain. A funeral was held the next day, 8th October, attended by only four mourners, including Herring and Neilson Poe.

Griswold's
Obituary and
'Memoir of the
Author'

An obituary appeared in the *New York Tribune* on 9th October 1849, signed "Ludwig", the pseudonym of Poe's long-standing adversary Rufus Wilmot Griswold, which stated that "few will be grieved" by Poe's death since "he had few or no friends". At this time Griswold also claimed that it was Poe's wish that he (Griswold) be made his literary executor – whether this is the case or not, it is true that Maria Clemm transferred power of attorney to Griswold on 20th October. As a result, a three-volume collection of Poe's works was published from January 1850, edited by Griswold, James Russell Lowell and Nathaniel Parker Willis. The third volume was prefaced by a vituperative 'Memoir of the Author' written by Griswold, which contained many fabrications – including that Poe was expelled from the University of Virginia and that he attempted to seduce his foster father John Allan's second wife – and in which he represented the author as a lunatic, a drug addict and a drunkard. Although it was denounced by many who had known Poe, including Sarah Helen Whitman, Charles Frederick Briggs and George Rex Graham, Griswold's character assassination coloured the writer's posthumous reputation throughout the nineteenth century.

Edgar Allan Poe's Works

Poe published his first, forty-page book of verse, entitled *Tamerlane and Other Poems*, at his own expense in June or July 1827, with the help of a Boston printer named Calvin Frederick Stephen Thomas, about whom little is known. Only one hundred copies were printed, and the volume received no critical attention during the author's lifetime. Indeed, so small was the volume's print run, and so limited was its distribution, that, writing in 1850 – the year after Poe's death – the editor and critic Rufus Wilmot Griswold questioned whether it had existed at all. (A copy was eventually found in 1859.) The book contained ten poems, including the long title piece, about the Turko-Mongol conqueror Tamerlane (1336–1405). In the book's preface the anonymous author (called simply "a Bostonian" on the cover), referring to himself in the third person, asserted that "failure will not at all influence him in a resolution already adopted".

Tamerlane and Other Poems

Al Aaraaf,
Tamerlane and
Minor Poems

The author's second collection, *Al Aaraaf, Tamerlane and Minor Poems*, which included revised versions of five of the poems from the first volume, was published by the Baltimore firm of Hatch & Dunning in December 1829 and ascribed to "Edgar A. Poe". The extent of the print run is unknown, although it is likely that five hundred copies or fewer were produced. The book contains the first published version of Poe's longest poem, 'Al Aaraaf' (422 lines), which took as its inspiration the discovery in 1572 by the Danish astronomer Tycho Brahe of a supernova, which Poe equated with Al Aaraaf, a place described in the Koran as, in Poe's words, "a medium between Heaven and Hell". Critics mostly reacted negatively to the volume, although John Neal, editor of the *Yankee and Boston Literary Gazette*, opined that if the author "would but do himself justice he might make a beautiful and perhaps a magnificent poem".

Poems

Al Aaraaf, Tamerlane and Minor Poems was followed just over a year later, in the spring of 1831, by a third collection of poetry, entitled simply *Poems*, printed by Elam Bliss of New York, probably in a run of between five hundred and a thousand copies. Poe dedicated it to his former colleagues in "the US Corps of Cadets" – some of whom had contributed seventy-five cents each towards the cost. The book described itself as a "second edition", since it contained many poems that had appeared in previous collections, notably 'Tamerlane' and 'Al Aaraaf', as well as six previously unpublished pieces, including early versions of 'To Helen' and 'Israfel'. The volume also included a preface, 'Letter to Mr —', in which Poe outlined his belief that a poem "is opposed to a work of science by having, for its immediate object, *pleasure*, not truth".

The Narrative
of Arthur
Gordon Pym
of Nantucket

Having switched his attention to fiction in the early 1830s, partly for pragmatic reasons, Poe had begun to devise a plan for a volume of short stories under the title *Tales of the Folio Club*. However, the collection was turned down by the publishers Harper & Brothers, who suggested to Poe that "a single work" – that is, a novel – might appeal to "the ordinary comprehension of the generality of readers". Thus he began composing what would be his only novel – a seafaring adventure yarn with supernatural elements about a stowaway aboard a whaling ship – arranging with his employer, Thomas Willis White, editor of the Richmond-based *Southern Literary Messenger*, to have the story, titled *The Narrative of Arthur Gordon Pym of Nantucket*, serialized in the periodical. However, only two instalments appeared before Poe was fired from his position on the *Messenger* in January 1837. Economic necessity later forced Poe to complete the novel, which was published in two volumes by Harper & Brothers in July 1838, presented as an account by Pym himself – Poe's name did not appear. Contemporary reviewers were unimpressed, with many criticizing its violence as well as the attempt to trick readers into believing it was a true story. Poe himself called it "a very silly book". Nevertheless, *Arthur Gordon Pym* has proven to be a highly influential work, with eminent authors such as Jorge Luis Borges, H.G. Wells and Arthur Conan Doyle among its admirers.

In late 1839, the Philadelphia firm Lea & Blanchard produced a collection of twenty-five of Poe's short stories, comprising those that were to have been included in the abandoned *Tales of the Folio Club* – including 'MS Found in a Bottle' and 'Metzengerstein' – plus several more, notably 'The Fall of the House of Usher', 'William Wilson' and 'Ligeia'. All of the pieces included in the two volumes, titled *Tales of the Grotesque and Arabesque* and dated 1840, had previously appeared in print, in a variety of publications including the *Southern Literary Messenger* and *Burton's Gentleman's Magazine*. "If in many of my productions terror has been the thesis, I maintain that terror is not of Germany, but of the soul," Poe wrote in his preface, responding to the criticisms of "'Germanism' and gloom" in his fiction. The author was beginning to receive considerable praise for his own work at this time, something that he craved, and many of the reviews of the collection

Tales of the Grotesque and Arabesque

were positive: Poe had "placed himself in the foremost rank of American writers", according to the reviewer of *Alexander's Weekly*. The book failed to sell, however, and Poe received no payment. A year later he approached Lea & Blanchard with a proposal for a second, expanded edition – to be titled *Phantasy Pieces* and incorporating newer stories such as 'The Murders in the Rue Morgue' and 'A Descent into the Maelstrom' – but the publisher declined.

Tales   The next collection of Poe's fiction to be published was *Tales*, which appeared in June 1845 under the imprint of the New York-based Wiley & Putnam. The selection of twelve stories – which, as well as 'The Murders in the Rue Morgue', included two other adventures featuring Poe's detective C. Auguste Dupin, 'The Mystery of Marie Rogêt' and 'The Purloined Letter', as well as now-famous pieces such as 'The Gold-Bug' and 'The Black Cat' – was made by an editor, Evert Augustus Duyckinck, although Poe expressed dissatisfaction with the choices, believing that they represented an insufficient "diversity of subject, thought and especially tone and manner of handling". Nevertheless, the collection was a critical success, with the *American Review* hailing it as "one of the most original and peculiar [volumes] ever published in the United States".

The Raven and   Only four months later, in November 1845, *The Raven*
Other Poems   *and Other Poems*, the first collection of Poe's verse to be published for fourteen years, appeared, courtesy again of Wiley & Putnam. The title work had appeared in the New York *Evening Mirror* on 29th January 1845, and had proved wildly popular, enabling Poe to enjoy a taste of the popular and critical approbation he felt so keenly that he needed. The new volume, which contained thirty poems, reprinted several works that had appeared in previous collections, notably 'Tamerlane' and 'Al Aaraaf', alongside a number of hitherto unpublished pieces. In his preface Poe wrote: "With me poetry has been not a purpose, but a passion." Anticipating brisk sales following the success of *Tales*, the publisher increased

the print run of *The Raven and Other Poems* from 750 to about 1,500 copies. The collection, however, failed to make a significant commercial impact.

The last of Poe's works to be issued in his lifetime was *Eureka: A Prose Poem*, which appeared in July 1848, published by George P. Putnam (the successor firm of Wiley & Putnam). A work of non-fiction, it was based on a lecture titled "The Cosmography of the Universe" that Poe gave at New York's Society Library on 3rd February of the same year. Two months after the lecture, Poe approached Putnam with a proposal to adapt its contents into a treatise on the origins, expansion and ultimate collapse of the cosmos, a work whose impact would eclipse that of Newton's theory of gravitation. Putnam was impressed, and agreed to print five hundred copies (a tenth of the quantity suggested by Poe). Poe presented it in his preface "as an art product alone: let us say as a romance – or, if I be not urging too lofty a claim, as a poem". Despite its eccentricity, and the fact that Poe had no formal scientific training to draw on, some see *Eureka* – and the lecture – as predicting aspects of modern cosmology, including the Big Bang theory (in Poe's description of a "primordial particle" created by God) and relativity (in Poe's claim that "space and duration are one"). Poe considered it his greatest work, although the critics failed to agree, with many dismissing it as baffling and absurd.

Eureka

Edgar Allan Poe's Works

Correspondence:
The Collected Letters of Edgar Allan Poe, ed. J.W. Ostrom, B.R. Pollin and J.A. Savoye, 2 vols., 3rd edn. (New York: Gordian Press, 2008)

Biographies:
Peter Ackroyd, *Poe: A Life Cut Short* (London: Chatto & Windus, 2008)
Hervey Allen, *Israfel: The Life and Times of Edgar Allan Poe*, 2 vols. (New York: George H. Doran, 1927)
Jeffrey Meyers, *Edgar Allan Poe: His Life and Legacy* (New York: Charles Scribner's Sons, 1992)
Una Pope-Hennessy, *Edgar Allan Poe, 1809–1849: A Critical Biography* (New York: Haskell House, 1934)
Arthur Hobson Quinn, *Edgar Allan Poe: A Critical Biography* (New York: D. Appleton–Century, 1941)

Additional Recommended Background Material:
Kevin J. Hayes, ed., *The Cambridge Companion to Edgar Allan Poe* (Cambridge: Cambridge University Press, 2002)
I.M. Walker, ed., *Edgar Allan Poe: The Critical Heritage* (London: Routledge, 1986)

Websites:
The Edgar Allan Poe Society of Baltimore, available at eapoe.org
The Poe Museum, available at poemuseum.org

Index of Titles and First Lines

EVERGREENS SERIES

Beautifully produced classics, affordably priced

Alma Classics is committed to making available a wide range of literature from around the globe. Most of the titles are enriched by an extensive critical apparatus, notes and extra reading material, as well as a selection of photographs. The texts are based on the most authoritative editions and edited using a fresh, accessible editorial approach. With an emphasis on production, editorial and typographical values, Alma Classics aspires to revitalize the whole experience of reading classics.

For our complete list and latest offers

visit

almabooks.com/evergreens

GREAT POETS SERIES

Each volume is based on the most authoritative text, and reflects Alma's commitment to provide affordable editions with valuable insight into the great poets' works.

Selected Poems
Blake, William
ISBN: 9781847498212
£7.99 • PB • 288 pp

The Rime of the Ancient Mariner
Coleridge, Samuel Taylor
ISBN: 9781847497529
£7.99 • PB • 256 pp

Complete Poems
Keats, John
ISBN: 9781847497567
£9.99 • PB • 520 pp

Paradise Lost
Milton, John
ISBN: 9781847498038
£7.99 • PB • 320 pp

Sonnets
Shakespeare, William
ISBN: 9781847496089
£4.99 • PB • 256 pp

Leaves of Grass
Whitman, Walt
ISBN: 9781847497550
£8.99 • PB • 288 pp

MORE POETRY TITLES

Dante Alighieri: *Inferno, Purgatory, Paradise, Rime, Vita Nuova, Love Poems*; Alexander Pushkin: *Lyrics Vol. 1 and 2, Love Poems, Ruslan and Lyudmila*; François Villon: *The Testament and Other Poems*; Cecco Angiolieri: *Sonnets*; Guido Cavalcanti: *Complete Poems*; Emily Brontë: *Poems from the Moor*; Anonymous: *Beowulf*; Ugo Foscolo: *Sepulchres*; W.B. Yeats: *Selected Poems*; Charles Baudelaire: *The Flowers of Evil*; Sándor Márai: *The Withering World*; Antonia Pozzi: *Poems*; Giuseppe Gioacchino Belli: *Sonnets*; Dickens: *Poems*

WWW.ALMABOOKS.COM/POETRY

101-PAGE CLASSICS

Great Rediscovered Classics

This series has been created with the aim to redefine and enrich the classics canon by promoting unjustly neglected works of enduring significance. These works, beautifully produced and mostly in translation, will intrigue and inspire the literary connoisseur and the general reader alike.

THE PERFECT COLLECTION OF LESSER-KNOWN WORKS BY MAJOR AUTHORS

almabooks.com/101-pages

ALMA CLASSICS

ALMA CLASSICS aims to publish mainstream and lesser-known European classics in an innovative and striking way, while employing the highest editorial and production standards. By way of a unique approach the range offers much more, both visually and textually, than readers have come to expect from contemporary classics publishing.

LATEST TITLES PUBLISHED BY ALMA CLASSICS

www.almaclassics.com